AN

ENDLESS

SKYWAY

An
Endless
Skyway

Poetry from the State
Poets Laureate

Edited by Caryn Mirriam-Goldberg,
Marilyn L. Taylor, Denise Low,
and Walter Bargen

Ice cube Books
North Liberty, Iowa

An Endless Skyway:
Poetry from the State Poets Laureate

Copyright © 2011
All Rights Reserved

Editors—Caryn Mirriam-Goldberg, Marilyn L.
Taylor, Denise Low, and Walter Bargen

ISBN 9781888160529

Library of Congress Control Number:
2010939900

Ice Cube Books, LLC (est. 1993)
205 North Front Street
North Liberty, Iowa 52317-9302
www.icecubepress.com
steve@icecubepress.com
1-319-558-7609

Printed in Canada

The paper used in this publication meets the
minimum requirements of the American
National Standard for Information
Sciences—Permanence of Paper for Printed
Library Materials, ANSI Z39.48-1992

Background photo on book cover:
weaoo148, NOAA's National Weather
ervice (NWS) Collection.

Thanks to Jerry Sipe for his gorgeous
photo. Steve Semken for making dreams
come true for writers, all the poets laureate
for their contributions, and our esteemed
reviewers for their kind comments.

*To all who love the power of poetry in
our home states and throughout the world.*

TABLE OF CONTENTS

PREFACE

Thirty-eight states in the United States currently have a State Poet Laureate. The position hearkens back to the European customs of including a poet in the royal retinue, such as the *versificator regis* (King's Poet) of King Richard the Lion Heart. In England, in the 1370s, Chaucer served King Edward III unofficially as a poet; three centuries later in 1668, John Dryden became the first officially appointed Poet Laureate of England. He was paid in cash and good Canary Islands wine for writing commemorative odes for New Years, birthdays, and state occasions.

In the United States, the tradition may have derived from courtly pleasures, but it has adapted over the years to reflect the contemporary community and what it wishes to celebrate. Not only have we had a National Poet Laureate since 1937; since the mid-twentieth century, more and more individual states have also begun to honor its poets by appointing State Poets Laureate.

The duties and terms of these appointees vary widely from state to state. They sometimes compose poems for their governors. William Stafford, former Poet Laureate of Oregon, always opened the state legislative sessions with a new poem. Denise Low composed a poem for the re-dedication of the state legislative chambers in Kansas. Most often, however, State Poets Laureate travel throughout their regions to share the art of verse with schools, libraries, and community organizations. Some have one-year terms, and some serve for life. Some have small salaries but large stipends for mileage, and some have no funds available to them at all.

Some serve under the auspices of state arts councils, humanities councils or state offices, and some are appointed by small groups of individuals. No organization exists to unite all the State Poets Laureate, although occasional conferences have been held.

This collection grew from a gathering of midwestern State Poets Laureate organized by Kansas Poet Laureate Caryn Mirriam-Goldberg in Lawrence, Kansas, in the spring of 2009. The five Poets Laureate who attended this gathering were inspired and energized not only by the formal presentations, but also by having the opportunity to share their experiences. From this—as we sat together one evening after dinner at a local restaurant in downtown Lawrence—two ideas were sparked: first, the possibility of creating an anthology of State Poets Laureates' work; and second, of putting together a larger conference, open to all State Poets Laureate, past and present. Both sparks caught fire and blazed into this anthology and an event titled *Poet Laureati: A National Convergence of State Poets Laureate*, held in March, 2011, in Lawrence.

When we put out the word for the anthology, we had no idea of the sheer splendor, veracity, and diversity of the poetry that would come in. This collection brings together the work of thirty-eight talented and versatile poets in the United States, all sharing their strongest poems. Some are of the poets are well-known beyond their states, some are not as famous, but all have devoted themselves to cultivating the audience for poetry, bringing together writers and their communities, and helping people of all ages and backgrounds in their states discover their truest voices and most generous visions. This is a book of activist poets: poets committed to organizing projects, events, campaigns, and programs around poetry. We believe poetry has the potential to enhance lives, bring communities together, and shift an entire culture's understanding of how we can best live.

The torch that is passed from Poet Laureate to Poet Laureate can be seen as the signature of our humanity, to be carried around each of our states as an example of what we feel, think, and do. We hold poetry up to illuminate, to mirror, to show us who we are in the moment, suggesting a commonality, a shared space. Poems calls us to look again, to pause, and to reexamine the difference between a life lived, and a lived life.

Again and again, State Poets Laureate offer their citizens the opportunity to take refuge in words, in images, in metaphors, and to return from the poem invigorated and enlightened. How often have we heard a man or woman come up after a reading to say, "You know, I'm eighty years old and no one ever introduced me to poetry, and now I regret that." Or overheard a husband say, "My wife dragged me here this evening and I thought I'd never like poetry, but you know, I really enjoyed this." Many people crave the enthusiasms and insights that poetry offers, but it is not until the State Poet Laureate whistles through town that a shimmering silence of listening is born.

William Carlos Williams probably said it best when he wrote:

It is difficult
to get the news from poems
yet men die miserably every day
for lack
of what is found there.

Here in this volume is a splendid supply of, "what is found there."

We are certain that you will enjoy, revisit, and come away from this collection of poetry consistently renewed.

Caryn Mirriam Goldberg, Poet Laureate of Kansas
Denise Low, Poet Laureate of Kansas (2007-2009)
Walter Bargen, Poet Laureate of Missouri (2008-2010)
Marilyn L Taylor, Poet Laureate of Wisconsin (2009-2010)

December, 2010

AN
ENDLESS
SKYWAY

SUE BRANNAN WALKER

ALABAMA

Incredible Incomparable Urchins

(For Denise Marcucci)

Sea urchins eat nothing but kelp and algae,
so the use of them is often hard to see.
They have no legs, no eyes, no nose
so humans, in arrogance, sometimes suppose
that because they can talk and even sing
they're superior. They criticize the urchin's sting.
It's said humans have a developed mind,
but they're only urchins of a different kind.
Their mouths emit venom and spit verbal stings
and the pain is equal to what a sea urchin brings.
But of course there are folks who refuse to see
how singularly imperfect a human can be
when given to gluttony, lust, greed and pride,
sloth, wrath, and envy—this Jekyll and Hyde.
Beneath the appearance of how something seems
lies the hope and promise of unrealized dreams
waiting in some 7000 genes that all urchins share.
Land-living denizens should be environmentally aware
that sea urchin research could soon bring about
a cure for Alzheimer's, cancer, and gout.
Let's offer great praises and undying devotion
for sea urchins that dwell in the depths of the ocean.

If You Would Like To View Storm Report Images For A Previous Day, Type In The Date You Wish To Retrieve (e.g. 990704).

You could see it coming,
see its intent across miles
of water, see it make its way,
see it gather momentum,
and it would be in the papers,
it would be on tv—the colors
would spread, purple and red,
and its fury would churn
the waters: category 1,
cat 3; then 5, and orders
would be given to evacuate.
Still nothing could be done
to stop it from entering
the mouth of the bay;
nothing could prevent it
from coming ashore,
from washing away houses,
ripping roofs off buildings,
tearing down trees, killing,
and though people would flee,
hide in shelters, board-up
if they could, nothing,
nothing could be done;
no one would be arrested,
no one put in jail, no sentence
served, and the culprits,
year after year—Ivan
and Katrina, Ida and Hugo,
Andrew and their kind
would go free, and people
would talk, speak of courage,
claim heroes as they might,
and yet in August, September,

even November, there would be
another watch—and then waiting
for chaos, devastation, destruction,
and nothing could be done.

Sue Brannan Walker is the Stokes Distinguished Professor of Creative Writing at
the University of South Alabama and Alabama's Poet Laureate. She has published
seven books of poetry, numerous anthologies, critical works on James Dickey, Flannery
O'Connor, Carson McCullers, and Marge Piercy. She has also published fiction and
drama. She is the recipient of a Fellowship from the Alabama Council on the Arts as well
as awards from the Medical Society of Alabama for her work in literature and medicine.
She is the publisher of Negative Capability Press, which for twenty years published the
literary journal, *Negative Capability*.

PEGGY SHUMAKER

ALASKA

Long Before We Got Here, Long After We're Gone

In the season blue-white sun
barely lifts above the ridge,
limps along the horizon
then dives out of sight,
we're changed each day by light.

Someone who's gone before
broke trail, set tracks.
With the right kick wax,
we make our way among birch
breathing hard rare frosted light.

We make of light arpeggio crystals,
caribou dance fans, shush
of bristles. One moment made
alive, human, unafraid.
All that's lost not gone.

In Praise, Ephemera

At dawn feeding swans, upended
by the ice shelf, black beaks
champing half-thawed weeds,

draw us to the riverbank. Grizzled feathers,
echo of boots over rotting snow. Far between,
few, tundra swans step out on late ice.

Glacial melt, snow melt
hustle downstream--
ice dams hold tight

jostled swathes of half-lace ice.
Knife-edged narrow
leads open, sliced river swollen.

Muskrat and beaver gnaw
new shoots of red willow,
open winter lodges. Fresh water, air.

Pollen, lavish, carpets the
quick and the dead, blessing the
revived, blessing the remade.

Season of cold broken. Season of ice broken. Season of
tattered shirtsleeves. Bare hands
useful again after burrowing all winter.

Voles gather first shoots of new grasses,
weave fresh sheaves to put by, chew new roots, shoots, and
xylem, drunk on the season's sugars risen

yesterday and today, this hour
zipping by, lifting off, wild swan in clear sky.

Chatanika

High, the Chatanika,
high this year, surges
the flats, soaks
the valley. Chatanika

spreads wide
where gravel braids.
Where banks
snug close,

where rock,
earth, and root
gang up, high water
scours, carves,

its own image
changeable.
Chatanika, in pools
deep green, in eddies

steeped tea, freezes
and thaws, makes its way on,
full of grayling
flashing like thoughts

among the millions
of mirrors at Minto.
What brought me
exactly here?

Is my flowing
through the world
a fit gift? Have I nourished
more roots than I undercut?

Gnawed Bones

If language is bones, hard parts
of speech, what do skulls of pack rats
crushed into owl pellets
have to tell us?

If this delicate pelvis
once balanced a gravid
javelina, what word passes on
to her shoats?

If cicada shells hang on
like single mothers starved
for touch, what does hot
wind whisper through them?

If every day
re-enacts creation,
if we live
here, now

in the first world
and the last,
let us speak
in our bones

languages of water
from all skies, from
deep underground.
Let our bones quench

the thirst of history,
thirst for all we yearn
to sip, marrow
of each dry tongue.

Mother Tongue

In a language recently
disappeared, god
is talking.

No one knows anymore
how long the leaves
keep silent

how deep
the stones' truth
lies buried

what silent kinship
glints off blond fur
where grizzly cubs graze.

In the far time, nearly
everyone could speak
with salmon,

water,
clouds, stars.
Every body.

Now no one sees the ocean
though it lives in every tear.

In a language lost to us
god is singing.

Peggy Shumaker is the Alaska State Writer Laureate. Her new book of poems is *Gnawed Bones* (Red Hen Press). Her lyrical memoir is *Just Breathe Normally* (Nebraska). She's currently working on a manuscript of poems set in Costa Rica. Professor emerita at University of Alaska Fairbanks, she teaches in the Rainier Writing Workshop and at many writing conferences and festivals. In 2008, Peggy founded Boreal Books (www.borealbooks.org) to publish literature and fine art from Alaska.

DAVID
MASON
COLORADO

Fog Horns

The loneliest days,
damp and indistinct,
sea and land a haze.

And purple fog horns
blossomed over tides—
bruises being born

in silence, so slow,
so out there, around,
above and below.

In such hurts of sound
the known world became
neither flat nor round.

The steaming tea pot
was all we fathomed
of *is* and *is not*.

The hours were hallways
with doors at the ends
opened into days

fading into night
and the scattering
particles of light.

Nothing was done then.
Nothing was ever
done. Then it was done.

Fathers and Sons

Some things, they say,
one should not write about. I tried
to help my father comprehend
the toilet, how one needs
to undo one's belt, to slide
one's trousers down and sit,
but he stubbornly stood
and would not bend his knees.
I tried again
to bend him toward the seat,

and then I laughed
at the absurdity. Fathers and sons.
How he had wiped my bottom
half a century ago, and how
I would repay the favor
if only he would sit.

                    Don't you—
he gripped me, trembling, searching for my eyes.
Don't you—but the word
was lost to him. Somewhere
a man of dignity would not be laughed at.
He could not see
it was only the crazy dance
that made me laugh,
trying to make him sit
when he wanted to stand.

Home Care

My father says his feet will soon be trees
and he is right, though not in any way
I want to know. A regal woman sees
me in the hallway and has much to say,
as if we were lovers once and I've come back
to offer her a rose. But I am here
to find the old man's shoes, his little sack
of laundered shirts, stretch pants and underwear.

Rattling a metal walker for emphasis,
his pal called Joe has one coherent line—
How the hell they get this power over us?—
then logic shatters and a silent whine
crosses his face. My father's spotted hands
flutter like dying moths. I take them up
and lead him in a paranoiac dance
toward the parking lot and our escape.

He is my boy, regressed at eighty-two
to mooncalf prominence, drugged and adrift.
And I can only play, remembering who
he was not long ago, a son bereft.
Strapped in the car, he sleeps away the hour
we're caught in currents of the interstate.
He will be ashes in a summer shower
and sink to roots beneath the winter's weight.

A Bit of Skin

Across an aircraft aisle
a mother, young, in jeans
beside her children, leans
to pick up a dropped doll,
and at her reach, the blue
of her brief jacket lifts.
My glance furtively shifts,
acknowledging the view:

only the small of her back,
but lovely, olive, then
a realization—*skin*—
and I shyly bend to my book.
That teasing notion, touch,
transferred from eye to hand
six miles above the land
has shifted me to such

an adolescent state
when skin was everything
ecstatic, every sting
relieved by a hot date,
but now it's not so clear.
The mother across the aisle
indulges space with a smile
I can only describe as pure.

That too is skin, as is
the hand that holds my pen
depicting this little scene
like notes for an altarpiece.
Often I think our skin
is deep enough for love.
We wear it like a glove
until we wear it thin.

Outworn, its aging nerves
relay in the faintest brush
with other skins, the hush
of the advancing years.
This is our passage, bound
by all the laws of flight
through turbulence at night
until the wheels touch ground.

And as we disembark,
dragging our offices
or households past the eyes
and uniforms, the dark
above the parking lot
does not distinguish skin
from skin, woman from man,
who's loved from who is not.

Marco Polo in the Old Hotel

Marco. . .
                    . . . Polo

Marco. . .
                    . . . Polo

Pour another glass of sunlight,
tasting an after-dinner hour.
This is not a time for reading.
Wait a while. A meteor shower
may fall about your head tonight
and children in a nearby pool
are laughing in late summer air,
happy to be free of school.

Marco. . .
                    . . . Polo

Marco. . .
                    . . . Polo

You are the only dinner guest.
The meal is finished, but the wine
will last until the dark arrives.
The children in the pool incline
their bodies, leaping from the waves,
their voices calling to each other,
traveling through the evenings, years
and decades of late summer weather.

Marco. . .
                    . . . Polo

Marco. . .
                    . . . Polo

Across the parking lot a flag
is flapping, thin as Chinese silk
the camels caravanned through deserts.
Voices fall into the dark.

You breathe the last mouthful of wine
and seem to float into the air
as they call to eternity,
the unenclosing everywhere:

Marco. . .

        . . . Polo

Marco. . .

        . . . Polo

David Mason's books of poems include *The Buried Houses* (winner of the Nicholas
Roerich Poetry Prize), *The Country I Remember* (winner of the Alice Fay Di Castagnola
Award), and *Arrivals*. His verse novel, *Ludlow*, was published in 2007, and named best
poetry book of the year by the Contemporary Poetry Review and the National Cow-
boy and Western Heritage Museum, and it won the Colorado Book Award. It was also
featured on the *PBS News Hour*. Author of a collection of essays, *The Poetry of Life and
the Life of Poetry*, Mason has also co-edited several textbooks and anthologies, including
Western Wind: An Introduction to Poetry, *Rebel Angels: 25 Poets of the New Formalism*,
Twentieth Century American Poetry, and *Twentieth Century American Poetics: Poets on the
Art of Poetry*. He has also written the libretti for composer Lori Laitman's opera of *The
Scarlet Letter* and her oratorio, *Vedem*. He recently won the Thatcher Hoffman Smith
Creativity in Motion Prize for the development of a new libretto based upon *Ludlow*.
Mason's literary memoir, *News from the Village*, has just appeared. A second book of es-
says, *Two Minds of a Western Poet*, will appear in 2011 from the University of Michigan's
Poets on Poetry Series. A former Fulbright Fellow to Greece, he lives near the Garden of
the Gods in Colorado with his wife, Anne Lennox.

MARY CROW
COLORADO

Darkly

To some the world is given in hills,
their haze color and texture of canvas, hills
that stack up as the bus rises slowly from the station
and hills flood the view, hills and their haze—pronounced
like graininess above a fire tickling the throat, hoarseness
full of wheel cadences and road dust—hills' solitude greater
than barbed wire's shadow on the horizon, used syringes
scattered in debris—autumn hills growing colder, lamps covered
because of snipers, powder coming down from clouds like pollen
in yellow threads, black swamp rubbing its belly forward as
it sloughs a skin toward a new given, somewhere, in the farthest hills.

Duchess

i.
wind gusts bow the treetops
as my father bowed my mother—
his "duchess" whose stricken face
proclaimed her rebellion—
her delicate uselessness—

how I fought off the sight
of her torment, how my father
bent her will with distances
while I poured into my music
solace of mourning

ii.
to wake up years later
snowfall so heavy I see
only a circular sunglow
remember the loud
snap as the snow
let loose a white cloud
tumbling me over
over edges white feathers
brushing the slope

and I fell and I fell
in quiescence of white
in the sudden shock
of your betrayal till
my nerves told my arms
to swim upward to where
I struggled to breathe
to stretch out frozen hands
toward the little torch
blurred above me

Premonitions

Now I turn toward my music
while you turn toward the world..
Now the weight of the uniforms in the street
flickers inside me.

And I can't wake from the tingling density,
swing of grief ripe with epaulets,
the nude smell of brass buttons.
And though I pull myself toward music,
I can't enter—

                I leap from myself—

grasses polishing themselves around me,
sun rubbing color from new dandelions
into the dagger-glint of sidewalks—

While I hold myself together,
my music's architecture
bright with terror rows out again and again,
oar-beats rolling in.

Bagan Ferris Wheel

how some small gesture swells with images
this night that holds your hand   floating
sky turning like a ferris wheel   dizzy
with shrieks of laughter   scratchy song

wheel whose weight pulls it down   till it turns
lifting again toward a crowd   the world
upside down   under it the small red ponies
of a nearby carousel prancing in their mirrors

why don't you turn   give up what's
below   if I unwind the horoscope   fold up
shadows   suddenly everything slides
empty of you as the wheel halts at the top

Mary Crow was raised in Loudonville, Ohio, and educated at the College of Wooster, Indiana University, and the Iowa Writers Workshop. She came west to begin a creative writing and teaching career at Colorado State University. She also served as Poet Laureate of Colorado. Along with teaching Creative Writing and Contemporary Poetry, Women Writers, Latin, South American and World Poetry, Crow also served as director of CSU's Creative Writing Program. Now Emeritus Professor of English at Colorado State University, Mary Crow has been awarded Poetry Fellowships from the National Endowment for the Arts and the Colorado Council on the Arts.

DICK ALLEN
CONNECTICUT

Out of the Blue

Lion, tyger, panther, figured wheel,
the carriage, *La Belle Dame sans Merci*,
small rain, hunted hare, ball-turret gunner,
flea on a bonnet, witness tree,

starry night, Daddy, groundhog, Grecian urn,
west wind, my cat Geoffrey,
hurt hawk, pool player, Thomas the Rhymer,
coy mistress, jar in Tennessee—

they all come out of the blue, they spin,
prance, whisper, wound, tease, run away,
settle for a moment, then are gone
out of the mind and from this day—

Julia's clothes, country churchyard, darkling thrush,
windhover, Lake Isle of Innisfree,
Musee des Beaux Arts, earth's imagined corners,
red wheelbarrow, papa waltzing, Annabel Lee,

daffodils, London snows, a noiseless patient spider,
trout on a hook, three ravens, Apeneck Sweeney,
proud music, cuckoo song, the Metro station,
Jenny's kiss, chambered nautilus. . . this light blue elegy.

An AIDS Alphabet

A is for Alex, who painted ghost faces
on subway car windows, leaving no other traces.

B is for Brenda, who loved beautiful clothes
and jittery bracelets and sheer nylon hose.

C is for Charlie who could cook like a chef
and blow thirty-five candles out with one breath.

D is for Donald, that thin handsome man
with his wonderful smile and his marvelous tan.

E is for Ed and the way that he danced
on the edges of sidewalks and laughed when we glanced.

F is for Frank—all the books that he read,
all the poems he wrote, all the nice things he said.

G is for Ginnie, and for Ginnie's two kids,
and the meanings they found under coffee can lids.

H is for Henry, who cast his first vote
for President Clinton, and watched balloons float.

I is for Ivoree's way with a song;
all though his life, he just hummed along.

J is for Jackson. He once saw a bear
step over a campfire and claw up a chair.

K is for Katlin, Wall Street's best broker,
the craft of her hands as she beat you in poker.

L is for Larry. He wanted to star;
you saw him Off-Broadway before he went far.

M is for Mike who bombed down a road
so high on reefer, he *knew* he saw God.

N is for Nicholas—Nicholas, Nicholas;
whatever you said, he couldn't care less.

O is O'Connell. His first name got lost
in the flash of his eyes and the drinks that he tossed.

P is for Paula, her store on the corner,
her shrugs and her frowns and her *O Jesus* laughter.

Q is for Quentin. Quentin would walk
fifty-eight miles to hear library talk.

R is Roberto's. He cried when he saw
how well Larry could act and Alex could draw.

S is Stan dreaming that one day he'd stand
in the halls of the Senate, a flag in one hand.

T is for Thomas, who wanted no more
than to live in a house with a sliding glass door.

U is for Uldine. She hated her name,
but she loved carrot sticks, and listening to *Fame*.

V is for Vic and for Vikki and Val
Vanesa and Vinnie and Vinnie's best pal.

W stands for how William would die
for a stroll in the rain or a piece of Lime Pie.

X is the name of one I don't know
who left us an angel laid down in the snow.

Y is Yvonne. She's lighting a fire.
She's washing the dishes. She's singing in Choir.

And Z is for Zackary, gone. Zack's gone.
All of them gone. All, all of them gone.

Poetry Editors at Dawn

They wake up, sweating. Out there, they know,
a young man has fallen in love
with a young woman's nose. An early commuter
has found magnolia blossoms on his sunroof,
a teacher starts crying. Shakily, the editors
rise from their beds like swans. They've been dreaming
of beautiful snowstorms, lonely lakes, fathers and mothers
dying with their poet sons and daughters
beside them, taking notes. . . . The morning news
is as surrealistic as it's always been, the coffee
sugary hot. The editors look in their mirrors
and whimper; they wonder what kind of sex life
a gynecologist has—or if, after many years,
accountants hate numbers. Out there, somewhere,
a middle-aged woman is staring at an El Greco
that just breaks her heart; a middle-aged man
has felt a sparrow's joy; an old codger
remembers children jumping in the leaves
and takes out his pen. *Seashores*, think the editors,
raindrops, hills and horizons,
stickball on city streets, newspaper headlines,
overwhelming sorrow and increasing pain,
windows and window frames,
the crow, the forsythia, storms banging shutters,
the solitary heron and the subway shooting
echoing for years—all the familiar words, all the images
lines, stanzas, thoughts, feelings . . . growing, forming, frothing
splashing, cascading, overwhelming, *I'm coming for you,*
in the mails toward them.

Bravo

For how you've lived this long. *Bravo*
because the trees around your house have not yet fallen
and the sun's running the sky. *Bravo, Bravo*
that you've remembered to put the key in upside down
so the door opens,
that the first word you said this morning was "Good."
That you clink bottles together just to hear the "clink."
That someone screwed your head on wrong.
Bravo. Bravissimo,
that you're still walking
and your hands do more than you'd expect,
that birdsongs sound crazy, like tying bubbles in knots,
Bravo for ye gods and little fishes,
turns in the road and the signs that mark these turns,
spumoni, African violets, Apple computers,
and *bravo, bravo, bravo,*
the lifting of the curtain and your solo voice on stage,
your shout, your cry,
Ave Maria. Ave, ave dominus, Dominus tecum,
this incredible journey you took and still are taking,
that the universe is not an empty dodecahedron,
for all that befalls us: rain, snow, spiders, moonlight. . .
and for rice pudding, *Bravo.*

Poem in Memory of the Big Bopper

Far more than once,
you have to listen to whatever music you've always hated,
extracting from it
a plum, a dark rose, a fish hook, an earring.

You have to ask yourself, several times a day,
"What am I doing wrong?"
You have to teach yourself to take your own advice
and not go hammering nails into the wrong buildings.

You have to sign up for long walks through nowhere,
in the winter especially, alert for strange tire tracks,
their white on white along a country road.
In the heart of nothing, a direction.

You have to linger over something until it hurts:
a dictionary word with umlauts,
some Rothko where you slip from ledge to ledge,
any beach pebble.

You must order your life
not only a good cheese omelet in the afternoon,
but buckets of sunflowers,
and as many grains of salt as will fill a baby's crib.

And this above all: each Spring,
you must buy yourself a pair of new white shoes
and not slip them on until the height of summer,
singing, *"Chantilly Lace."*

Sea

What is ridiculous about the sea
is the huge size of it, the way it mocks the sky,
how it keeps turning itself over and over,
flaunting its amoeba shape, wandering off
into its pseudopods of tidal rivers,
coves and bays. How preposterous
are the little vessels that ride on it,
the capsules it swallows whole, the seeds
of dolphins and whales that glide in its underbelly.
And how laughable, how outside the Tao
you and I must be to it—little swimming things,
meaningless details,
asplash on its coastline this bright August day
the sea is so calm it almost seems to want us.

Dick Allen's most recent collection, the Zen Buddhist-themed *Present Vanishing: Poems* (Sarabande Books), received the 2009 Connecticut Book Award for Poetry. His previous two books, *The Day Before: Poems*, and *Ode to the Cold War: Poems New and Selected*, were also published by Sarabande. Allen has received poetry writing fellowships from the N.E.A. and Ingram Merrill Foundations and a Pushcart Prize, among other honors. His poems have been included six times in *The Best American Poetry* volumes. He has new poems just out or forthcoming in *American Scholar, Ploughshares, Cincinnati Review, New York Quarterly,* and *Georgia Review,* among other publications. Allen lives near the shores of Thrushwood Lake, in Trumbull, Connecticut, with his wife, poet L.N. Allen. They have two grown children. He is addicted to bluegrass music, to driving around the U.S.A., and to breakfasts at Holiday Inn Express and Hampton Inn breakfast bars. In June, 2010, he succeeded John Hollander as the Connecticut State Poet Laureate.

JOANN BALINGIT

DELAWARE

Speaking of Snow

for Fred

Did I tell you it fell
around ten that night,
time I look out
tea water heating?
Not long, long enough
　　　　to say *snowing*
as if the sky could talk
sowing hyphens
like half-spoken words.

The kettle caught me
short of breath, night
sky burnished the
red-gold of summer
ripe peaches, how
　　　　can this be?
The times I have needed
it to snow, to tell
the snow to someone—

that is when I knew
what you'd become to me.

Your Heart and How It Works

Your heart is a pump not much bigger than a sweet potato.
It weighs about half a pound. It is a hollow
      ball of muscle of butterflies of stone
connected to your arteries and veins.

Your heart is a steel wrecking ball, glove
unbuttoned at the wrist. Slip it off, see your heart
dented flat in places. Winking,
      a mirror ball all night tossing stars

Until pound becomes gush and sigh and heart settles
      down to feeding cells, firing the dark
regions of your hungry brain, moving blood
steadily, without fail.

But we are all so deceived by the heart as a pump we forget
the heart itself is alive! Odd to think, the heart must pump
      blood to the heart. Feed
its own lush cravings. Dream no matter

      how fast your heart beats it's how
hard your heart beats that's wildly important.
(For while everyone knows that the heart beats,
very few of us know why.)

Your heart is tough but it can suffer
      injury, like any other part of the body. Luckily
given half a chance, a healthy heart will heal itself
if the cause of the hurt is lessened or removed.

Did you know, if all the work your heart does in one day
could be used to lift you off the ground, it would raise you
twice as high as the Empire State Building, twice as high
      as the lowest clouds in your sky on a brooding day?

Julian's Lullaby

I love you more than the numbers keep going
When you ask, What degrees is a red giant's core?
I love you more than *delicious* in Spanish
When you launch that hot laughter my fingers hunt for.

My love stretches long as a ribbon of wrens
That twists and gathers, smocks and sweeps.
But I shake like a dove in a hawk's fierce clutch
When you tumble untamed, all force into me.

It's dark outside. Before long, morning.
The sun will knock once as it enters the door.
Yes the stars burn out slowly, and numbers keep going—
The time it will take to know who you are.

History Textbook, America

I'd search for Philippines in History class.
The index gave one page, moved on to Pierce.
The Making of America marched past
my enigmatic father's place of birth.
The week he died some man we didn't know
called up. *This is his brother,* one more shock,
phoning for him. "He died three days ago."
The leaden black receiver did not talk.
My uncle never gave his name or town,
we never heard from him. Was it a dream?
The earpiece roar dissolved to crackling sounds,
a dial tone erased the Philippines.
And yet my world grows huge with maps, crisscrossed,
my history alive with all I've lost.

Song of a river

I am a mouth pried
    slowly open

swallowed
by a wider mouth

sipped
    from

soaked
    into

rising out of its
banks the way

words rise
    into words

of others or drown
in others' words or

drink them
    in.

I am a daughter
with seven sisters

    who course
from a single mother—

little tributes,
    tributaries,

we tarry, go
    we tarry, go.

My praise,
    my running

ends in mother—
widest song I know.

The Blue Spotted Salamander

does not flinch as my boot rolls the pine limb over
The night is wet with icy stars sprinkled down its ribs
Not one muscle would I move if God rolled my roof open
I'd lie curled, an unborn word, awake inside his skull

JoAnn Balingit grew up in Lakeland, Florida. She lived and worked in Morocco, Portugal, California and Kentucky before settling in Delaware in 1990. She is the author of *Your Heart and How it Works* (Spire Press, 2009). Appointed Delaware's poet laureate in May 2008, she teaches poetry in schools and community organizations throughout the state, most recently to teens at the Cleveland White School, a reform and secure care facility. Her work has appeared in journals and anthologies such as *DIAGRAM. 2*, *Harpur Palate*, *Smartish Pace*, *Best New Poets 2007*, and on *Verse Daily*. She was a 2009 Mid Atlantic Arts Foundation creative fellow, selected for a residency at the Virginia Center for the Creative Arts.

FLEDA BROWN
DELAWARE

Night Swimming

We are without our men, hers dead
ten years, mine far away, the water
glassy warm. My old aunt already stands
half in. All I see is the white half,
her small old breasts like bells,
almost nice as a girl's. Then we hardly
feel the water, a drag on the nipples,
a brush on the crotch, like making love
blind, only the knives of light
from the opposite shore, the shudders
of our swimming breaking it up.
We let the water get next to us
and into the quick of losses we don't
have to talk about. We swim out
to where the dock goes blank,
and we are stranded, abandoned good flesh
in a black of glimmering. We each fit
our skin exactly. After a while
we come out of the water slick as eels,
still swimming, straight-backed,
breasts out, up to the porch,
illuminate, sexy as hell, inspired.

For Grandmother Beth

Just one scandalous year past our
grandmother's death, the second wife
stood homely and trembling ankle-deep
in the lake, taking on water and family
at once. Once, she told me, your grandfather
found the box of hair your grandmother
saved when she had it bobbed. She said
he cried, and I tried to imagine both
wives working it out in heaven. He took
this second one, taught her theories of
economics, gave her his grown children
and grandchildren, money and houses. They
used to sit at the kitchen table and eat
prunes, the same table where he ate
prunes with my grandmother. Regularity
took him to ninety-five, although
the last year in the nursing home
he couldn't remember who she was, and even
years before that, at the lake, he'd
call her by his dead wife's name. No,
Harry, she'd say, it's Beth, Beth,
and lead him back to where he meant
to go. She never touched the money
he left her, saved it for his children,
took in roomers and lived on interest.
Now she's dead all Garth Avenue
is gone from me, from us, the house,
the lilies of the valley on the north side,
oh, it would be a long list,
and who cares now but us. This
is what I have to say for her, who held
a place and saved everything as if
she had no needs or wishes, except
to be no trouble at all, and to die quickly,
a light turned out to save electric bills.

Chipmunk of a Rock

1

I read, "The chipmunk of a rock dropped
in a stream," before I saw "chimmuck," a word
exactly right for the sound. But then there was
the rock, missing its chipmunk, the chipmunk
that had depended upon the rock and held onto it,
perhaps, as part of itself, so familiar it was
with the contours, ragged edges and smooth
surfaces. And the rock, feeling the cold
for the first time, feeling its crystallization
as a burden, a weight headed for the stream,
one giving, the other displacing exactly,
the geometry of cells arid as a dead planet,
indifferently chimmucking into watery space.

2

Among the magenta paintbrush,
cinquefoil, and heather of Mount Rainier, I sat
on a rise, and chipmunks emerged, six of them.
They came almost to my hand, little brush tails
like surprised rudders. It seemed painful,
to have to remain on Orange Alert both for good
and for bad: bits of sandwich dropped in the cracks,
and the huge, shadowy forms inexplicably arriving
and leaving with some morality of their own.
I had nothing to give, so I sat like a rock,
except for my breathing, which I kept smooth,
for diplomacy. In this way, we set up our relationship,
which I miss even now, its electric fragility,
the meanings that could shift second by second.

The Kayak and the Eiffel Tower

The white sheet I remember, flashing across
the bed and I was watching my mother and the crying
and the bed disappeared and all was white
but it was not snow, it was my mind, and then, oddly,
she took us in a taxi to the movies, I think
it was *Ben Hur*. It was his postcard, now I know,
from that woman in the Philippines, back when
he was a soldier. All this, a movement
of shapes, nothing to hold onto. The kayak
is like that. It slides through the water and the paddle
goes on one side then the other, and there is the sway
of the boat and then the correction. It was
like that, and it was like the Eiffel Tower, all filigree
and lace, because I couldn't see anything solid,
but of course it was night and the movie was over,
I guess, but I remember the feel of her body,
her coat against my coat and the sidewalk rough
the way a child remembers the sidewalk: closer
than it will ever be again, grain after grain, and down
inside the grains, the press of earth that made
the grains, and the grinding that broke them apart,
and there were cracks in the sidewalk, and I swayed
a little as if I were in a kayak, not breathing but
sliding through with my mind so far away it was
on a lake, far out, and the shore wasn't the wool coat
my mother wore, not the coat, not anywhere.
And where was my father? Home, maybe, while
all this was rising from the bottom like a log, or a huge
gar, all the way to the top of the Eiffel Tower, while
my kayak dreamed its way off into some other story.

Venus de Milo

The moon is a bleached marble the color of the Venus de Milo.
It gets so full of itself it breaks through whole centuries.

In this twenty-first one, I am called upstairs by my grandson Noah
to see the full moon over Paris. I tell him about the centuries

inside the marble, layers and streaks. How the sculptor studies
the grain. How even then it can break out of control. Jab the chisel

too far, it leaves a white bruise. Mystery is that erotic, I'm thinking,
if you stay with it, as Noah and I do on the balcony trying to take

a picture that didn't come out, that resisted us, the way the Venus
de Milo did in the afternoon, with her missing arms, holding

herself in, turning us back toward details. I explain to Noah
how rasps and rifflers are used for the final shaping. I explain love

and beauty in the language of work, what else is there to say?
Why mention how much is free-fall—accident—the combination

of genes and skill that turn them to face each other like two mirrors
making their long corridor of escape? I just climb the 64 stairs

to the balcony, panting. I say it's nothing. But then we step
into the dark and enter beauty, where there never was a foothold.

I could have told him that, but just then we were looking at the moon.

Roofers

Five roofers are wedging off the old,
scraping it over the edge. Great black birds
diving in front of the window.
In another place, a nail gun goes off in patterns
of four, sometimes five. They're nice guys:
one has a funny beard that sticks
straight out, one has a lip ring. One is pounding,
testing for rot. One is flipping sections of shingles
down; I hear them slap like clown's feet,
something out of Shakespeare. They know
what they're doing and they do it,
great rolls of thunder, the roof
of heaven cluttered with gods: Homer's
Tityus, Leto, Tantalus, the ones
who work the obscure jobs, who come
when called, the ones before Milton's great-
voiced dignitary, before Hopkins' rod-bearer,
the ones from the old days, from my old days,
when over my head, there was music
in the air, the pitch of my church-camp voice,
raised out of the heat and the breeze
and the sun on the spillway rocks, all of it
holding me in, as if I were in a shadow-box,
the kind someone looks through
a peephole and everything is 3-D, so the eye
is like the Important God. It fills me
with tenderness, the little world I had going on
inside, my grief that it was not the world.

Fleda Brown's new book is *Driving With Dvorak*, released in March 2010, by the University of Nebraska Press. Her most recent collection of poems, *Reunion* (University of Wisconsin Press, 2007), won the Felix Pollak Prize. The author of five previous collections of poems, she has won numerous prizes, among them a Pushcart Prize, the Philip Levine Prize, the Great Lakes Colleges New Writer's Award, and her work has been a finalist for the National Poetry Series. She is professor emerita at the University of Delaware, where she taught for 27 years and directed the Poets in the Schools program. She was Poet Laureate of Delaware from 2001-07. She now lives in Traverse City, Michigan, and is on the faculty of the Rainier Writing Workshop, a low-residency MFA program in Tacoma, Washington.

KEVIN STEIN
ILLINOIS

The Afterlife

As a priest marries the Church   so I wed work.
The union's tin ring, a fin per   week and nothing
down. Trouble was, everything   *was* down:
the line, my pay, the pickup's   windows in rain.
The blonde in shipping couldn't   keep lunch down
or her pants up. Damp her sloppy   tears, damp the shirt's
pits, damp the Chevy's back seat   where rum and Cokes
broke the ice. Her lesson? Never   operate heavy machinery
with lips and zipper. My hands   made feral love
to chill metal, worksong of parts   you'd never see whole
so boys, smoke 'em if you've got   'em. Smokes made ash,
the dust from which ye came and   to dust ye shall.
Dust upon the riven garden. Dust   at neck and sleeves
of my black pocket tee, dust etching   each night's second
shower, my chest the archaic torso   of unionized Apollo.
School's velvet poet counseled me,   "You must change your life."
Though I wished his face so near   I could punch it,
language I understood I could not   understand
changed me for the price of student   loans and Latin.
I'm living the afterlife – these hands   uncalloused,
tweed houndstoothed, my dust become   the stuff of
stacked books. I'm living the afterlife   for those who cut
then polish, lug and heave, who stack   mortise and miter
swing shift. They don't need my guilt   or your pity.
Change is what's fisted back from our   broken dollar.
Change is stashed by the door in a   cracked Ball jar.

On Being a Nielsen Family

We pocket five ones when we agree,
fingered cash our soul's ransom.
And a Family Viewership Record Book
for each TV, of which we've three.
We are the Postmodern Descartes,

pledging, "I watch, therefore I am."
We're the grand experiment that was
America, both scientist and the mouse
with a human ear stitched to its pink back,
checking the appropriate idiot-box boxes.

We're our own Peeping Tom, peering in.
On stage, we're culture's disguise,
the way a bickering couple makes nice
once the bell ding-dongs neighbors in
for cocktails and unsalted Cheese Nips.

Though it's Oprah, we circle BBC News.
Though Jerry Springer, we mark Charlie Rose.
No no no. Not South Park, not Cops,
not World's Funniest Animal Tricks,
but History Channel and Discovery,

NASA Live, Nightline, and Devotionals,
the Food Network's Thanksgiving Day
Vegan Special. We are watched watching,
watching ourselves watched. We are never
enough, so the lie is as we wish to be.

Autumnal

Lofting the Molotov cocktail into the church's
empty lot was, in retrospect, a political act.
Back then it was only three guys I didn't like
unhanding the girly mags, fevered to spectacular action.
Friday night and no driver's license gave us this license.

In the graveyard we slunk behind granite markers,
thumbing cloth down the Coke bottle's high octane throat.
Strange, how doing something marks your life,
hard and permanent as stone, as years later,
driving home from the hospital after something

they called our baby had died, I thought I'd turned
the corner when no I'd not. It had turned on me.
Wittgenstein says you can't see the periphery
of your world because you're in it. He penciled
a sketch in his *Tractatus* just to prove it, buddy,

which is what, in a way, the cops said to me.
Molotov, what's it like to have a weapon named after you?
You're the world's word for insurrection. Emerson says
words themselves are actions, though bless him,
in his dotage he forgot even how to ask for a glass of _____.

Some words you can't say without invoking action.
Against them, there's cultural or moral injunction,
but "dead baby" you say only in the bathroom
with the water running. It's what's not said each time
you blow out the candle. It's what nothing's named after.

Some things you do you wish you hadn't.
Some you don't you wish you had.
It's years before you know the difference,
so what good's remorse? At the hospital
with my wife, what prayer could I have spoken

to what forgetful god? In time, we break things,
stupid and unreflective. In time, we're broken
by things, stupid and unreflective. After I'd tossed
the Molotov, I ran like water through dark alleys.
I never looked back for flames I didn't believe in either.

Sufficiency of the Actual

Had I freed the one-legged cricket twitching in the roses'
      spider-webbed twilight,
I'd become Patron Saint of One-Legged Crickets Twitching
      in Spider-Webbed Twilight.
I'd be Saint of Cracked Song, Patron of the Incomplete
      and Longing.
But then, saintly though I might be, the spider goes hungry.

Anyway, there's already a multitude, patrons of the broken web,
      unrisen bread,
lost keys – so many, this book says, their duties overlap, say,
      Patron Saint of Fractions.
(See Incomplete and Longing.) That's who The Who prayed to,
      trashing instruments
as "Pop Art Auto Destruction," this, Pete Townsend's phrase,

his name a line and demarcation. The young like to break things,
      even themselves.
The young like a summer drum you put your foot through:
      thump worship.
Jon Entwistle, The Who's bassist, stored all his parts
      in a wooden
coffin box, until middle-age donned its knee-high socks.

Then he undid the undoing, cobbling five guitars into one
      he dubbed "Frankenstein,"
whose name my friend Frank and I shared with it and, well,
      with Wollstonecraft's
romantic sci-fi tragic victim hero. Together, we made a creature
      the smarty pants party drunks
called "Frank-and-Stein" from the keg-drenched kitchen.

Aren't we all cobbled of pieces, glued and screwed and strung
      together,
ready to snap? Are we instruments some huge hand plucks?

       Are we the roses
or a cricket's cracked song? And redemption? – in the end
       Entwistle's estate
auctioned "Frankenstein" for a cool $100,000.

Frank did ten years in the county orphanage. (See Incomplete
       and Longing).
His mother remarried a furnace whose pilot wouldn't stay lit.
       You've heard about
the stutterer who falling from a ladder is cured of his affliction
       but made suddenly
blind. What he no longer sees he sings about instead.

Blue Tuesday

I want to invent a thing as beautiful and useless as the Slinky.
Because it's Blue Tuesday, second Tuesday of February,
a tradition invented by my mother who's fond of puzzlers,
say, Did the first inventor invent the notion of "new

and improved"?, or Given a philosophical tree's falling
in unpeopled woods, was there sound? Class dismissed.
Because it's Blue Tuesday I want to be Richard James
and wife Betty, all pumps and pearls, tinkering

a machine to harness ships' horsepower when *plink*
a spring skitters out and walks down the laboratory's
metal steps. Aha, they burped, over meat loaf lunch,
indigestion the mother of invention. The Slinky's pure

sprung pleasure. It doesn't feed nor clothe nor house
the poor, but it won't put your eye out either.
I have, in a fit of wayward fatherliness, spent all
afternoon walking a Slinky up the stairs so my son

could walk it down again. Good boy. The Slinky's
inventor invented this, too, a game to be played
by willing surrogates like you and me – not unlike
pilot Charles Sweeney, the unlucky surrogate

who delivered Oppenheimer's invention to Nagasaki,
Fat Man the first bomb he ever dropped.
That was 1945, same year the Slinky's invented.
If a plane drops a bomb that no one hears

and afterwards there's no one left, did it happen?
I too have ridden the moral high horse,
fingering Sweeney even more than Tibbets
who banked over Hiroshima not knowing

what mushroom would sprout. Sweeney knew,
and never the sour apple of regret. He didn't
sing the Blues, though both the singing
and the not are original American art forms,

the way "I want" becomes the Blues
when a chorus answers "You can't have it!"
Sweeney, because it's Blue Tuesday,
second Tuesday of the second month,

coldest but shortest, metaphor of the human,
I wish I'd invented the Slinky. I wish you and I
were beautiful and useless together, dropping a big
fat Slinky from the blue sky of never happens.

Kevin Stein has published ten volumes of poetry, criticism, and anthology, including the
book of essays, *Poetry's Afterlife: Verse in the Digital Age* (University of Michigan Press,
June 2010). His most recent poetry collections are *Sufficiency of the Actual* (University
of Illinois Press, 2009) and *American Ghost Roses* (University of Illinois Press, 2005),
winner of the Society of Midland Authors Prize. Since 2003 he's served as Illinois poet
laureate.

NORBERT KRAPF

INDIANA

A Blank Piece of Paper

Between dark hills
somewhere in this land
a boy sits at a table
next to a dim light.

He stares at a blank
piece of paper,
holding a pen
filled with enough ink
to tell a good story.

What the boy can't yet
tell is where he began
and where he will end

but even though he is
somewhere not quite
in the middle of
whatever story is his

he knows the time
has come for him
to let the ink flow.

He can feel the first
line poise on the
tip of his pen.

Let the story begin
wherever the tip
of his pen touches
the piece of paper.

Even though our boy
will spend several
lifetimes trying to
move his pen
toward the ending
of the story,

each time he moves
halfway there more ink
will come into the pen.

Though he will never
tell the whole story,
in the telling
of every new half
of the story
always left to tell

the boy will
make his life
twice as large

and ours as
full as it
can become.

The Day John Lennon

The day John Lennon...
we were living in Germany,
had recently adopted a baby girl
from Colombia, and were happy
even though I was laid up in bed
with a painful sinus infection.

The day John Lennon...
we did not listen to the news
on the radio or turn on the TV
or talk to any friends on the phone
or neighbors in the apartment building
because I was sick in bed and we
just tried to take care of ourselves
and nurse our little world back
to routine health so we could
get ready for Christmas in Germany.

The day John Lennon...
it was the eighth of December,
the feast of the Immaculate Conception,
a holy day of obligation for Catholics,
but we did not leave our apartment
and I made it no farther from the bed
than to tiptoe to the bathroom
or to the kitchen table to sip
a bowl of chicken noodle soup.

The day before John Lennon...
our dear friend in New York
who was planning to visit us
when the German winter was over
went out and bought a Christmas tree
that she propped in the corner
of her studio apartment.

One day later she wrote a letter
in which she told us she would
not be able to put one single
ornament on her Tannenbaum.

The day after John Lennon...
I went in to work, stopped
to buy a newspaper, and read
the headline boldly proclaiming
that John Lennon had been....
When I reached my office,
I picked up the phone, dialed
our apartment number, and told
my wife something terrible
had happened: John Lennon had been....
"That's not supposed to happen,"
she said after a painfully long silence.
"No it isn't!" was all I could add.

All day after the day John Lennon...
all I could hear was the tune
and the lyrics of a song I loved
in which John Lennon tried to imagine
the kind of world I wanted to give
to my daughter, and now that she is
twenty-six years old, I still hope and pray
that our children and hers will dream
and that we can learn to live as one.

Someone Who Misses New Orleans

"Do you know what it means to miss New Orleans?"
           —as sung by Louis Armstrong

I know someone
who knows what it means
to miss New Orleans,
the visits to relatives
who lived in a small shotgun house
on Freret Street, in Uptown,
played canasta there with cousins, slurped
snow cones from a neighborhood stand.

I know someone
who knows what it means
to miss New Orleans,
who as a college student
drove down Robert E. Lee Boulevard,
not far from Lake Ponchartrain,
to a college that no longer exists,
looking at pink oleander in bloom,
someone who loves crepe myrtle
and camellia and magnolia
and still believes summer begins in March,
though March is a cruel month up North.

I know someone
who knows what it means
to miss New Orleans,
who married a young man from Indiana,
which happens to rhyme with Louisiana,
who waited for him to fly down to meet
her Cajun family for the first time,
eat crawfish stew, Mississippi River shrimp,
gumbo, okra, and stuffed eggplant,
sip strong coffee from a family demitasse

and just made it back out of the airport
on the very last flight before
Camille hit with her full fury.

I know someone
who knows what it means
to miss New Orleans,
who felt a diamond ring being slipped
on her finger on a bench in City Park,
under the live oaks and Spanish moss,
who brought her new husband to stay
in her brother's apartment
in the Pontalbo Building, on Jackson Square,
near St. Louis Cathedral and sip café au lait
and savor beignet in the Café du Monde like
a new communicant, as jazz oozed and pulsed
out of every building in the all-night French Quarter.

I know what it means
to know someone
who misses New Orleans,
someone who married a young man
who brought her to live far away
from home, in New York, leaving
her mother sad but too proud to complain.

I know someone
who knows what it means
to miss New Orleans,
because when her mother and father
married they moved to the city
from the country and lived
on Tonti Street in Mid-City and ate
read beans and rice every Monday for dinner;
and one day many years later,
in another part of the United States,
as Katrina whirled across the Gulf,

she turned on the TV, watched the waters
of the Lake and the Gulf batter the levee,
and silently sobbed as the waters rose
up the sides of houses and buildings,
winds howling through the live oaks.

I know someone
who knows what it means
to return to New Orleans
and drive up and down streets
in Lakeview, Bucktown,
the Lower Ninth Ward, and Arabi
and see houses blown off
their concrete blocks, trees twisted
and crashed onto roofs, windows
blasted out by winds, everyday
objects of ordinary lives scattered,
piled and heaped everywhere like
rubble in a war-ravaged country.

I know someone
who knows what it means
to miss New Orleans and come back
and see painted on the wall
of a condemned house, on the front porch,
a red, white and blue American flag,
with a hand-painted caption below,
GOD BLESS AMERICA.

I also know what it means
to come back with someone
who loves New Orleans
and finds jazz the heart beat
of a Sunday mass celebrated
by an African American priest
with a Cajun name, in Tremé,
in St. Augustine Church,

in a parish the Catholic authorities
had decreed would be eliminated,
before the people refused to let it die
because the spirit of God
shook their bodies to the core as,
to the backing of trumpet, saxophone,
guitar, banjo, bass, piano, and drum,
they sang hymns and spirituals
that lifted their spirits and made them
believe deep in their hearts that
we are all children of God
who want to be among that number
and whose spirits shall rise higher
than the waters and winds of any storm
named after any man or woman,
or generations of injustice,
could ever bring down to
the ground and keep down low.

Norbert Krapf, a native of Jasper, Indiana, taught for 34 years at Long Island Univ.,
where he directed the C.W. Post Poetry Center for almost 20 years. In 2004, he moved
with his family to Indianapolis and served as Indiana Poet Laureate 2008-10. A hallmark
of his laureateship has been collaborations with photographers and musicians, including
the collections *Invisible Presence* (2006), with photographer Darryl Jones, *Bloodroot: Indi-
ana Poems* (2008), with David Pierini, and a CD with jazz pianist and composer Monika
Herzig, *Imagine – Indiana In Music and Words* (2007). He has also published a prose
memoir, *The Ripest Moments: A Southern Indiana Childhood* (2008), and has been part of
the Hoosier Dylan show that has played in old Indiana theatres.

JOYCE BRINKMAN
INDIANA

Neighborhood Travel Renku

Old bricks and new wood
hold a building together.
Come child meet your past.

Building life where other lives
hammered out an existence.

The smell of sawdust,
the echo of steel hammers
permeate the air.

Breathe. Take in air that touches
the lungs of those around you.

Feed on green foliage
nurtured in your neighborhood.
Test your strong rootstock.

Don't ask, Who is my neighbor.
Find the past, the now, yourself.

The travel brochures
shout in multi-color scenes,
call you to partake.

Today taste brown bread baked here
for you. Savor the flavor.

As tomorrow's bus
arrives, new destinations
arise from fresh yeast.

Invitation to Dance

Let's tanka together!

I'll devise fives,
flirty and fiery.

With a dominating weave,
you choreograph sevens.

Red-hot music flows
in staccato yet touching
Buson and Basho
joining words in wild tango
on a dance floor white-hot paged.

Dancing to heaven
with stars and the moon
we'll tanka forever!

Joyce Brinkman, Indiana Poet Laureate 2002-2008, believes in poetry as public art.
She creates public poetry projects involving her poetry and the poetry of others. Her
own poetry is on permanent display in a twenty-five foot stained glass window in an
airport, in lighted glass at a library and on a wall in the town square of Quezaltepecque,
El Salvador. Joyce has received fellowships from the Mary Anderson Center for the Arts
and the Indianapolis Arts Council.

MARY SWANDER

IOWA

Crazy Eddy on the Judgment Day

Great goblins, this ain't the Promised Land.
I don't see no bright lights,
don't hear no trumpets sounding,
don't feel no angels hovering round.
What we got ourselves stuck into here, folks,
is muck. Yessir, a muddy, messy,
snake-infested swamp.
I'll be tetotaciously exflunctified.
This ain't the way they said it was going to be,
but how about that?
The Lord played tricks on us before.
You bet. Ain't we used to this sort of thing?
The river rising and falling,
us never knowing what was where
and when was what.
So here we is, sure as you're alive,
all of us Pompeii dead gathered together
in the Bayou. Believe me,
what else could this be but the Judgment Day?
Look at it this way,
ain't we been floating downstream all our lives?
Here at the end, that Old Devil River,
he just gave us the extra push.
Old boy, he snuck into our boneyard

and pried us loose, popped us up and out
and pitched us into the black night.
Coffins carried along by the current.
Yessir, it all comes back to us, don't it?
Can't you hear your Mama and Papa
and every old schoolmarm you ever had say it?
Life ain't no free lunch.
Little did they know that Death ain't
no peanut butter sandwich, neither.
But Death could be free public transportation.
Whoa, we just sailed along,
the old Devil rushing us,
riding fast and free,
us heading south, trying to navigate
around boulders and dams and
the wrecks we've made of our lives.
Now, I've been a low-livered,
moonshine-shimmying hell-raiser all my life,
but never too drunk to steer.
The lucky ones: we coasted right on into New Orleans.
King and Queen of Cajun Country.
Mumbo-jumbo-gumbo.
And all that jazz. *Ha-ha-ha.*
The unlucky ones: why their coffins became
runaways beached on sandbars or
hitting snags and busting into a billion bits.
Those guys didn't have a chance,
dropping down to become a meal for the catfish.
Fiends of the fathoms.
So long, fellas.
Regrets?
My only regret is we're hitting
the Apocalypse on the off-season.
Great goblins, now I never figured the end
would come in Voodoo Land.
Not this morass of a marshland,

this stinking, sinking swamp.
If we're going to rise up again,
you'd a thought the good Lord at least
could've launched us from solid ground.
And why in the middle of the summer
when we're all dripping with so much sweat
that we're flooding the river,
fixing it to rise even more?
Why not Mardi Gras?
You know, with the parades
and people carousing the streets
all dressed up in masks and such,
the band playing
When the Saints Come Marching In.
Next day, ashes on the forehead.
Remember, man, you was dust once't,
and you damn well will be again.
Now, ain't that more like it?
Not a horn, not a clarinet, not a trombone
or bass drum in sight in this quagmire.
A shame. Well, I suppose we ain't nothing
to toot about, but just the same . . .
Folks, we'll forge ahead without no accompaniment—
rich and poor, men, women and children,
Protestant, Catholics and Jews,
tall and short alike.
For tonight in this bog
we is equal in sorrow.
We is equal in woe,
for the Mississippi has washed over all
and stripped us to the bone,
bones that never rise again
'cept out of the mouths of gators.
Yessir, we gave our bodies to the earth
but the earth didn't save us.
The worms crawl in,

the worms crawl out,
the worms play pinochle on our snouts.
The Old Devil River lapped at the banks,
lapped at the sandbags
and bashed again and again at the levee
until Joshua fit the battle of Jericho
and the walls came tumbling down.
The levees.
These are the walls of dirt,
the walls of our blessed labor,
piled up higher and higher each year.
Silt, loam, clay—
nothing can keep the Devil out.
Each time, we built the walls back up again,
no matter what the cost,
no matter what the pain.
Why don't we just move the whole town?
The Devil already done that for us,
changed the lay of the land.
Why, one year we lived in Missouri,
the next Ioway,
then thank the stars above,
I think the next we was back
in the Show Me state where you
could still buy liquor by the drink.
Old Beelzebub, he turns our world upside down.
Last spring, he sent a season more full
of rain and mud and *crackle-dee-pop-siss* lightning
than any we'd ever seen.
All the calves was born
in one downpour or another,
most just too soggy to suck.
That's right, didn't know their mother's teat
from an old broken-off limb of a tree.
Why, the wind would blow
and the branches would break,

and hell's bells, down would come
baby, cradle and all.
Well, I knowed a guy had two prize bulls.
One got struck by lightning, see,
and the other come down with
Post Traumatic Stress or some such.
The second bull, why, he couldn't stand it
without his buddy. Got real depressed,
hanging his head down and all.
Then whenever another storm hit,
lightning or no,
he'd snort through his nose ring
and leap over the fence,
charging around the whole neighborhood,
pawing the ground and looking
real mean toward anything that moved.
My friend goes looking for his bereaved bull
to shoo him home, *toro, toro,* hoping against hope
that critter don't run him through with his horns.
Now, this same fella
took and sold off that deranged bull
and set up a string of farrowing sows
in little huts right there in the same field.
Was that dumb.
But this fella just couldn't figure the rains'd
keep up the way they done.
Well, if he weren't tetotaciously exflunctified.
Down came the rain, up rose the creek
that weren't never more than a drop
of spit before. Great goblins,
up rose that creek and washed away
them huts with all them little piggies inside.
You could huff and you could puff
and you could blow them huts down
but the last little piggy would never go
wee-wee-wee all the way home.

So long, fellas.
Another guy, he lost it all—
house, dog, and the junk
he'd piled up in his garage,
not nothing left but a cave of mud
where his house once was.
He sets hisself down in a boat
and starts rowing, rowing through
the cornfields out of town
toward the Kwik 'N E Z.
He woulda rowed all day
and rowed all night if he didn't
get hisself hung up on an old outhouse.
There his boat stopped,
dead in the water,
not going nowheres,
but the guy, he just kept rowing,
rowing and rowing.
Finally, a couple of his sons come along.
Daddy. Let's go home, Daddy.
Ain't got no home. Kids ain't got no shoes. Wife
ain't got a pot to cook in.
Let's go, Daddy.
I ain't got a pot to pee in.
Daddy. . .
Everything's under water, everything I ever
believed in.
Daddy. . .
Everything I ever loved.
Let's go, Daddy. . .
The other boy, he fingers a cigarette,
puts it in his mouth and searches for matches.
But when he pulls them out of his pocket,
they's all wet.
Daddy. You got a lighter, Daddy?
That's about all I got. That's about all I got.

Old Satan River, he broke our hearts.
He broke our backs, and this time around,
he damn near broke our spirits, too.
Great goblins, I stand here before you, folks,
reviewing my life, and I sees that I stood up
to worse things. I stood up to everybody
calling me midget and runt and squirt.
I stood up to everybody patting me
on the head like a six year old.
Coochie, coochie, coo.
Why, onc't I even stood up to
Whiskey Jack and his crew.
That's right.
Big seven foot tall Jack
who floated down on a raft from up north.
Kraut with long flowing blonde hair.
Samson of Wisconsin.
Well, Jack, he thought he could outwit
Eddy, see, and one day he and his boys
anchored in near the café.
They're real thirsty but ain't got no money.
Finally, one of the crew comes in and slaps
down a whopping big catfish on the counter,
asks if I'd make a trade for a beer.
Seemed like an okay deal to me,
and real nice-like, he says
he'll take the catfish on back to the kitchen.
He takes the fish on back to the kitchen, all right,
but I don't see him keep going
out the door where there's another guy waiting
to pick up the fish and start the whole thing again.
Will you trade this whopper for a beer?
Sure.
Well, this keeps up until I got Jack
and his whole crew drunk
before my very eyes.

Then I goes back into the kitchen
expecting to find a whole mess of catfish.
When I only sees one, I'm mad,
madder than that loony bull without his buddy.
I slips out the back, cuts the cord
on Jack's raft and it goes *rock-a-bye-bye* downstream.
Then I goes back into the café
and serves up another round of beers.
It's on the house, boys. It's just a pleasure to do
business with you.
Well, Jack and his crew, they gets so soused
they's slopping and sliding over the table,
and I sneaks up behind Samson of Wisconsin
with my knife and cuts his hair.
That's right, the pygmy gives the giant a pixie
and returns him to the Philistines.
Ladies and gentlemen,
in this life, we cannot lie down
and pretend we're dead.
We must rise up,
rise up out of our coffins,
out of the damp chains of this swamp
and keep rowing.
Even on the Judgment Day,
we must keep rowing,
no matter how futile it may seem.
We must keep rowing
with a destination in mind.
We must know that we will come again
and that justice will reign supreme.
We must know that even if we gets
hung up on the outhouse,
we can, if we tries hard enough,
make it to the Kwik 'N E Z.
Today, the rains will stop.
The piglets will come home to roost,

and the Whiskey Jacks of this world
will have buzz cuts.
Keep the faith, folks.
Today, the lame shall walk,
the meek shall inherit the earth,
and the dwarves shall tower over
Old Devil River, Old Beelzebub,
Old Satan of the Mighty Mississippi.
So long, fellas.

Mary Swander was appointed Poet Laureate of Iowa in 2009. She is the author of over ten books of poetry and non-fiction. She is a Distinguished Professor of Liberal Arts and Sciences at Iowa State University.

MARVIN
BELL
IOWA

This Library

A library is where they live—words that burn
or freeze, cajole and tease, that sound of
barks, bawls, hollers, whispers, mutters,
and storms. Here you may hear a fish sing,
observe a man walk a ladder over a gorge
to reach a summit, or meet a woman who
discovered radium. There is dancing in the stacks
you cannot see except in your mind's eye.
Socrates teaches, Aristotle studies, and Marco Polo
departs for Asia. Where is the Caribbean? Who
was X? How many tribes of Native Americans
lived here? Who are you? How many languages
are left? How many species? I hear whispering
among the shelves that sounds like, "How about
this one?" and, at the front desk, a hopeful
"How long may I keep it?" May this our library
prosper, for life without it would be smaller.

*"This Library" was commissioned by the Iowa City Library Board to
commemorate the expansion of the library in 2004.*

Writers in a Café
- Iowa City, Iowa, U.S.A.

Amid semi-trailers hauling produce
grown in the deep blue-black topsoil
left mid-country by an inexpressible Ice Age,
there is known to be a place where words
have dirt on their shoes. Where sky reaches
to girdle the globe, the earth is etched
by signs and portents. Many have bowed
to their writing in attics and basements,
at rest by the river or paused on a bridge,
in the shadow of winter or eclipse, voicing
local lives and affairs of state—as much by
the reflections of leaves and the glow
of prairie grasses left to live in the mind
as by shapes in clouds or the dark news.
They were here who made the sentence
behave and misbehave, who added
chapter and verse, and recast the myths.
The café grows quiet as they write.
The espresso machine lets go the steam
someone may write in on the mirror.
It is an impulse that survives disaster.
The guns fail when surrounded by writing.

"Writers in a Café" was commissioned to accompany the petition of Iowa City in 2008 to be designated a Creative City of Literature by UNESCO.

The Case for the Arts and Humanities

We begin with the body, our instrument.
We begin with the limbs and torso of a dancer,
the cadenced breath, the voice of a poet,
the eye and dextrous hand of a painter,
the sculptor's skin against sculptor's clay,
the ear where melody and harmony play.
Our long discourse is corporeal, be it
of philosophy or society, law or the psyche,
events physical or metaphysical.
We know by how a thing smells, we learn
by sweet and sour, by rough and smooth,
by every common sense, and by heart, too,
and by brain, that soft-tough muscle,
wherein we seek those truths beyond our Age.
While warships move slowly and world events
sway our conscience and pain our hearts,
let us think what we shall leave to entropy.
We who use the world must revisit it.
Let our works, like our words, express in time
the truth of our nature, for good or bad,
for the jury is out and the foreman has asked
for a fully detailed, illuminated transcript.

"The Case for the Arts and Humanities" was commissioned by Humanities Iowa in celebration of the State of Iowa's "Year of Arts, Culture and Recreation" and the University of Iowa's "Year of the Arts and Humanities," July, 2004 to July, 2005.

Marvin Bell served two terms as Iowa's first poet laureate. His 19th and 20th books are *Mars Being Red* and *7 Poets, 4 Days, 1 Book*—the latter, co-authored by poets from five countries. His next three will be *Vertigo: The Living Dead Man Poems*, from Copper Canyon Press in 2011; *Whiteout*, a collaboration with the photographer Nathan Lyons, from Lodima; and a children's picture book, from Candlewick Press, based on his poem, "A Primer about the Flag." A song cycle, "The Animals," commissioned by the composer David Gompper, premiered in 2009. Long on the faculty of the Iowa Writers' Workshop, he teaches now for the brief-residency MFA based in Oregon at Pacific University and lives in Iowa City and Port Townsend, Washington.

ROBERT DANA
IOWA

A Short History of the Middle West

Under this corn,
these beans,
these acres of tamed grasses,

the prairie still rolls,

heave and trough,
breaker and green curl,

an ocean of dirt tilting and tipping.

Its towns
toss up on the distance, your distance,
like the wink

of islands.

And the sky
is a blue voice
you cannot answer for.

The forked and burning wildflowers
that madden
the ditches
nod without vocabulary.

Your neighbor
is out early this morning—the air
already humid as raw diamond.

Drunk or lonely,
he's scattering large scraps of white
bread for the birds

as if it were winter.

He'd give you the sour undershirt off
his back—
sweet, bad man.

Does he remember
rain salting down from that flat, far shore
of clouds

slowly changing
its story?

On this shore,
the trees all babbling with their hands?

The Morning of the Red Admirals

for D & L

We saw them first
    last evening—two,
spiralling up,
    a column of late
sunlight, then,
    tilting away
from each other
    in a floating stagger
through the early
    summer leaves—
a jittery dipping,
    dropping, rising—
one coming
    to rest a moment
on the still warm
    roof of our fat
pagoda lantern,
    the other on weathered
deck rail;
    the tips of its
long antennae
    beaded and bright;
wings black,
    white dot
and blue dot,
    and barred aslant
with orange red,
    laid flat,
then clicking shut
    to dull grey sail,
then opening again.

Now, it's morning;
        You've gone to work.
The air gleams,
        dry and clear,
almost Greek,
        and a half dozen
admirals sip
        from the lilac blossoms,
still signalling
        their unsayable
story. One
        lights on my shoulder
as I hang the day's
        laundry on the line,
shirts and drawers,
        dull socks,
our flapping colors
        answering his.
He's weightless,
        this migrant—
a small, wild
        scrap of grace—
and I'm his resting
        post on the way
to whatever far
        edge of creation
breathes at the tips
        of his wings.

Starting Out for the Difficult World

This morning, once again,
I see young girls with
their books and clarinets
starting out for the difficult
world. The wind has turned
into the north. It picks a few
leaves from the trees, leaves
already curled, some brown.
They scatter. Even so, their
circles under maple and hack-
berry thicken. The light,
clean as juice to the taste.

Great art, someone said,
rides on the backs of the poor.
Perhaps that's so. But this
is not Long Island. No packed
white waves leap yelping on the shore.
Here, the nights are cold and starry.
Three solitary clouds pig along
the near horizon. And you could
mistake this autumn for Keats's
or your own, or the
autumn of someone you once knew.

Chimes

Mid-August. Evening. Rain falling.

Cold, bright silk where the street fronts the house.

Out back, it laves and slicks the parched leaves of the trees.
Ragged hang of summer's end.

I lean against the doorway of the poem,
listening to the old patter.

My cat, Zeke, lays himself out imperially.
Eleven pounds of grey smoke
                with tufted ears and a curved plume of tail.

Now, a slight wind,
and The Emperor of Heaven's chimes intone like distant bells,
his court musician's 4000-year-old pentatonic scale
                     pealing in slow, clear ripples.

Occasionally, a chord.

Every day I live I live forever.

Robert Dana was born in Boston in 1929. After serving in the South Pacific at the
end of World War II, he moved to Iowa where he attended Drake University and The
University of Iowa Writers' Workshop. Dana was appointed Poet Laureate for the State
of Iowa 2004 through 2008. His poetry has won several awards, including The Delmore
Schwartz Memorial Award from New York University and two National Endowment
for the Arts Fellowships. He revived and edited *The North American Review* in the sixties

and also operated The Hillside Press. Retired from teaching after forty years as Poet-in-Residence at Cornell College, he also served as visiting writer at Stockholm and Beijing universities and at a number of American colleges and universities. Among his ten books of poetry and three of prose are: *New & Selected Poems: 1955 to 2010* (Anhinga 2010), *The Morning of the Red Admirals* (Anhinga, 2004), and *Starting Out for the Difficult World* (Harper & Row, 1987). He died in February, 2010, of pancreatic cancer.

CARYN MIRRIAM-GOLDBERG
KANSAS

The Dreaming Land

I dream of spring, when the sky dampens
the seeds of gathering heat, the diving crow
aims toward what was just born, and
even the driveway gravel glitters in the stark
white light between storm and night.
I dream of the winter's black-and-white landscape
scribbled green, punctured by the maroon tip of root
in a field cleaned black with fire while
the cottonwoods unfurl their pale green hearts.

This land dreams sky, a shifting infusion
of shadow on cloud, despite the unreliability
of rain or clarity. The deer dream fawns.
The fawns dream flight as they walk the through-line
of the horizon. The horizon never stops dreaming,
its sleep a progression of filtering color through space.

The dream always dreams possibility
juxtaposed against decay, lightning, first
redbud blossom or starling feather stuck on a rooftop.
The rooftop dreams, belly up, to the sky,
its dream a song of shelter and risk.

The sky dreams light rolling away from dark,
dark rolling away from light, expansive as sorrow
that permeates the porous souls of everything
from weather to the dog left alone in the living room
while I step outside into the dizzy of bird call,
flocks pouring down onto branches
swollen with the hard dreams of blossom.

Just-Doing-That Moon

The cupboards licked clean by grief,
I open the front door anyway.
Ice wind, hot sun – too much or too little.
I close the door.

Give me an hour, and the cupboards
fill again with cans and boxes ready
to warm the belly, add weight
to the thin blue glass dinner plates
while the wind turns balmy,
the sky seamlessly white,
both of which scour the ground
which wants something planted
but not just yet.

Close my eyes, the dreams bleed
and quicken, just like this March weather:
a rush overhead as if the bare sycamore
is a canopy of faces, all the ancestors
at their tea party. Open my eyes,
and I can't remember anything
but this old dog grief, chasing rabbits
in his sleep, always hungry.

When I open the night door to the
Just-doing-that moon, I forget all but
the surprise of snow at midnight
that falls so lightly, it can rest on
the lip of the first daffodil.

Downward Dog

I do not like you, downward dog.
I see right through your resting pose status
to how you're just wind trying to keep
steady in the enveloping storm,
you supposed triangle, you landing base
that keeps climbing through variegated
fears of dying. Turn my pelvis upside down
and bring whatever rusting squirrels
spring from the center of my body
back to the mama spine.
Stop biting the undersides of my earnest
knuckles, the pads of my feet, my forearms
straining toward failure. You think
I can't tell what you're doing with me
between those graceful planks and sullen child poses?
Between the heat from what hurts most in close
or far-off memory and the humidity of this moment?
Between the leaf falling outside the lines
of this pose and these walls, and the weather
that keeps going to the downward dogs?

Oh, downward dog, scatter me high and low,
here and there, breathing unsteady as a lost flock
caught in an abrupt wind, and wherever you take me,
get me back to the forgiving mat ready to exhale
peonies out of their knotty buds, and then
do it all over again.

Self-Portrait as Pond

I turn my back and a million wings
shiver across my surface. I stop
but the beveling echo doesn't.
I float a half-brown leaf as if
I'm made of open hands.
I hold myself quiet where
the sand parts, each molecule
a tiny ocean, and the old fish sleep
cooled by the blank sheets of
my moving bottom. Nothing not
in motion, I'm as fearless as
the weather I mirror and distort.
I'm as rough as any old fighter
half asleep who jolts up swinging.
Don't cross me. I can outrun you
even in the stillest air and all the
trembling swirls on white fire.
I eat wind and breathe out crossing
angles of passing memory. Don't forget
I am perfectly set in the center
of whoever you think you are.

In the End, There Is Only Kindness

for Gene

When the floor slips and the time comes,
when interventions falter, there is only kindness,
a lantern to hold at journey's end, then hand over
so someone else can lift the light enough
to illuminate where to step next, and how.

In this kindness, there are always stories:
Telling the checker who rang up his milk twice,
don't worry, everyone makes mistakes.
His long wait among aging magazines at the VA
so a homeless vet could get his medication.
Gravel on our walkway because he didn't want
us slipping when we brought home the new baby.
Jokes about being old and decrepit while he
cooked everyone dinner. How he power-rocked
the babies to sleep, his heart beating through theirs.
Christmas stockings and grandchildren to wake up early,
coins to collect for each one. Oxygen in one hand,
a cane in the other so he could see a grandchild
in orchestra or band, graduation or swim meet
even when his back and memory hurt.
The dishes or long drives, reaching for the check,
and taking the time to greet the stranger eating alone.
Only kindness matters in the circle of love
he made out of this world.

In the end, there is always the beginning,
a seamless turn from here to there
even if everything is different from
the irreplaceable loss shining and aching at once,
a kind of river running alongside our lives,
or weather reminding us that
we love, were loved by a man here only
for kindness, which is not just a kind of love
but the only love there is.

Self-Portrait as Grown-Up

They said this would happen.
Clothing would stay and not go. Cars
would break down or hit other cars.
Boys would become men, and men would not
return calls. Sex would become a declaration,
then a sport, then a minefield, then not anything
static enough to be named. Touch would be too much
or not enough, what to wear would be as existential
as weeding gardens or jump-starting cars, and
dark chocolate would eclipse milk chocolate.
In the morning, she would become the waker-upper
instead of the one woken. In the afternoons,
coffee would be needed along with many distractions
falling across the rooms and cubicles like
early autumn leaves. Money would change
from something needed for the swim club
to a magician's hat that never holds enough rabbits.
Dusk would become night, dishes would be done
or heavy with remnants of animated conversations.
But dreams wouldn't move out of the child house,
a dead father would still be arguing with her
that she said something she didn't and wouldn't,
and when awake again, walking down the street,
stopping to lean on a tree to tie her wild shoelace,
she would still be all the concentric circles at once.

The Last Moment

On the corner, the accordion player
infuses the humid night with a darkness
sweet and grieving in perfect hue
with the green neon fish two stories up, over the bar,
you crossing the street, a nighthawk diving,
and the cobalt blue of the sky, almost turquoise
at the edges of a leafy horizon.

This is your town on a hot June night.
You reach the other side, turn away
from the swaying musician and tattered linden tree.
Down the block, you see only one room lit
at the top of the loft apartment building;
in that room, a potted ficus tree and a chair
someone may or may not be sitting in.
You turn toward the alley, aim yourself
between decay and limestone,
stairs on one side, blue dumpster on the other.
A breeze pours down from the rooftops, and
you realize this could be the last moment
you remember, decades from now, as you lean
into death or stop leaning away.

This could be the line between the life you've lived
and the life you will live as you step across
the parking lot, toward your husband and sons,
already in the car with the new books
you will have long read and forgotten
by the time this is a memory,
by the time so many you love are gone,
so many you don't yet imagine are here.

You reach for the car door to join
the present, the blue chord of your life,
the pulse of time and music,
the quick fire, the wide water of home.

Caryn Mirriam-Goldberg was named Poet Laureate of Kansas for the years 2009-2012 by then-governor Kathleen Sebelius. She is the author of 10 books, including the memoir *The Sky Begins At Your Feet: A Memoir on Cancer, Community and Coming Home to the Body* (Ice Cube Books, 2009); four collections of poetry, *Landed* (Mammoth Publications, 2009), *Animals in the House* (Woodley Press, 2004), *Reading the Body* (Mammoth Publication, 2004), and *Lot's Wife* (Woodley Press, 1999); *Write Where You Are* (Free Spirit Press, 1988), and several anthologies. Her poetry and prose have appeared in dozens of literary magazines, and anthologies. She founded Transformative Language Arts – a master's level concentration in social and personal transformation through the spoken, written and sung word – at Goddard College, where she teaches. She also facilitates writing workshops for many populations, and, with Kelley Hunt, singing and writing workshops through their business, Brave Voice. Caryn's songs, co-written with Kelley Hunt, have been performed by Hunt on Prairie Home Companion, and around the world. A founding member of the Kansas Area Watershed Council, the Continental Bioregional Congress, and the Transformative Language Arts Network, Caryn makes her home south of Lawrence, Kansas, with her husband, the ecological author Ken Lassman, and their children, Daniel, Natalie and Forest.

DENISE LOW
KANSAS

Kene: Bald Eagle

For Buddy Weso
        "O day and night, but this is wondrous strange!" Horatio (Hamlet)

My grandmother said we travel to stars
when we die. This dawn a bonfire hisses
blue flames against banked snow
guiding Uncle's journey from life
to unknown sky. Clouds obscure
heaven's embers. Around us white pines
collect tears from the driving wind

Across the Wolf River a faint cry
and someone says *"kene"* just as softly
so I barely pick out both the bird's sound
and the spoken Algonquin word
from the burning, breaking splinters
and explosion of popping orange sparks—
familiar fireplace sounds I recognize—

but just as quickly I doubt soft voices
until again, in full daylight, the sound *"kene."*

Two Gates

I look through glass and see a young woman
of twenty, washing dishes, and the window
turns into a painting. She is myself thirty years ago.
She holds the same blue bowls and brass teapot
I still own. I see her outline against lamplight;
she knows only her side of the pane. The porch
where I stand is empty. Sunlight fades. I hear
water run in the sink as she lowers her head,
blind to the future. She does not imagine I exist.

I step forward for a better look and she dissolves
into lumber and paint. A gate I passed through
to the next life loses shape. Once more I stand
squared into the present, among maple trees
and scissor-tailed birds, in a garden, almost
a mother to that faint, distant woman.

American Robin

Nothing would give up life:
Even the dirt kept breathing a small breath.
　　　—Theodore Roethke

Cold sun brings this mourning season to an end—
One year since my mother's death. Last winter thaw
my brother shoveled clay-dirt, she called it gumbo,
over what the crematorium sent back. Not her,

but fine powdery substance, lightened, all else
rendered into invisible elements. That handful
of a pouch, un-boxed, was tucked into plotted soil,
the churchyard columbarium, a brass plaque the only

permanence, and the brick retaining wall. So finally
my mother is a garden, day lilies and chrysanthemums
feeding from that slight, dampened, decomposing ash.
Her voice stilled. One ruddy robin in the grass, dipping.

Anniversary

One perfect mallard
doubling itself
in afternoon reflection,

two curved heads dabbling
reappearing, disappearing
into water-bowl lake:

slide and blur
until just the tails
touch, tip, shatter,

Dear, like us
two images folded
into a single pose

slipped into dark
earth's rest
held only by breath

until to awaken
to kiss and uncover
two touching, touched skins.

Buried City

1.
Spiro Mounds. A buzzard
slides into clouds like a ghost
and then returns to our view.

We read the guidebook:
"Imagine a living city
with children and running dogs."

But around us: silence.
The plaza is a broken surface
empty of ball players.

A spring warbler pierces
churring wind while off trail
we leave tobacco offerings.

Then among mole diggings
a chipped black stone appears
and a flat black plume:

the living earth raising
dark forms even now
into balance of the sky.

2.
Over the ridge, tucked
into its final roll
lies an armadillo—

its shell patterned
with lozenges and diamonds,
tiered and sectioned—

like patterns etched

on conch shells, on copper,
on dugout canoes, on pipes.

It lies on an earthen bier,
ornamented in gray armor
motionless to our eyes

but it travels through grass
to the buried city beneath us
hidden from daylight.

3.
What lies below:

> blankets of buffalo yarn,
> Mexican parrot feathers,
> capes of turkey plumes,
> sunflower seeds, maize,

> charcoal smell of cookfires,
> echoes of clackers and rattles,
> low voices and lullabies,
> a child's first breath.

Lotus Garden

The fetid ponds
turn magical: pads
overlap silk-floss knots
of buds, striped cerise,
and then one arises—
a Buddha figurine
come to life within.

Minnows flutter
inside dank shallows,
and eddies where bass
attack water striders
and fall back, turtles
raise question-mark necks,
and herons dip beaks—
the cacophony of feeders
under parasol leaves.

Lily roots seek
the anchor of mud
and spew sap upward
into explosion of silk,
each bloom a quiet saint.

Golden Triangle Elephant

Alone the mammoth animal steps
shoulder first down the soft mountain,
padded feet braced against muddy gravity.
The Grand Canyon mule trails
have switchbacks but this elephant
walks straight down the mounded height.
My son tells me it is a hotel elephant,
let loose to forage, but it looks wild,
ranging alone, a bull. Banana trees cover
the incline, not granite or basalt
or tilted sediment. No fences. We could
run into it.
          The elephant is deliberate
like a bulldozer. It plans each
move like a driver turning sharp curves.
It knows exactly the next twist, the heft
of its weight, the angle of descent.
It is a huge piece of furniture
moving itself, a wardrobe maybe,
in a house of corners and thin doors.
The flaring ears are Victorian ornament.
It faces us a hundred feet away,
drifts sideways into waves of leaves
so high they enfold the gray giant,
the close clouds, the rims of far mountains.

Denise Low, Kansas 2007-2009 Poet Laureate, has 20 books of poetry and essays, including *Natural Theologies: Essays on Literature of the Middle Plains; Words of a Prairie Alchemist: Essays; Ghost Stories of the New West,* and *Thailand Journal: Poems,* a *Kansas City Star* notable book. *Three Voices* is a text, image, and videography project. She is vice president of and a board member of the Associated Writers & Writing Programs. She has taught creative writing at Haskell Indian Nations University, the University of Kansas, and the University of Richmond. Awards are from the Academy of American Poets, The Newberry Library, Lannan Foundation, and National Endowment for the Humanities.

JONATHAN HOLDEN
KANSAS

Tornado Symptoms

As you step outdoors you'll enter a hot barn
with a moist haystack inside.
The cardinals will dart like embers, *pierce*
pierce your nerves with their bent sabres.
You'll be intimate with traffic for miles around.
But if you look up where the twigs
all stiffly point, you'll see silent
pandemonium, ugly rumors,
vagrant clouds loitering at loose ends.
It's a schizophrenic air.

By supper the sky will be uprooted,
a garden hopelessly gone to seed.
Gray broccoli will float by disconnected
from the ground, fat sooty toadstools,
a species you've never seen before,
will sprout beside swollen fungi
and other gray growths, strange weeds trailing
their severed roots, flowers the color
of bad bruises just opening into blossom,
slowly moving areas of combustion.
Even cauliflower as it rolls past
will be misshapen
before the forest comes.

Shoptalk

I like this low, comfortable kind
of conversation which the rain's
been having with itself all day
as it goes about its business,
deftly assembling its tiny parts,
confident, in no great hurry,
discussing, perhaps, the different
gutters it has seen, the taste of rust
in New York, the rust in Chicago.
Or perhaps comparing notes
about the finer points of roofs,
where best to creep to find
flaws in asphalt shingles,
or maybe it's murmuring in rain-jargon
over different grades of redwood,
the rate they rot. No end of stories
that it could be telling—
the drudgery of cycling in a monsoon,
monotony of equatorial assignments,
the same steamy party each afternoon.
Or maybe the gossip's of some great
typhoon, the melee of another
grand convention. Or is it muttering
about the way some thunderstorms
rig their elections, the social
life of rain in some bayou,
as the rain keeps up its quiet
shoptalk—the level, reassuring
talk of people who are comfortable
again, sure what they're doing,
graceful in their work, and accurate,
serious in the way that rain
is serious,
given over to their task
of touching the world.

Kansas Fair

Sorefooted, sunburnt, I escape
the hot pelt of the crowd for a little
shade, to watch from the sidelines
people trading places. A baby,
eyes bugging, bobs by in its knapsack.
An old couple, in pursuit
of something severe and private,
hesitate, then find their narrow
seam through the traffic.
And as I sit there, pulled
by the argument of every smell—
cigar smoke, french fries, suntan oil—
by the whole, complex, bittersweet
scent of the gathered human—I wonder
what it would take to convert
these farm hands with mustard streaks
on their beards, so they might believe
in history. A scuffle? An explosion?
The helicopter, a dark locust swarm
spinning down over the trees?
I do not believe in one history,
but that among us the believers
are the dangerous ones.
Their minds are elsewhere.
When they eye a crowd from the side
they are counting the bodies.
And that it's lucky to be in the shade,
to be so prodigally bored,
resting one's feet, certain that
all this afternoon and the next, nothing
important will happen.

Western Meadowlark

Through the open car window
seven needles in a haystack
BoPEEP-doodle-our-PEOple!
snatched by ear out of the moving
prairie, like you
already fading, passed, gone.
BoPEEP-doodle-our-PEOple!
If I could find it, it would be
points of sunlight glancing
off a brooch so near shades
of gold in these moving
grasses I could scarcely distinguish
it from the grasses. Like you
it is always gone.

BoPEEP-doodle-our-PEOple!
The bird pulled it off like a string
of catches on this flying
trapeze which keeps swinging
back. If birds' songs simply mean
I'm here! I'm here!
then why a song so baroque?
How many notes did it have?
Which notes were extra?

In the Beatles' "Blackbird"
you again hear a meadowlark, its song
canned as the slow-motion replay
of a pass-reception on TV:
Love studied into pornography,
Bo-PEEP-diddle-diddle-her-PEEP-hole!
The bird falls off a see-saw,

hesitates, picks itself
back up on the rising board,
completes its song.
It does it again.

I prefer the song that eludes me,
this one which we are passing,
banjo wind and distance
already falling behind

gone and not gone.

—*for Ana*

Jonathan Holden was the first Poet Laureate of Kansas, serving from 2005-07. His book *The Sublime* won the 1995 Vassar Miller Prize in Poetry; *Against Paradise* won the 1989 Utah Competition; *The Names of the Rapids* won the 1985 Juniper Prize; *Leverage* was co-winner of the 1983 AWP Award Series for Poetry; and *Design for a House* won the 1972 Devins Award. Holden is also the recipient of a National Endowment for the Arts Creative Writing Fellowship and numerous other awards. He teaches at Kansas State University.

BETSY SHOLL
MAINE

Belmullet

To see where I came from, I'm looking at stones,
at *Johns* and *Marys*, at twenty-eight *Nearys*
in a County Mayo graveyard, each with a pot
of primroses, a plot with white chips of gravel.

If the Irish love talk, my family's silence
seemed to ask, Who wants to go back
to rotten potatoes and patched-up boats,
horse thievery and peat? Who needs long roots

and old wars? Those sealed lips clearly said,
Better to shrug it all off, scrap the sod
from your boots and glad hand the new world,
let mild winds drift above gravity's grip.

But what wind doesn't come from elsewhere?
Now that those *Nearys* are nearly gone,
and there's no one to ask whose history
is swelling my knuckles, crimping my face,

I want to be part of a line tethered somewhere,
if only by sea swells, by gusts I love best
when they batter. So I stand among stones
cut deep with my name, not knowing

if the bones rusting here in this ground
are related. But since my family left

no word, I tell these *Nearys*, if they'll have me,
I'd be pleased to be ghosted by them

in their wellies and wool, their prayer beads
and pints, their eyes creased by sea glitter
and those minor chords with bent notes
piercing the soul. I'd be pleased

to root myself in this town where tides rise
and sink into sludge, this river mouth littered
with bike frames, clumps of mussels,
and plastic paint buckets—my roots in this junk

the water will nudge and cover again,
as it pours through the inlet, swirling with foam.
Is this where I come from? I kneel down
to finger the gouged letters and half-think,

half-say to this long line of *Marys* and *Johns*,
these twenty-eight *Nearys*: If we all come
to the same end, surely it's not just malarkey
and lark song spiraling up, then plummeting

silently down, surely by sun glint and gull,
by that long ago swallowed sadness,
by sea gut and gravel and wind-wild sky,
these stones that name you name me as well.

Elegy with Spiders

Across the fields, like a troop of gypsies
hundreds of spiders lay out their wares.
And if there is music in those strings,
if we could hear them sing, maybe one
would step forward to ask in plaintive voice,

"Why are we so despised, when night
after night we spin the world,
retie its threads—night after night
reweave the morning you'll walk through,
never noticing what filaments you break?"

For weeks after my friend had taken
his life, I couldn't shake his nightmares
still coiled in my phone, his red shirt,
sad eyes, his green car disappearing
around curve after curve, awake or asleep,

until the morning those spiders reeled me
to the field's edge where they were camped,
basking in early light, having spun all night
their bright God's eyes. I didn't know
God had so many, that the world was faceted

with such brilliant corners endlessly
improvised, so many marvelous sectors
and slots, intricate mazes, airy prisms
beaming the day's first light from stalk to stalk—
which soon the farmer will plow under, yes,

and before that, the three rowdy shepherds
will race through, tearing the gauzy threads.
But what those spiders said to me,
as they set in motion their hundreds
of silken gears, and filled the valley

with eyes, on that one October morning
as the sun rose above Stone Mountain,
was all about this making and remaking,
casting lines to shape the invisible air,
so for all the damage, not everything is lost.

Lullaby in Blue

Now the child takes her first journey
through the inner blue world of her mother's body,
blue veins, blue eyes, frail petal lids.

Beyond that unborn brackish world so deep
it will be felt forever as longing, a dream
of blue notes plucked from memory's guitar,

the wind blows indigo shadows under streetlights,
clouds crowd the moon and bear down on the limbs
of a blue spruce. The child's head appears,

midnight pond, weedy and glistening.
It draws back, reluctant to leave its first home.
Blue catch in the back of the mother's throat,

ferocious bruise of a growl, and out slides
the iridescent body—fish-slippery
in her father's hands, plucked from water

into such thin densities of air,
her arms and tiny hands stutter and flail,
till he places her on her mother's body,

then cuts the smoky cord, releasing her
into this world, its cold harbor below
where a blue caul of shrink-wrap covers

each boat gestating on the winter shore.
Child, the world comes in twos, above and below,
visible and unseen. Inside your mother's croon

there's the hum of an old man tapping his foot
on a porch floor, his instrument made from one
string nailed to a wall, as if anything

can be turned into song, always what is
and what is longed for. Against the window
   the electric blue of cop lights signals

somebody's bad news, and a lone man walks
through the street, his guitar sealed in dark plush.
   Child, from this world now you will draw your breath

and let out your moth flutter of blue sighs.
Now your mother will listen for each one,
   alert enough to hear snow starting to flake

from the sky, bay water beginning to freeze.
Sleep now, little shadow, as your first world
   still flickers across your face, that other side

where all was given and nothing desired.
Soon enough you'll want milk, want faces, hands,
   heartbeats and voices singing in your ear.

Soon the world will amaze you, and you
will give back its bird-warble, its dove call,
   singing that blue note which deepens the song,

that longing for what no one can recall,
your small night cry roused from the wholeness
   you carry into this broken world.

Night Vision

I thought city hall might be blown up, but not my street.
The bombs are smart, they can tell what's residential,
can find a building at night after its workers have gone,
just papers left to fly out of steel cages, wheeling like gulls,
only silent, no rusty hinge, no old fan belt of a cry.

I thought the courthouse's wood panels might be curled
by the heat, names of accused and accuser mingled in ash.
Maybe the police station, chunks of concrete collapsing
on the garage full of confiscated cars, thin plumes
of smoke rising through skeletal beams.

But not my street with its flower baskets,
its seven schools, two pizza shops, its butcher
selling gourmet food, its shoe repairs, its sewing shop
run by two Koreans. I didn't expect to see
lawns seared, porches charred, windows blown out,

our family portraits scattered on the street in pools
of water from the firefighters' anxious dousing.
I didn't expect people wailing, shaking their fists,
bent over limp children who'd been walking to school.
But I was wrong, wrong. None of this happened,

not here on this street, not downtown. None of it
occurred anywhere outside the green night lens
of my own troubled sleep's lit-up synapses,
my foolish dream which couldn't tell fear from truth,
could not distinguish between *here there us them.*

Betsy Sholl's seventh collection of poetry is *Rough Cradle.* Her previous collections include *Late Psalm* and *Don't Explain.* Her awards include the Felix Pollak Prize and the AWP Prize for Poetry. She is the recipient of grants from the NEA and the Maine Arts Commission, and was named Poet Laureate of Maine in 2006. She teaches at the University of Southern Maine and in the Vermont College of Fine Arts MFA in Writing Program.

DAVID CLEWELL
MISSOURI

Goodbye Note to Debbie Fuller: Pass It On

Whoever this Debbie Fuller is in your poems, she ought to
be collecting royalties. — a loyal reader

When we passed those notes to each other and laughed
behind Miss Jago's back in Hamilton School, we were flirting
with real danger. The secret insults and atonement
that passed for our friendship seemed effortless in cursive,
too easily could have become a part of our Permanent Record.
Those days we got away with more than we ever imagined,
so many ways of saying I'm sorry again, I won't do it
anymore, and I promise not to get you
into trouble from now on. As if we could help ourselves.

If I've named names under pressure in my life since then
in the late-night interrogation rooms of the heart,
if I've had to write out one more doctored confession,
give up on maintaining my innocence one more night
and your name is the one I keep coming back to,
I'll admit it: you're the alibi I've needed, the only one
who can place me miles and years away from the dried blood,
the chalked outline of childhood on the sidewalk. Otherwise
I'm looking at some serious hard time, and you know
I'll be taking you with me.

Say I fell hard for those dirty blonde bangs, those doleful eyes,
those corduroy skirts and OK, finally, even the way you moved
to Basking Ridge, New Jersey that December of '65
without breathing a word to anyone, not even to me
in the holiday assembly when I was the top of the wobbling
human Christmas tree and you placed that cardboard star on my head
with a kiss we never practiced in rehearsal.
How could you know what you were lighting up forever,
improvising one last piece of business that was nowhere
in the script? Maybe no one told you either,
or you didn't know how to say it. Maybe that day was
your rendition of uncanny grace under pressure.
I was ten and thought I knew everything
I could possibly want for Christmas for the rest of my life.

I wanted you earlier in the alphabet, or taller, depending
on any given day's meticulous instructions for lining up
on our way to whatever came next. My faintest hope was always
rained-out gym, huddled inside, boy-girl-boy-
girl for almost an hour, no questions asked. God, I wanted you
to realize how much it mattered too. Those were the days
before love knew its own name, almost before hormones
in their nervous skirmishes at the borders of wherever we were.

I don't know why, after so many years of everything
I've put you through in words—silent partner
in a thousand schemes, or worse, my unwitting accomplice—
you still keep coming back to me. As if it's been in your power
to refuse, as if you've had anything to say. I'll confess again:
I've used you, but I guess I'd like to think I haven't
used you up completely. So here's my promise at long last:
you won't have to get dressed on short notice, hurry out of a house
full of people who love you more for whatever you've become.
No more questions of *what do I wear* in this poem, *what
can he possibly want from me now?* I'll leave you alone
to look me up in your own quiet version of time.

And people who insist on reading this before it gets to you
can sigh and shake their heads if they want to, as long
as they keep it moving while the world drones on
through its baffling arithmetic, geography without end,
through its far-flung chalky sense of history
while the radiators hiss and the clock lops off another minute
you're too far away to whisper all this in your ear.
As long as they know this one's for Debbie Fuller,
for old times' sake, for all the good it does,
from the kid still making any promise he can get away with:
it won't happen again, I swear,
or your name's not Debbie Fuller. Debbie Fuller,
it won't ever happen again.

In Case of Rapture

Warning: in case of Rapture, this car will be unmanned.
     —bumper sticker

And with my usual brand of luck I'll be in the car
right behind, cursing, leaning on the horn, as always
getting nowhere fast. And this time the old man
so ubiquitous in his homburg will stop completely,
roll down the window, and slowly bail out of his Chevrolet
to join hands with a woman already rising above the corner bakery.
Say the word and there goes the entire fish-fry contingent
from the local Kingdom Hall, called home somewhere between grace
and potato salad until the sky's so full of old-time religion
broad daylight's common sense is utterly eclipsed.
In case of Rapture, I'll try not to stare. Clearly
these people can't help the way they suddenly appear.
Besides, looking directly at a spectacle like that
could mean going blind. These things always seem to happen
on the road to somewhere. Saul and his Damascus. Me and my A&P.

No wonder there's no shortage of preachers when you're driving,
more than ever occur to you on the radio at home.
Minutes from my nightcap at the Idle Hour I'm blessed:
we'll float upward just like helium balloons is the way
this gospel man guarantees me. The balloon's his idea
of a metaphor, but not the being lifted. That's belief itself,
more for what it is than what it's like: to be that literally
exalted, that assuredly lighthearted.
To have that much faith in the promise of thin air.

It isn't long before I'm leaning on the jukebox
and laughing it up with the regulars, telling them exactly
how I heard it, word for unbelievable word.
The guy shooting pool knows better, says he's here to testify:
no matter how many can't-miss shots he still has in him,
he's learned to count only on the money in his pocket right now,

believes even if the Rapture comes tonight, tomorrow's likely
to be just another day on the planet.
And after all, he's the man of old-fashioned science,
the professor of gravity. He figures what rises
has to fall sometime: the lazy fly to right,
whole civilizations, the balloon some kid attaches a note to
before she lets go, fully expecting it one day to come down
anywhere but in her own backyard. He chalks it up
to history, to how he's seen it happen so often
to even the slightest hope, genuine faith's fainter sister.

If he's turning a little too solemn, blame the serious drinking,
a lot of nights mostly like this one, waiting
for a stiff wind the spirit could positively soar in,
not so much like a bird or a bright-colored leaf or a kite
or a lighter-than-air balloon. Surely there is no comparison,
no way of saying what it's like. Metaphor is an assurance
we'll know something when we finally feel it,
but we could wait a lifetime for wind strong enough
to get that completely carried away.

* * *

For now it's clear skies. Not a soul in sight.
There's no illumination beyond the ordinary
light from stars that have made it this far through the dark,
not another car on the road. Maybe the Rapture's come
and gone while the good people lay home in their beds,
manning their dreams until they were roused way out of them.
Maybe they're already rising to some dimly imagined occasion,
and we who remain behind are finally left alone
to our own God-forsaken devices, wearing the conspicuous smiles
of the damned, the ones so far removed from any saving grace
that we might yet make a kingdom of it
here, in the rest of the only lives we can swear to.

I'd really like to leave it at that. I've got a cold six
pack in the icebox tonight, just in case of Rapture.
In case I feel the need to stay up late celebrating, not believing
I'd ever live out my days like the way-too-faithful,
ever carelessly mistake whatever isn't hell
for part of heaven: a glass of house brand whiskey,
a postcard in the mailbox, a car noise that I can actually make
my doubting mechanic hear. But there have been nights so long
the heart sputters, running on empty promises again,
and I've said whatever I've had to say, talking it up
on the chance I'd somehow rise above those nights, radiant, once
and for all. Be plucked from behind the sweaty wheel
of too many harrowing miles in a row. Be lifted clean away.

Driving home this far past midnight I'm not above conceding
there may be some goings-on in the boondocks of what's possible
that pass for the miraculous, no matter how inflated,
things that happen so far beyond words
there'd be simply no telling. Try
and you could end up looking wildly for all the world
like someone you'd never believe, even at high noon
with you and your down-to earth frustration right behind him,
watching him with your own eyes, undeniably floating
out of your life. And you'd have to insist it's nothing
you ever expected, not on those days you need to get through
in a hurry. Not when horns are blaring for miles
because suddenly you're the one inexplicably stalling,
holding everything up. It's your face, frantic, looking back
in the rear-view mirror. But no one else has any idea
what's next, exactly where you're supposed to go from here.

Wrong Number After Midnight

When I pick up, the voice on the other end is already off
and running: *You were right, man, you were so
incredibly right, and now I'm more than sorry I didn't believe you
when you claimed that the only way to keep their voices out of our heads
was by using heavy-duty aluminum foil, the kind
our own mothers were crazy for when it came to preparing leftovers
for their deep-freeze oblivion. You tried to tell me:
regular foil's too thin for making any kind of proper headgear—
a ponderous buffer-zone helmet, or something less obtrusive and more
stylish, say, a wave-deflecting beret. Next time I visit,
I'll be sure to bring enough of the extra-strength for us both.*

And although this sounds like something I certainly might have suggested—
perhaps only to my closest friends, it's true—it happens
that I didn't, and finally he stops to worry up a whisper: *This isn't
my friend Stuart, is it?* And I say *No,* and he says *Oh my God,
man, they've gone and gotten through to you, haven't they?* As if
he's the one who can't believe what he's hearing, who's never felt so
disconnected, standing in the middle of whatever room he's renting
in his suddenly less-than-accommodating life. There's no way
he can appreciate how accidentally he's reached me, how sympathetic
I really am—the one other person who might think it's worth trying,
this last-ditch defense against the aliens or the in-laws or those
frightening late-night infomercial people.
                                    It's after midnight again,
when everything that comes along is that much harder to resist,
and where I've come to live, more often than I'd like,
just a single touch-tone button away, apparently, from the madhouse.
I'm so wide awake now in the dark, it's not funny, and there's nothing
left to say along the miles of open line, nothing to do but quietly lay down
the receiver in its cradle, take the long walk back to sleep. And if I make it
that far again tonight, you can be absolutely sure that's when
the Venusian scout-ships will be closing in, or Patricia's mother,
and somewhere Mr. Car Wax Guru will be setting a Chevrolet on fire
to the paid-off astonishment of his TV-studio audience—one more

brilliant lesson in the virtue of sheer resilience—and he'll swear
nothing else on Earth can stand up to that kind of heat.
But three of us, more or less, in our foil-wrapped, American-as-baked-
potato wisdom, will know better. There's me, my wrong-number friend, and
Stuart, wherever he is right now. May his meds make him unbreakable,
and doctors never talk him fully out of his half-baked, hard-won silence.
May his friends wait until the morning before ringing through to him there.

And let the plans of the space people and our relatives and anyone else
who would come to us in our woozy sleep, on this night at least,
come to naught. May they be foiled, with any luck. And with our blessings
or our curses, foiled again. May it turn out they've been looking,
all along, for someone else. And if they find us instead, certifiable
wrong numbers, may they have to tell us exactly how sorry they are.
And for how much.   Given the crush of increasingly unstable particles
in the universe, it's no small thing: how surprisingly undisturbed
we actually are, how quiet it so often is on our end of the line.
And whenever we get to thinking that's OK, there's quite enough
still ringing in our ears for one more night or for a lifetime,
here comes another one of those voices out of nowhere, saying
in so many words we haven't heard anything yet.

David Clewell is the author of eight collections of poetry—most recently, *The Low End of Higher Things*—and two booklength poems, *The Conspiracy Quartet* and *Jack Ruby's America*. His work regularly appears in a wide variety of national magazines and jour-nals—including *Poetry*, *Harper's*, *The Georgia Review*, *New Letters*, *The Kenyon Review*, and *Boulevard*—and has been represented in over sixty anthologies. Among his honors are several book awards: the Felix Pollak Poetry Prize (for *Now We're Getting Somewhere*), National Poetry Series selection (for *Blessings in Disguise*), and the inaugural Four Lakes

Poetry Prize for *Taken Somehow By Surprise*, his new collection forthcoming in Spring 2011 from the University of Wisconsin Press. He is currently the Poet Laureate of Missouri. Clewell teaches writing and literature at Webster University in St. Louis, where he also directs the English Department's creative writing program.

WALTER BARGEN
MISSOURI

Back Roads

Desert dwellers will argue all roads
are back roads, and some go so far back
they lead to alien crash sites, their emaciated
remains: ratty, feathered, elastic hides,
now stored in secret military hangars,
not to be confused with Roadrunner and Coyote's,
Yes, so far back even fission finds a safe place
to expose itself.
    Today a roadrunner, large, ground-loving
bird, that looks nothing like the cartoon character,
the one that always one-ups the wily cartoon
coyote, that looks nothing like a coyote,
unless four legs and a tail are all that's needed
to belong to that class of visionary buffoons
who survive their own and our worst catastrophes,
and then do it again, falling a thousand feet
from a cliff, stepping in front of a second
speeding truck, swallowing twice just-lit dynamite
then belching the acrid smoke of an explosion.
    It's obvious, the obsession to possess
or be destroyed. Maybe it's not what we think,
not hunger but the hunt, the challenge,
the risk. There beyond the lava beds of *Jornada
Del Muerto*, is the sun-flattened Trinity Site,
the first atom-blasted crater, still closed

to the public, where Father, Son, and Holy
Ghost were fused into a Rube Goldberg
trap that Coyote now plans for Roadrunner
some Saturday morning soon.

    We stop, to miss and not miss on the hardscrabble
road, what we see through our sun-blasted faces
reflected in the windshield, a roadrunner cutting
in front of us, rattlesnake in its beak.

To Put By

He walks to the back of the house he's lived in all his life and finds a room that he's never entered. He opens the door and feels along the wall for the light switch. How strange to work both his palms over something cold, flat, vertical, and in the pitch of darkness, extending to the infinity of corners. For a moment, he's falling upward, sideways, and down. He secures his feet to the floor and turns. Something long and thin brushes his cheek. He spins from vertigo to fear. Quickly stepping back, he swings his arm to defend himself and his hand tangles in the pull chain. A dusty bulb shrouded in cobwebs ignites, as if a clod of earth were glowing from the low ceiling.

He coughs from the musty odor of things sealed and undisturbed. From floor to ceiling, he is surrounded by shelves. On each shelf he sees old glass canning jars. Thousands of Ball jars crowded into rows and labeled, the hand-lettering faded beyond reading. He looks for pickles, peas, pears, parsnips. It's not what he finds. From the top shelf, he pulls down jars packed with cirrus, cumulus, nimbus, stratus clouds, all of them sealed tight. He sees all the faces and animals and the grotesqueries that ever came to him, lying on his back in fields staring up at the passing days: the flocks of sheep, herds of buffalo, legends of Roman soldiers, flotillas, armadas; the islands, archipelagos, continents where he wanted to spend his summers and falls; and the dancing Katchinas, the spirits that surely must be behind it all.

On the lower shelf are jars of wind. There's the one that softly dissolved him as he sat on the porch one long late afternoon. In the next, the wind that pushed waves into his boat as he crossed a lake, and the gust that caught his kite, breaking the twine, releasing him to blow across a field. The other jars aswirl with what hasn't arrived.

There are jars of snowflakes, each classified according to its intricate frozen lattice. There are sunsets packed like colored sand in shot glasses sold in stores along the highway in Tucumcari and Yuma. Jars of light rain and mists, deluges and floods. Forty days and forty nights of jars. Jars of extinct bird songs, jars of grackle crackle and sparrow twitter, so many he can't reach, sitting too far back.

He finds the shelf full of his breathing: the very first one that burned his lungs into life, the longest one when he fell from the oak breaking his arm, all of those from the hospital waiting for his father to die, all those inhaling the fragrance of another's hair, the new jars appearing at that moment to take in the breathing of this room.

Manifest Breakfast

In a house buttressed by books and slanted morning light
slicing across the grain of the kitchen table, Lieutenant Colonel
George Armstrong Custer's 1876 orders to pursue the Sioux,

Cheyenne, Sans Arcs, Blackfeet, sits beside an emptied bowl
of Grape Nuts. The document is randomly punctuated with crumbs
from half-burnt toast, difficult to read the general's elegantly looping

Nineteenth Century signature and the limits of force given Custer's command.
My wife has printed over in her typewriter-meticulous style a grocery list
of olive oil, cilantro, garlic, tortellini, supplies for this evening's company,

but not the 7th Cavalry last seen surrounded near the banks of the Little Big Horn.
There's also a lengthy paragraph to herself, notes on rehabbing
the upstairs bathroom and the rest of her destiny. She's scribbled

calculations, an attempt at reviving a diminishing bank account,
and an addendum to the Christmas card list, and it's only February.
This morning my wife sits down to rewrite Custer's orders to pursue the Sioux.

Civilized Sacrifice

I have climbed the backs of gods too. It's not so
strange, dressed in heavy coat and boots, hat
pulled down to the eyebrows, cheeks windburnt,
gloved fingers numb, and each brief breath prayed

upon, each step thrown onto the loose altar of stone.
Blinded by spires of light, I've looked away
as the unblemished blue splintered in all directions.
And I've backed away from the sheer

precipice, the infinite suddenly a fearful measure,
the way down to tundra and the jagged maze of
granite, leaving only a crevice in which to cower.
I've lain on the steep slopes of night under spruce,

wrapped against rain and cold, and watched clouds
explode in my face. Stark boughs reached
then sagged back in a sweeping, resolute silence.
I was shaken loose by thunder and lightning,

like the small girl, named Juanita by strangers.
She tumbled a hundred yards down
Nevado Ampato peak, her whereabouts unquestioned
for five hundred years until a nearby volcano

began a festering eruption, thawing the slope,
and wrapped in her *illiclia* shawl woven in the ancient
Cuzco tradition, wearing a toucan- and parrot-feathered
headdress, her frozen fetal posture a last effort

at warmth above tree line amid ice fields, there
to address and redress for rain and maize, for
full vats of fermenting beer, plentiful llama herds,
for the civilized sacrifice, to be buried alive and wait

in private, as we all do to speak with our gods, hoping to appease, to know, to secure the illusive cosmic machinery, and in that last numb moment her left hand gripped her dress for the intervening centuries.

Minor Gods

Another roadside bomb, another suicide
bomber, another dozen blind-folded, hands-tied-
behind-the-back bodies found half buried at the town dump,
it's how a Saturday explodes until I turn off
the radio and look out the east window at a tabby
crouched in explosive morning light and acting strangely.

I hurry outside to rescue an eight-inch long, pencil-thin,
ring-neck snake before it is playfully eviscerated.
A hundred yards into the woods, the palm heat
of cupped hands has pacified its coiled panic
and I scold it to be more careful before it calmly
slithers into a brush pile and into another ambush.

Balanced between two flood lights on the west wall,
phoebes again build a nest out of moss and spittle,
and I build a four-feet high fence on the ground below them.
They quickly abandon their efforts as if not understanding
what I'm trying to keep out and keep in. Occasionally,
I see their bobbing drab-gray tails on a nearby branch.

I leave the fence standing. I blame the cats
without evidence of guilt. Weeks later,
the phoebes return, the same pair or different,
I don't know after so many seasons of failed attempts
on every wall of the house, including the black snake
that scaled ten feet of siding to eat the hatchlings.

From the kitchen window, I watch them fly back
and forth through the gauntlet of clawed hunger,
too early to know ends except this flying.
Either the gods are omnipotent and not good,
according to Epicurus, just look at this world, or they are
good and not omnipotent, look at these phoebes.

Beirut

Machine guns inhabit the rooftops
like hungry crows.
Bullets peck the library
city hall the cobble streets
Allah's forehead.

To the east
the mountains belch dust
as artillery fires into the city
planting the bloom of brown orchids
on the beach apartments
on the Hilton
in courtyards filled
with the shattered rosary of bricks.

People are opening their bodies
for the world to read
the print still wet and so red
it pours out a stoplight
on Broadway and Ninth
in downtown Columbia, Missouri.

Walter Bargen has published thirteen books of poetry and two chapbooks. The latest are: *The Feast*, BkMk Press-UMKC, 2004, winner of the 2005 William Rockhill Nelson Award; *Remedies for Vertigo* (2006) from WordTech Communications; *West of West* from Timberline and *Theban Traffic* (2008) WordTech Communications. In 2009, BkMk Press-UMKC published *Days Like This Are Necessary: New & Selected Poems*. His poems have appeared in *Elder Mountain, The Gingko Tree Review, Margie, New Letters, Pleiades, Poetry East, Rattle, and River Styx*. He was appointed to be the first Poet Laureate of Missouri (2008-2009).

W. E. Butts
New Hampshire

Porcelain

Early Saturday afternoon, in winter,
Mother and I are walking
down Elm to the gray and white house
of the Stevens sisters, who were so frail,
I remember, the dust-swirled light
passed through them. "Be careful,"
Mother warned when, in the curiosity
of a four-year-old boy, I picked up
the Boston terrier from the mantel
and turned that tiny figurine
slowly over in my palm. It was then
one of the sisters reached for the collie
and beagle, and when she placed them
on the lace doily draped over the rolled arm
of the button-tufted high back chair,
I saw how the inside of her wrist
had become a small, colorless leaf.

I sat down and soon they were
gathered by me: the Austrian shepherd
and chocolate Siamese, the bulldog
and English setter. And a golden palomino
stood near a grazing brown foal,
while a barn owl, a blue bird,
and a white-throated sparrow
quietly rested. Even the turtle dove
and humming bird were there, and then

I was raising the birds above my head,
and I sang for them too. And I barked
for the dogs and whinnied for the horses,
and the room filled with flight and the new
sounds I had made for them all,
as those three women watched over me.

Later, while they chatted over tea
and I drank hot cocoa from a thin china cup
painted with tiny roses, snow fell
endlessly outside the frosted window,
and I had held those many things
which I knew now would not break.

Boys at the Saturday Matinee

We were happy those afternoons,
with our boxes of Dots,
watered-down sodas, and bags
spilling over with popcorn,
even as the sudden dark
and slow slide of curtains
silenced our laughter
and screams, while we waited
for a Saturday matinee serial to begin:

Black Arrow and *Captain Marvel*,
Buck Rogers and *Flash Gordon*,
The Green Hornet and *Dick Tracy*,
Red Ryder and *The Lone Ranger*,
or any one of a dozen others
our saved quarters let us follow
for twenty minutes each
into new episodes of heroes, villains,
kidnappings and impossible escapes,
and always a beautiful woman
who had to be rescued.

But sometimes it was hard to figure
who the criminal mastermind really was.
And despite how many times we saw
a chapter end with the hero
trapped and certainly doomed,
we argued his fate until we returned
to be captured again
by those metaphors of good and evil
that rose up like truth, like faith,
before our cheers and applause,
our eternal and communal praise.

Radio Time

"Is low the moon, but high the wind"
    —Chuck Berry

A howling dog, transistor radio crackling,
Chuck Berry: cars, girls and school,
and there, from the nightstand in my bedroom,
something close to revelation.
Ex-con – Kansas City joyride, broken down
car and jail, yet this skinny black man
and his guitar knew how to be sixteen.

And here, too, the gravelly voice
of George "Hound Dog" Lorenz,
who each evening on WKBW – "the greatest
station on your dial" – proclaimed
"The Hound's Around," and reminded us listeners
if we were "hangin` around the corner,"
we were "doggin` it." And I was transfixed

as that DJ spun those forbidden records
through the airwaves: Fats Domino,
LaVern Baker, The Moonglows, The Five Satins,
Ann Cole, Joe Turner, The Clovers,
Little Richard & The Upsetters, Etta James
lamenting "All I Could Do Was Cry."

And so it was I came to hear again
those historians of desire, prophets
of a change that would soon be mine.

Ash

Here, the sheet rocker mourns, the bipolar son
of a mystic stays in a room far away, speaking in tongues,
the widow quietly folds her hands,
children of the father who last week became ash
sit together in their loud silence,
women deliver trays of food
and place them on tables draped in white cloth,
friends gather in their small groups of memory,
then it's my turn to speak. I know nothing of death.
I remember once, years ago, the daughter of ash,
having been called by the quick signatures of lightning bugs,
brought me to an open field, where she discovered her name
among a constellation of stars.

Odds Against Tomorrow

Kallett Theater, 1959

Here are three men driving through the fast fall-off
of noir light and shadow, following the Hudson River
toward a small town bank outside Albany
that the disgraced former policeman swears will be an easy score,
and you can tell by the look in their eyes
and grim set of their mouths they need to believe it:
the Harlem musician tired of crooning to the ofay crowd
in smoke-filled bars; the racist war vet, just out of the joint
for hitting a man so hard he killed him but, he reminds his girlfriend,
he didn't mean to do it. Something snapped and he can't remember.
Now they're at a lake's gray shore, close-up
of a half-submerged and ruined china doll, the ex-cop
tossing stones at a crumbled can. In the nearby woods
the veteran points his shotgun at a startled rabbit,
and we have to wonder why he hesitates, until
the frightened animal scurries away, he shoots,
and then we understand. Of course, the robbery goes wrong.
We already knew this plan wouldn't work: the ex-cop dead in an alley,
the musician and veteran running past the rail yard into the looming rows
of oil terminals, and a confrontation that had to happen.
But it's what the camera shows us next that makes us
sit up straight. In a scene reminiscent of Cagney's finish
in "White Heat," they climb on top a tank and fire simultaneously
at each other, the screen exploding in flame and rising smoke,
in the aftermath, their scorched bodies laid side by side.
And in this time out of time we know failure,
desperation, even greed, each of us unrecognizable
in the darkened theater of our collective breath:
student and teacher; housewife and sales clerk;
grocer and mechanic; the teenage couple
necking in the last row. And "Who,"
the first detective to arrive is asking,
"can tell the difference?"

The Gift of Unwanted Knowledge

Because every evening, ten miles east,
small men guide their nervous horses
to the starting gate, afternoons in our town
my father leans over a pockmarked bar,
checks the history of losses and wins
posted in the latest racing form, collects
the folded slips and wrinkled bills of barroom regulars.

Here, at the dust-twirled Eagle Tavern,
it's 1958, and light glows amber in their glasses
of Pabst Blue Ribbon, Black Label and Genesee.
Where else could faith assemble when the factory's gone,
but in this dark cathedral of last chances? They know
the odds are never with them, but place their bets
like a devoted Sunday congregation.

Outside, the sun is gleaming proudly on the hood
of a new Edsel driving slowly down Main Street.
A few loud boys waving Hubley cap pistols
run from the 5 & Dime, falling then quickly rising
into the repeated resurrection of their play,
as troubled, speechless shoppers step back now,
worried in their sudden search for safety.

And I am one of those running, screaming kids,
toy gun in my hand, freed from school to an afternoon
that needs killing. We had learned what doesn't survive:
Sputnik a cinder descended from the atmosphere
of stars and other planets, Roy Campanella,
once called the best catcher in baseball,
crippled by his car's bad slide and crash.

We heard our fathers, late at night in their darkened houses,
sleepless and bitter, so many things already gone.
We skip flat stones across the surface of the murky creek,

lie shirtless beneath a lowering sun and cool breeze.
If we have questions, they are here in whatever light
is left to hold us, each one his father's son,
and to know what's next is not what we expected.

W.E. Butts is the 2009-2014 New Hampshire Poet Laureate, and the author of *Radio Time* (forthcoming from Cherry Grove in 2011), *Sunday Evening at the Stardust Café*, winner of the 2006 Iowa Source Poetry Book Prize, and several other collections. The recipient of two Pushcart Prize nominations, he has poems recently published in *Café Review*, *Cider Press Review*, *The Fourth River*, *Poetry East*, and *Saranac Review*. He teaches in the low-residency BFA in Creative Writing Program at Goddard College.

MARIE
HARRIS
NEW HAMPSHIRE

**On our 25th anniversary I
add the surf scooter to my life list as**

we walk a thin strand between two of the rocky, pine-studded outthrustings
that poke into Penobscot Bay, not talking much, but now and then
noting the visual shouts that reverberate from this megaphone
of an absolutely clear November afternoon: the sight of a single sloop
under sail, a pair of diving ducks—black bodies, brilliant white
on the nape, bills orange as...*yes! that lobster buoy*—surfacing together
to reveal themselves separate from the blue-black sea.

Valentine

This squall
of redpolls
blowing down
onto the hard earth
from bare branches
lifts my heart
as certain memories do
like the one involving
a rude porch
on a bright morning
blue bowl of white yogurt
blue berries
white ceramic spoon
and the unmistakable spring whistle
of a chickadee.

Bird Blind

Because all I can see
through clouding eyes
is flicker and flash,
the woods disconcert
and Sound—sibling
who had always deferred
to Sister Sight, the oldest, the boss,
scribe of the sheet music,
the one with the last word—
has her way with me:

teacher teacher teacher drink your tea your tea
poor Sam Peabody sweet sweet sweet
witchity witchity thief thief thief thief
come to me here I am
kong-ka-reee
fee bee
caw
caw
caw

Onward!

Marie Harris, NH Poet Laureate 1999-2004, is a writer, teacher, editor and business-woman. In 2003, she co-produced the first-ever gathering of state poets laureate. She has served as writer-in-residence at elementary and secondary schools throughout New England and is the author of four books of poetry. Her books for children are *G is for Granite: A New Hampshire Alphabet* and *Primary Numbers: A New Hampshire Number Book.* Her upcoming picture book from Penguin is called *The Girl Who Heard Colors.* She is currently writing a story for young readers on the life and time of American composer Amy Beach.

LARRY WOIWODE
NORTH DAKOTA

Neighboring Contrary

Sleeplessness, sleeplessness, sleep-
lessness,
draw your eye down now
in dim panes,

pry it there,
trying for surcease as
carrying cottonwood
all cross the sea.

First to be before tomorrow
Sleeplessness sleeps inside
imperfect memory.

A quotient, a pose, a rock
that's a turtle
racing toward sleep and its
neighboring contrary.

Sleeplessness, sleeplessness
Prince in the Night,
pass over my daughter and
die here in me.

Desert of Snow

I watch the blizzard rise
And blind my dew-wet eyes
In whining risers far below,
And recognize the hour when I
Give to an inner desert of snow.

One thing I know, I know
That my existence is
A desert of snow.

White lids, black hair, black eyes,
The devil you want to know
The way a stormy filly set me flying,
Staring at starry sky, my back
Backed into a desert of snow.

One thing I know, I know
That her existence is
A desert of snow.

The valley of shadow is surly, steep,
Littered with lousy lover's lies,
I been in it and I ain't going back,
I hear her say from far below,
Her cry a distant desert of snow.

One thing I know, I know
That our existence is
A desert of snow.

Bitter snowy valley black and wide,
Bleak blizzard blinding me to my
Filly, my black and white bride,
While all I hear is the blow by blow
Covering us in a desert of snow.

One thing I know, I know
That all existence is
A desert of snow.

A Deserted Barn

I am a deserted barn,
                my cattle robbed from me,
    My horses gone,
Light leaking in my sides, sun piercing my tin roof
    Where it's torn,
    I am a deserted barn.

    Dung's still in my gutter;
It shrinks each year as side planks shrink,
Letting in more of the elements,
                and flies.

Worried by termites, dung beetles,
    Maggots and rats,
        Visited by pigeons and owls and bats and hawks,
Unable to say who or what shall enter,
              or what shall not,
    I am a deserted barn.

    I stand near Devils Lake,
A gray shape at the edge of a recent slough;
    Starlings come to my peak,
Dirty, and perch there;
           swallows light on bent
    Lightning rods whose blue
    Globes have gone to
A tenant's son and his .22.

    My door is torn.
It sags from rusted rails it once rolled upon,
    Waiting for a wind to lift it loose;
Then a bigger wind will take out
    My back wall.

But winter is what I fear,
                    when swallows and hawks
Abandon me, when insects and rodents retreat,
        When starlings, like the last of bad thoughts, go off,
        And nothing is left to fill me
Except reflections—
                    reflections, at noon,
        From the cold cloak of snow and
Reflections, at night, from the reflected light of the moon.

Venerable Elm

convener and celebrant of
every everyday breeze disheveling your shade,
rocked by amber thought, syrup flung

in stringy yarn toward
carved scars, torn stems, and the needlepoint of stars;
gulping ground whiskey, drunk in the sun, assuming quaking poses

and slurred susurrus that provokes
busybody birds; provender to
rooters above and below, raccoons and moles

and leaf miners and borers and ants attuned to
your whiplash scenes and spooky phases, plus
woodpeckers rattling inside

in red rages. No nodding new growth at this,
your last leaves as far from
you as the rows printed on my camo

cap, O multitude of one,
Lakota
dancer stilled

by a light-
ning hit,

shedder
of shade to
the ages,

its proof
incised in
inner rings,

now I, my
chain saw
crying blue

as the sky,
must dis-
member

you.

Larry Woiwode is the author of five novels, including *Beyond The Bedroom Wall*. Of his dozen books, six have been chosen "notable books of the year" by the *New York Times Book Review*. His poems have appeared in the *Atlantic Monthly, Harpers, The New Yorker, Transatlantic Review*, etc., and Farrar Straus published his collection, *Even Tide*. His most recent book is the memoir, *A Step From Death*. Woiwode is the Poet Laureate of North Dakota and Writer in Residence at Jamestown College.

JIM BARNES
OKLAHOMA

Five Villanelles

"—and, toward the end, it glimmered with enticing rumors of tranquillity."
—Anthony Lane, The New Yorker, 4 July 2005

There was one witness: his name was Robinson
or so he said. The day was gray and wet
and he had a crooked eye and a long coat on

that must have cost a good god-awful sum.
This Robinson's story made no sense. Yet
there was one witness: his name was Robinson,

a fictive lie for a bit of fame or fortune
is my guess and one thing for sure, no bet,
is he had a crooked eye and a long coat on

that was not his. Not long before he'd gone
on across the bridge, he bit his lip a bit.
There was one witness: his name was Robinson.

He'd told us he lived in Sausalito, none
the worse for him, but he lied about it
and he had a crooked eye and a long coat on.

He lit a cig and let the Zippo burn
and gave a description that exactly fit
our man. One witness: his name was Robinson,
but he had a crooked eye and a long coat on.

*

Somewhere in a foreign city a phone is ringing
soft as a lover's murmur. It never stops:
the whole long night is but a beginning

or an end you've lost the middle of. Something
quite other than you imagined now throbs
somewhere in a foreign city. A phone is ringing

and it's for you, but you can never bring
yourself to pick it up. The pillow flops
the whole night long. If this is a beginning,

let there be more of light and less the thing
that brought you south and safe from wife or cops.
Somewhere in a foreign city a phone is ringing

you will pick up someday. Let's say it's spring,
guitar in the street, a full moon coming up,
the whole long night is nada but beginning

to make you want to dance, and you could sing
if you could swing your old soul round and stop
somewhere in this foreign city, phones all ringing
the whole night long and you with a new beginning.

*

He said he saw him jump into the fog
rolling in with the tide and fishing boats,
and there was nothing else to do save jog

over and see him going down like a log.
Nothing human dropping that far would float,
he said. He saw him jump into the fog.

We didn't trust his looks: his hat was sog-
gy and ill-kept unlike his overcoat.
But there was nothing else to do but log

in the time and place and the witness's smug
remarks. Robinson's, that is. That was what
he said: He saw him jump into the fog.

His name was Kees, the registration tag
in the Plymouth's glove box read. We knew squat,
and there was nothing else to do but lug

our soaked selves back to the station and our jug.
We had Robinson's worthless cockeyed report:
he said he saw him jump into the fog:
nothing left for us to do but drink and shrug.

＊

He told Robinson his name was Robinson
after he parked the car and left the keys.
The case was cold before the heat was on

the cops to find the now missing Robinson,
not to mention the Robinson washed out to sea
who told Robinson his name was Robinson.

But how to find the bad-eyed Robinson
who saw this Robinson we know as Kees?
The case was cold before the heat was on.

He had disappeared into the fog beyond
our reach by the time we had found the keys.
Why tell Robinson his name was Robinson?

We needed another statement from our man,
for the poet left nothing in the car but keys.
The case was cold before the heat was on,

and then it heated up: the press was down
our throats. There was no Robinson, no Kees.
He told Robinson his name was Robinson,
and the case was cold before the heat was on.

      *

Meanwhile, somewhere down in Old Mexico,
at his usual spot in the shade of a mango tree,
an old man tries to recall three days ago,

fails, raises his hand to let the waiter know
he'll have another, though he had rather leave
for somewhere other. Down in Old Mexico,

he cannot remember, though he seems to know
what person it was he once wanted to be.
An old man tries to recall three days ago

and fails: it's hard to summon back a flow
of words he once had mastery of. They lie,
meanwhile, somewhere down in Old Mexico.

He looks back on his Robinson and, oh,
the lines he knew dissolve into the sea
an old man tried to recall three days ago.

His case is dropped again, and again. Though
persistent, it and he soon will cease to be.
Meanwhile, somewhere down in Old Mexico,
an old man tries to recall three days ago.

Deputy Finds Dean's Tombstone on Highway

—*St. Louis Post-Dispatch, 18 July 1998*

Over forty years ago, I saw you
in my mirror mornings before the slow
days dawned. Working the hootowl shift miles
above Bohemia and in love with smiles
anyone gave, I was you to the core,
looked like you even then. Hung my hands in
pockets lightly exactly the way you did,
and wore the light blue pants.

                         Our names the same
signaled something I tried my best to grasp.
Maybe I have it now. But for you, Jimmy,
I would have remained in the north country
and never have known the freedom of road
and will. I was a slow rebel, double
for you in the smoky taverns of Oregon
where lost women and mournful men spilled their
lives on Saturday nights.

                         You taught me how
to desire and what the desiring is for:
departure. The setting out must go on
and on. So I think of this these decades
late after reading the Reuters release.
In July there are shivers in Fairmount.
Someone's life somewhere is about to change,
the tailgate down and the bed empty and scarred.
Your name, our name, Jimbo, flat on the road
sliding west with traffic: that's the way it
ought to always be this far from Eden
or South Bend.

This far from the lumbering
towns or lots full of OICs, I see you
still, the standing shadow in every ditch
or curve someone sometime did not make
in a momentary reach for misguided
glory. The pickup reaches home toward
midnight. The two men, in late middle age,
lean their arms on the rim of the empty bed
and gaze into the nothing they have carried
to the sanctuary of the deep Indiana fields.

The Captive Stone

at Heavener, Oklahoma

Enmeshed in steel stands a stone,
near stunted ash and elm, cracked bones
of Yggdrasil, small trees of time:
the caged stone with ciphered runes
is part of Park where men once made
their mark with maul and biting bronze.

The aged stone, hard to hand's touch
when touch was still allowed,
has had its face forced clean:
lichen lies dead below washed runes.
Webbed shadows of encircling steel
now mark time on the lone stone.
Yet the stone stands as stone stood
when Odin still was king and came
with men to mark down lives and fates.

Now we who Sundays look long
on this stone's stark ruined face
see only stone and ciphered runes
under the steel's sharp shadows:
the whispering of wind through wire
carries scant legend, no hint of history.

Skipping

for all of us, our last day at LeFlore High

Something never quite returns when you want
the facts the way you'd like the past to be.
It was our last day together: the sun
was bright, the new grass up, the water right,
and no one cared that we had missed the day.

You can't quite remember getting there, or
which of you did this or that: skipping stones
was in our blood. This was our vague good-bye,
a salute to the world of the narrow stream
we frolicked in and the school two miles away.

You never get it right without the weather:
the May sun warmed our cheeks. We swam till noon.
Then the girls spread lunch on the bank under
the sycamore tree. Above us the Tarzan swing
was a thread of the sun, and we drifted

on a wave of small thought and talk, already
forgetting what we had been those walled years.
But still it's not quite right: you remember
more than was. The love didn't really happen.
You were too shy, or the others were wrapped

up in future selves. You know that someone
almost drowned: two others pulled him out by
the hair. He'd dived too deep. There was a knot
on his crown. Or maybe he'd just faked it
for the tears the girls almost didn't shed.

What is this life? We should have asked stones,
grass, stream. We idled down the sun. The songs
we sang should have echoed off whatever

doom or dance we still beat time to. But they
fade, and the faces come up wrong, the facts

a reconstruction of no consequence. Once
you've done it, you never lose the knack of
skipping flat stones. How smooth the rock feels
against thumb and fingers as you release it
into its final spin and brief buoyancy.

Military Burial, Summerfield Cemetery: A Late Eulogy

for J. C. Evans

An honor guard brought the gray box down from
Tinker Field the day of burial. A few
of us came up the hill as if we knew
this man death and the flyers carried home.

How easy it is when you are nine or ten
to let your body go into the night,
into a dream of glory that's just right
for you. When you are nineteen and a man,

the dream is still a dream but need is there.
Nearly fifty years have gone since they lowered
him to this still place, his wings sculptured
granite now aloft in an angelic air.

I remember echoes in the woods: the sound
of taps soft in the late afternoon sun,
the stilling volley, the ceremony done.
Deranged by the time, I felt the trees around

the drab cemetery shudder in the light
wind rising in the clear south, and from
the west I heard a high plane's engines thrum.
Now it is hard to name what his last flight

was for: honor, glory, right, or just war.
Others have ended near him, on this hill,
from later skies. For all who had the will
for wings I have only words I wish were more.

Jim Barnes is former Distinguished Professor of English and Creative Writing at Brigham Young University. Born in Oklahoma, schooled in the deep woods of western Oregon where he lumberjacked for ten years, and enlightened at Southeastern Oklahoma State University (B.A.), the University of Arkansas (M.A. and Ph.D.), he now makes his home with his artist-designer wife, Cora McKown, at the McKown family ranch near Atoka, Oklahoma, and at the hacienda in Santa Fe, New Mexico. He has received several awards, including an NEA Fellowship in Poetry, a Senior Fulbright Fellowship to Switzerland, two Rockefeller Bellagio Residency Fellowships, two Camargo Foundation Fellowships, a Schloss Solitude Fellowship, a Munich Kulturreferat Fellowship in Translation, and an Oklahoma Book Award. Also, he has published several volumes of poetry, including *Visiting Picasso* (University of Illinois Press), *On a Wing of the Sun* (Illinois), *Paris* (Illinois), *The Sawdust War* (Illinois), *A Season of Loss* (Purdue University Press), *La Plata Cantata* (Purdue), and *The American Book of the Dead* (Illinois). His *On Native Ground: Memoirs and Impressions* (University of Oklahoma Press) is now in a second edition. He served as Oklahoma Poet Laureate for 2009 and 2010.

PAULANN PETERSEN
OREGON

A Sacrament

Become that high priest,
the bee. Drone your way
from one fragrant
temple to another, nosing
into each altar. Drink
what's divine—
and while you're there,
let some of the sacred
cling to your limbs.
Wherever you go
leave a small trail
of its golden crumbs.

In your wake
the world unfolds
its rapture, the fruit
of its blooming.
Rooms in your house
fill with that sweetness
your body both
makes and eats.

Appetite

Pale gold and crumbling with crust
mottled dark, almost bronze,
pieces of honeycomb lie on a plate.
Flecked with the pale paper
of hive, their hexagonal cells
leak into the deepening pool
of amber. On your lips,
against palate, tooth and tongue,
the viscous sugar squeezes
from its chambers, sears sweetness
into your throat until you chew
pulp and wax from a blue city
of bees. Between your teeth
is the blown flower and the flower's
seed. Passport pages stamped
and turning. Death's officious hum.
Both the candle and its anther
of flame. Your own yellow hunger.
Never say you can't take
this world into your mouth.

Miracle

The wonder isn't that lightning
strikes where it does, but that it doesn't
strike everywhere. Specifically *me*.
It isn't the frequency of car crashes,
but their infrequency. Traffic flicks along
in its speed and perplexity, each move,
each surge a potential disaster.

The heart beats out its strange
litany of the enormously possible,
never excluding disease and stricture.
Why does my blood run so easy and warm?
This is the wonder: me approaching
the traffic light just turned yellow,
my foot pressing my trust down
into the brake, the car in agreement
coming steady steady to a stop.

Primed

It was middle June
during the duration
of a month that was a wait

for each day to come,
during that summer
when I would turn teen,

when I was almost something—
way past twelve and counting.
It was the middle of day,

mid-day heat halfway
between cool and hot,
a double-handed noonday

stroke: the clock's
count of twelve
reminding me of what

I was not. Still a multiple
of two, three, four, six,
I was a mere factoring

of too many baby birthdays—
crazy to be divisible by
only myself and one.

Resolution

Arms, legs, and head gone,
only his marble torso still tenses
under her touch—she of whom remains
a single marble hand grasping his chest,
her thumb a little above
the hard bud of his nipple,
forefinger pressed to the hollow pulse
of his smooth underarm, the rest of her
broken away at the wrist

where her body parted from his.
They are the history
of strife. She an Amazon,
he a warrior, the two fused in battle.
Scars, those wounds fresh or imagined: so much
is erased from their ancient struggle,
so much from allegiances
they bodied forth
is now irrevocably gone.

The heat remaining is that enduring
heat of war—but broken,
crumbled, ground to a pale dust.
Shoulders and belly and groin,
he strains at her touch, yearns toward her
phantom body. Of this,
his enemy, only what merges
with his own flesh is left.
They are lovers, at last.

To Dream a Lover Away

Let your dream carry him
away, and by that very
dreaming, put him
at arm's length where you may
examine at leisure
his exact shadowy shape,
maybe even come to terms
with his voice, its narcotic
ways and by-the-ways.

How dream you, Sweetness?
you might ask of him
as you dream right past
his swift, disarming glance,
moving on to explore
those ample lips,
his oh so heavy eyelids
half lowered—seeing all this
with your decidedly
undreamy, dreaming eyes.

Take him all in. Take his own
sweet time. Keep in mind
this dreaming lets you
linger on what's bound to be
too close, too wide
for the focus of your
open eyes. So linger along.
Have your way with him,
your own easy-does-it take
on what's waiting in
the wild awake.

When Meeting *the other*

Given arms, the sun
would choose to grow many.
Having many narrow arms,
the sun would—at each limb's end—
flare into a palm and fingers,
into the curves made for reaching.

Extremities of flame, of shine.
Hands that carry enough
heat and light to give away.

Be that sun. One small sun.

Paulann Petersen, Oregon's sixth Poet Laureate, has five full-length books of poetry:
*The Wild Awake; Blood-Silk; A Bride of Narrow Escape; Kindle, and most recently The
Voluptuary,* published by Lost Horse Press in 2010. A former Stegner Fellow at Stanford
University and the recipient of the 2006 Holbrook Award from Oregon Literary Arts,
she serves on the board of Friends of William Stafford, organizing the January Stafford
Birthday Events.

LISA STARR
RHODE ISLAND

Dear Reader

Today was so beautiful that I went out
and hunted down every damn thing
I could find. I started with grass,
blowing colors like bagpipes—
green sounding bliss,
and red so meaningful
I had to turn away.

Next, I tracked the sky. Don't tell me
you've grown used to clouds,
and how they shift from angel
to elephant like there is nothing to it,
never mind that the sky
is the only way the hawk knows
for finding you.

Oh, there was lots to see
but I kept up with it
and searched all through the day.
For an hour I even stalked
my own children and the dog;
they had no idea—
I appeared to be reading.

In the end, I tried to leave no traces
of myself, and took only what I needed
for the rest of the tribe. Then I cut
everything into good-sized pieces,

portioned them as evenly as I could,
and I've been trying to say that this
is the part that I brought back for you.

Prayer in April

Just this morning,
right as we clamored off to school,
in the driveway, the bird—
that startled baby bird...
He was so frightened he'd lost his voice;
his little, feathered head became more yellow
with his quivering.

We three took turns holding him.

The complicity of our awe
is what strikes me now
and I hope I'll always remember it:
how we dropped to our knees,
how we took turns cradling him,
how, for a moment, when he flew,
we lost our voices, too.

Hobbled

Years from now, I wonder if I'll be able to recognize the irony
of any of it, like how just when you had almost begun
to accept my leaving, I ruptured my Achilles playing
tennis with you, which was one of the only ways we knew
for managing time, and summer and Saturdays,
given this fact of my leaving.

Years from now, when I think of how ready I was to go—
to walk, run, fly, even swim, if I had to, away from the weariness
of what our love had become, I hope I will remember how,
when the time came, the only way to leave was slowly
and the only way to walk was to hobble, one wavering,
broken, brave new footstep at a time.

Investment

Just before the final final,
that is, about two weeks before she died,
I went on a shopping spree— sweatpants,
pajamas, new undies, I said,
snapping their ebullient waist bands
just to show her I meant it when I said I would stay
with her, and look square at everything with her
until the end, and my sister said, since one child
in every family must be the responsible one,
you know—I wouldn't go investing
in a lot of pajamas at this point in the game.

And I wanted to say what game?
There isn't any game.
And I wanted to tell her
about our mother's face, illuminated
with death, and a child's glad receiving—
how she held the velour, leopard-print ensemble
close to her chest as if to say mine, all mine,
and how she opened her arms again,
this time, at last, for me.

She wore them once.
They fit her beautifully.

Because

Lately she's been falling in love everywhere—
at the market, in the pharmacy, always in the cafeteria
sliding her tray over the metal rails,
last week with the hands of the attendant at a gas station.
It's not right, she knows, but still, she can't help it.
Sometimes it happens all day long.

Yesterday at the campus it was everything again—
The way the postmaster, on lunch break, went whistling past,
or how the frisbee players sing the quad.
The way some students stay after class, that usually gets her.
Cashiers, people who sing at stop lights—all fair game.
Cab drivers—forget it.

With ice cream scoopers, with their little paper hats,
it is often love at first sight,
and she will never forget the boy at the sandwich shop—
the way he said "miss, would you like anything to drink?"
to the 80-year-old woman in front of her,
then when it was her turn said "Ma'am" instead.

Later today, blessed by all this loving
she will make some tea and play a violin concerto
for her dog who is deaf.
She will play the music as loud as it will go
because she can, and because somehow, he'll hear it
and he will stand on the porch of the fine yellow house, glowing.

She will be all choked up
because the lawn chairs
have never been this white before
and because, tired ears flapping
in a soft Autumn breeze,
the old dog will bark back his joy.

In The End

For Eliot, September 7, 2004

And after everything, what is there to say, really,
to an animal whose death
one has long been expecting?
Perhaps it's best not to say anything.
Better just to sit with him—
to stroke the fur that no one's washed in months,
to scratch the ears which no longer hear,
to slowly shift that golden flop of a friend
to the spot he'd loved the best:
a little hilltop overlooking a harbor
where the boats are forever turning
toward the morning light,
where the heron is always just now landing, its ripple a whisper.

And careful with the legs, which stopped working, forever,
sometime last night, you turn him around gently
so that even though he can't see so well his body can remember.
And that's when he raises his fine head just one more time
to honor this slender, splendid patch of life—
the geese flying high and North forever,
the boats with their delicate dance.
He holds his head that way for several minutes though it hurts—
one more time smelling what's West,
and the breeze dallies one final time
in the soft fur of his chest.

And that's when you whisper, though you're weeping
"It will be okay, it will be okay."
And he shifts a thick, gentle paw, and somehow it finds your hand.
And may you have the sense, then, to sit with him in silence,
and to understand what he's been saying all along—
to know, at last, what it means to love the earth this way—
to endure this kind of pain

just for one more morning's breeze,
and the boats, and the blue,
so much blue.

Three For September

i. Birds
And when, dear one, you are so weary
you are ready to give up,
think then of the Canada Geese—
the way all day
they shout back at the beating,
broken heart of the world
"I am lonely too.
Keep flying. Keep flying.
I am lonely too."

ii. Bugs
These days, even spiders
have gone lovely and all day long,
I dodge their delicate webs,
and just today I walked the labyrinth with dragonflies.
I'd never noticed how they latch,
horizontally, to the flowers—
how they defy gravity,
how their needle noses
play the wildflowers like trumpets.

iii. Blessings
Whoever said God is a man was wrong,
just like whoever said God is a woman.
Clearly, God is September,
the apostles are goldenrod,
and the psalms are the breeze that stirs the field.
And if, even now, you still question your own belief,
maybe now is the time to take a look at your one, good life—
and the way you, too, sometimes shine and sway
just like those weeds in the meadow, gone mad with yellow.

Lisa Starr is an inn-keeper, a mother, a bartender, a coach and a teacher, who divides her time among a variety of interests, her children, and her passion for poetry. She is a two-time recipient of the R.I. Fellowship for Poetry. In her capacity as Poet Laureate, Starr has established dozens of poetry circles around Rhode Island in elderly communities (assisted living facilities, nursing homes, etc.), hospitals, shelters, the state prison, and agencies for children and adults living with severe mental and physical disabilities. In April of 2009 Starr assembled more than a dozen US State Poets Laureate in Rhode Island for Poetry for Hope, a series of readings, workshops, and public forums featuring the visiting poets and emerging and established Rhode Island poets and musicians at schools, libraries and cultural attractions around the state. Her books include *Mad With Yellow*, *This Place Here*, and *Days of Dogs and Driftwood*. She is the founder and director of the Block Island Poetry Project, a nationally acclaimed celebration of the arts and humanity, now in its 7th year. The brightest lights of her life are her two children, Orrin and Millie, and her dog, Brother. When time permits, she writes her heart out.

MARJORY WENTWORTH
SOUTH CAROLINA

The Art of Memory

in the blue hour   I wake
to remember   you   this day
in the heart of winter   sunlight
slowly seeping into a corner
of the sky   and I   continue
to pray   through decades in which
I have become   more
fatherless   but less alone
I can not explain   how
this happened   or why
I sense the mutable
interior of things   thriving
hidden   humming with life
like houses   lit up at the dinner hour
or letters written   even the stones
we stumble   over   here
beyond this color   filling
the air   there is nothing but
memory   restless   wandering
stars that fade   somewhere
in the back of the mind   a kind of
music   I want   to gather
each hour that bears your name
like holding rain or counting waves
at the beach with my children

you'll never know   we watch
for birds   lost in the cacophony
of dawn   your voice   oblivion
a shadow   drawn across the sea

Snow in the South

rarer than rainbows   hurricanes
or hail   startling
how this snow   fell   once
in decades   that came
and went as fast as this   winter
dream   that stayed
clinging in clumps   on
shaded sides of highway
despite midnight drizzle
and morning sun   so many snowballs
rolled out across cold fields
of cotton   snowmen stacked
in front of every home   around
the edges of town   that night
the hip-hop singer   dj
named buddha   preacher
in a pressed black suit   fiery wings
in a metal tray   above a bowl
of blue flame   that tall cousin
with the little boy   hip to ankle
nigerian pink tie-dye   leaning
on one crutch   her bright smile
on stage   baraka beating
the side of the podium
with a flat palm   still full
of hard earned anger
wool scarf wrapped tight around
his neck like some kind of armor

Corene

Inspired by the painting of the same name by Jonathan Green

summer flowing like a song
only she can hear   standing
in the tilting tall grass that is
singing also   a woman holds
a blue polka dot sheet
overhead   as if it is
a privilege to be   standing
in an open field   with wind
lifting her dress while she
dries baskets of clean laundry
beneath a sun filled sky

What Remains

white feathers   in the nest   like a dusting of snow
emptiness of birth   after prayers   paint drying
on the canvas   it is raining   blue egg
in a glass   Jim Crow   hidden in their hearts
a city divided   scars   in every home   the Gospel
truth   at the bottom of an empty puddle   silence
when the last breath is taken   days scratched
on the prison wall   shreds of silk   and sunlight
lining the abandoned   chrysalis   after the storm
the broken house   floating like a boat   a voice
filled with bells   bed of leaves   ashes
on the mantel   history is the container
buried beneath the killing fields   a white string
still tied to a baby's wrist   and bones   clinging
together   across the miles   in the hotel of stars
iron and straw   a field of winter   fields of milk
the permanence of snow   and the arithmetic
after childhood   that sack of small stones
we carry   a heart filled with scars   the sea
holding too many bones   despite genocide
so many creatures in the air   fluttering
over the graves   and the onion domes
inside   memories of what is found there

Into This Sea I Spill

clouds scattered like thought   the sound
the train makes   scars   that still pull
from within   words that matter
sleepless nights   childhood entire
all manner of birds   and what they have
seen   each forgotten
yet lingering dream   the skin
lining my heart   a small boat
filling   with winter   moonlight.

Marjory Wentworth was born in Lynn, Massachusetts. Educated at Mt. Holyoke College and Oxford University, she received her M.A. in English Literature and Creative Writing from New York University. Her poems have appeared in numerous books and magazines, and she has twice been nominated for the Pushcart Prize. Ms. Wentworth teaches poetry in an arts and healing program for cancer patients and their families at Roper Hospital in Charleston, SC. She serves on the Board of Directors for the Lowcountry Initiative for the Literary Arts (LILA), The Poetry Society of SC, and the University of SC Poetry Initiative. Ms. Wentworth works as a publicist. She lives in Mt. Pleasant, SC, with her husband Peter and their three sons, Hunter, Oliver, and Taylor.

DAVID ALLAN EVANS
SOUTH DAKOTA

For the Young Woman Who Cleans My Teeth

When I sit down and lie back,
your white rubber hands come
floating toward me as toward
a death mask stretched over
a crystal ball.

I gaze, or close my eyes,
and we hold a one-way
conversation as you scrape
and pick, accepting my aaaaa's
and silences as consent.

Sometimes you stop, lay down
your tool, squirt water
in my mouth; I slosh it
around a few times with
my spit and you insert
a plastic vacuum tube and
suck my cheeks dry as alum.

Then I rest my jaw.

But whenever your tool
appears above me, I
gape like a baby robin
to a dangling worm.

We might be pair-bonded
bonobos, one grooming
the other, who—stunned
by such routine joy—
stares into trees
or oblivion.

We are so close
and our room so private,
we might be lovers in bed.
"This way a little,"
you almost whisper, gently
pressing on my temple.
I obey every word
all the way through
flossing and polishing;
and I love and honor
once more the finishing
touch of your smile

which sends me—
with a new toothbrush
sticking out of my shirt pocket,
and a gritty, spearmint
taste—back to the corroding
daylight and job.

Cartoon Universals

Thinking Can Be Harmful to Your Health
Imagine the scene: you're literally way out on a limb
and your enemy is busy sawing

it off (or maybe you're the one doing
the sawing). Whatever you do, don't look
down. But of course you do, abruptly
ending the scene with your fall.

Luck and Muscles
You're a guy in a sailor cap with a pipe,
a gravelly, alpha voice, and super-sized forearms—

you're at a construction site just after being
cold cocked by the Paul Bunyan-sized fist of

another alpha male (in your ongoing arms
race over an hour-glass-shaped, black-haired girl

with a tedious voice), and you're walking—still
out cold—on a steadily-rising steel girder many

giddy floors up, and just as you reach the end of it
and are about to step off into oblivion, another

girder, ideally timed, meets your foot so all you do is
keep on walking and rising until, stepping off, another

girder replaces the last one so you continue walking,
now 50 or so floors up, and your power-source—

a can of spinach in your shirt pocket—begins to
bulge like your biceps, the sea fog clears in your head

(your testosterone level rising like crane-lifted girders),
and then in the final scene with a final *blamb* of

your famous fist you win back the girl for a night
on the town, or better yet, marriage, and a family.

The Triumph of the Inconspicuous
You're a remarkably resourceful coyote
that'll do anything to catch a nondescript,

beeping road runner with infinite speed
and plenty of gears, so to catch him you

shoot yourself out of cannons, zoom
across the prairie on jet skates,

mail yourself in a package marked:
"Road Runner" . . . and still, after all

your ingenious, hard work you're
nothing more than a loser. Meanwhile,

your boring, putative prey is effortlessly
speeding far, far away, *Bee beep*.

In This World, You Never Die
You're a cat that's been flattened
into its shadow by a mouse with an
outrageously oversized sledge hammer;
no problem: you're up in a jiffy on all
four paws and feeling fine in the next
scene, once again skittering mouse-

ward, spitting out your fate, while
your tiny enemy, now a furred

blurr . . . now hiding behind a wall,
is holding the hugest sledge hammer

in history—it's poised and waiting
for you, portending stars.

Turning 70

(Remembering Okoboji, Iowa, 1957)

. . . *click, click, click, click, click* went the wheels
of our little roller coaster car taking us slowly,
irrevocably upward to the top of the carnival until,
click   click   click—we slowed more, hesitated,

then, cresting out, began to fall, my guts whirling,
my primate grip strangling the safety bar,
my eyes locked shut on what we couldn't help
being headed for straight down—

then, picking up speed, the inevitable letting go
because we had no other choice, against a force
huger than carnivals, planets, universes—
so we all opened our eyes and reached as high
as we could for moons, for stars, then came
our avalanching screams. . . .

That's it—exactly what I need to get back to:
that letting go (minus the giddy guts), with my eyes
fiercely wide open, each day seconding Prospero's
"be cheerful, sir," and Lao Tzu's tree bending
in the wind, each day looking forward to enjoying
what's left of the ride, the carnival, the life.

Saturday Morning

Right out the door of
the Touch of Class
beauty shop strides
a giant woman
in sloppy jeans
and faded denim shirt
and a brand-new
double-decker bouffant—

back into her old Ford
she scoots, slides
but the hair's too high,
won't go.

It must be urged in,
gently,
with her left hand.

Sitting low,
the hair barely scraping
the ceiling,

she starts the engine,
revs up,
jerks into drive and
peels off toward tonight.

Bus Depot Reunion

just over the edge
of my *Life* a young sailor

bounds from a Greyhound's
hiss into his mother's hug,

steps back, trades hands
with his father, then turns

to an old, hunched man
maybe his grandfather—

no hand, no word goes out,
they regard each other,

waiting for something, and
now their hands cup,

they begin to crouch
and spar, the old man

coming on like a pro,
snuffling, weaving,

circling, flicks
out a hook like a lizard's tongue,

the boy ducking, countering,
moving with his moves,

biffing at the bobbing
yellow grin, the clever

head, never landing a real
punch, never taking one

until suddenly, exactly
together they quit,

throw an arm around each other
and walk away laughing

David Allan Evans, the Poet Laureate of South Dakota, was born in Sioux City, Iowa, in 1940. He married his high school girl friend Jan, and started college on a football scholarship. He has grants from the National Endowment for the Arts, the Bush Artist Foundation, and the South Dakota Arts Council. He was the 2009 recipient of the South Dakota Governor's Award for Creative Distinction in the Arts. A Fulbright Scholar twice in China, he taught at South Dakota State University for 39 years. He is the author of eight collections of poetry, the latest being *This Water, These Rocks*. He and Jan, who live in Sioux Falls, South Dakota, have three grown children.

PAUL RUFFIN
TEXAS

Frozen Over

In Mississippi I recall only once
how the cold came down like a lid of iron,
clamping the landscape, stilling the trees,
and all the ponds froze over: not
just a skim for crashing rocks through,
but thick and hard enough to walk on.

The gravel pit where we swam in summer
spanged and creaked as I edged out
toward the gray, awful middle where,
if I went through, no one could reach.
I moved like a bird coming to terms
with glass, sliding one foot, then
the other, holding back my weight
and breath until they had to come.

I could see, beyond the far shore,
cars moving on the highway, slowing,
faces in the window ringed with frost,
the little ones waving, pointing
to that child walking on water.

Gigging Frogs

There are some things on this earth
that may be fooled by two moons,
one still as a stone in the sky,
the other dancing. Not these frogs.
A moonlit night is not a night
for going after frogs. When your light
joins the moon, their clatter stops,
the pond goes dead: they are not fooled.

It must be done on a dark and dooming night
when yours will be the only light above
the rim of the pond. You must move
with the stealth of winter with your moon,
as slow as a stone sliding across the sky.

Then, as you see the eyes take life in
a seeming joy, moon-struck, you steady
the light, aim the deadly gig, and jab
the prongs through belly or head,
swift and sure as a cottonmouth.
When you have taken all you want, you
must ice them down for the trip home,
first cutting the hind legs, still joined,
from the upper torso, skinning them
like removing too-tight jeans
and laying them side by side
in the ice of your cooler,
the legs of so many lovely girls
collected by a moon-struck man
who slew them for his joy.

Burying

I found him stumbling about when the mother
died, an otherwise healthy calf, and fed him
by bottle until another cow came due, then
moved him in with her for suckling.
Third night she broke his neck.
It was a right and natural thing to do:
She reasoned her milk was for hers alone.

I found him barely breathing, head thrown
back, unable to rise for the bottle,
his eyes already hazing over; I could see
myself fading in them, backing into fog.
I brought the pipe down hard, twice, the
second time in malice: not for him or her,
but for the simple nature of things.
Blood came from his nose, his body
quivered. I dragged him from the barn.

The hole in the winter garden was easy, quick,
and the calf fit properly; but when the
first shovel of dirt struck his side,
he kicked, with vigor. I watched the flailing
foot strike against air. Nothing else moved.

There were no considerations: I did what
needed to be done. A few more scoops clamped
the leg and the earth stilled. I mounded
the grave and turned away, looking back once
to see that nothing heaved. I felt neither
fear nor sorrow, love nor hate. I felt
the slick handle of the shovel, slid
my thumb over its bright steel blade,
breathed deep the sharp and necessary air.

Sawdust Pile

A pile, they say,
will burn for twenty years,
seething with deep heat
those long years out,
cool enough on top
for weeds and barefoot boys.

Like early ice it lures
the unwary up a greening slope
firm to the foot, firm
and cool up to the very peak,
where the crust sags, gives way,
and legs, torso, and head
sink to the fierce core.

There are the tales:
Bo Simpson's horse, a pack
of pure-blood coon hounds,
Sarah Potter's little girl—
all gone to a quick hell.

Out here the rattler warns, lightning
strikes from a growling sky:
each terror is given a tongue.
But the fire lies quiet in this pile,
a coiled thing, tongueless and waiting,
beneath the devil's cool shell.

Returning to the Luxapalila

The river is the color of earth, fed by runoff
from pastures and fields of cotton and corn
and forestland heavy with humus.
Kneeling by the water near a shale outcropping,
I shatter my face and settle my outspread hand,
palm up, until it fades from sight
like something drowned in history's dark pages—
now you see it, now you don't.
Watching the hand disappear, I see
the face of a girl eased down by the pastor,
her paleness and blond hair darkened,
held below that brown rush
until she broke the surface again,
arms flung wide in the flaring sun,
face shining like an angel's,
white marble with thin blue veins
trailing from her temples to blend
with water whispering off her hair,
dress sheer and tight on her tiny breasts.
Thank you, Jesus, he cried to the water and the woods.

Here as a boy I curled at the end
of a cable swing, flung out, released,
hung there, wingless creature floating on air
until gravity snatched me and I dropped
breathless to the river, the flash of green bank,
the sun a yellow something spinning on blue,
then my feet entering the water, my body
going down through that wet tunnel,
the color of weak whiskey across my eyes,
a darker stronger bourbon, then nothing,
slipping into the earth itself, and deeper,
until my feet touched the bottom,
the spongy primordial end of the world.
A thrust and I rose through the tunnel,

eyes uplifted toward the brightness,
hands and arms battering like wings
to burst breathless to green and blue,
the steady round face of the sun,
my vision bleared by water,
the taste of Earth upon my tongue.

My feet uncertain against the muddy slope,
I clamber back to the level of brush and briar
on the bluff, watch the brown ribbon below
weaving around a grassy bar, and see—
is it a simple slant of light
breaking from behind me?—
the girl's marble-white face rising free,
hair streaming, cupped by my hand,
her arms stretched out to the mounting sun.

Paul Ruffin, Texas State University Regents' Professor and Distinguished Professor of English at Sam Houston State University, is the founding editor of *The Texas Review* and founding director of Texas Review Press. He is the author of two novels, three collections of short stories, two books of essays, and six earlier collections of poetry. He is also a newspaper columnist and feature writer. His poems have appeared widely in journals in this country, including *Poetry, Paris Review, Southern Review, Georgia Review, Michigan Quarterly Review*. He has two books forthcoming: *Living in a Christ-Haunted Land* (stories, 13E Note Editions, Paris, FR) and *Travels with George, in Search of Ben Hur* (essays, University of South Carolina Press).

KATHARINE COLES
UTAH

Found Objects

In the mood of Atget

A skeleton, modeled
Half life size. A bust.
A mounted beetle.
Cultivated dust.

This bat wing, severed
From a life now flown;
Hinge and lever,
Articulated bone—

No: umbrella.
Mooding trumps my eye,
Invents details
To match memory—

A corset, empty
Of the shape it gave,
A passing city,
A fallen nest, a grave.

Say: how do
Your eyes still pin me flat,
When it's you
Laid down in black and white?

Out Like a Lion

A flock of tiny birds gusts
Wild—the wind made flesh,
　　　Feather and hard-flung heart—

And on every pavement beneath
Vivid glass facades, a body
　　　A quarter my fist's size

Twists its head
Too far, as if in wonder (the rush:

People step around
Small death, faces
　　　Lowered into the gale)—still

Eyes gaze at blue sky
Reflected so purely she gave
　　　Over to what moved her,

Believing in her last fling
She could blow right through.

Collector

One thing beside another with no reason
Beyond some taxonomic hallucination—
Ceylon broach, South African soapstone pipe bowl,

Azurite fetish, scrimshaw hairpin, then
At last a notional order: entire cases of heads,
human here, and shrunken; there

Avian: ear and ruff,
Corythaix persa's crest, showy green
Edged white, or, beyond ornament, beaks

Lamellated, conical, fissirostral, each evolved
Precisely for its function, which
The gloss declines to tell us. In this case

Feet, disarticulated to fix attention
Before we're free to see the birds entire
And frankly disappointing, dusty, posed, not up

To their fantastic names (Ascar fairy bluebird,
Crimson sunbird, ivory breasted pitta), though to see
Any such creature in full motion, flustering

Deepest canopy, silencing the jungle,
Would be something else again,
It would.

Happiness

Already at dusk the moon is so full of itself
It is about to fall into my arms,

I have never deserved
Anything like it:
The sky delivered nightly,

Emerging above the platter of light
The sun spreads on the horizon
As if to offer up heavenly bodies

First one by one then all
At once as dark swoons in, overflowing

With stars, little boomerangs
Visible and invisible, bodies

So massive they could draw me out of myself
And into an orbit I would never escape—no,

I've never earned a storm and whoosh
Of spheres, brilliant figures

Telling my fortune, a last evening
Warm enough to sit on the porch. But then,

I don't deserve even my earthbound life
On any winter afternoon gone
Gray and sullen, waiting for you to arrive

At last and take off your old fleece coat
And draw me to you, your hands
Cold, your breath on my cowlick

Still edged with cold, your heart warm
And beating—so, when

I lean against your chest, it pulses
Miracle after miracle into my ear.

Dog Days

Then there are the questions of the body.
What holds it together? What falls
Apart? All of us are faltering, all
In our own ways going rough and shoddy:

My love's arthritic foot and knee; my back
Doubly ruptured, and I was only sitting down.
But these two—they don't think to complain.
They just keep their noses to the track,

Tracking delights of passage, every smell
Of every passerby bearing the *now*
Along in its delicious ripeness, enough.
And could it be enough for us? Leave well

Enough alone, I always say. He says
Every dog has her day every day.

Katharine Coles' fourth collection of poems, *Fault*, came out from Red Hen Press in June of 2008. She has also published two novels. Her collaboration with visual artist Maureen O'Hara Ure has resulted in several joint installations and an artist's book, *Swoon*. Her commissioned works include *Passages*, a sequence permanently installed in Salt Lake City at the Gateway's Passages Park, for which Coles also served on the design team; and "The Numbers," permanently installed as part of Anna Campbell Bliss's *Numbers and Measure* in the Leroy Cowles Mathematics Building at the University of Utah. She is a professor in the English Department at the University of Utah, where she teaches creative writing and literature and co-directs, with biologist and mathematician Fred Adler, the Utah Symposium in Science and Literature, which she founded. She is currently serving a two-year appointment as the Inaugural Director of the Harriet Monroe Poetry Institute at the Poetry Foundation in Chicago. In 2006, she was named to a five-year term as Poet Laureate of Utah. During the winter of 2010-11, she traveled to Antarctica as a recipient of a National Science Foundation Antarctic Artists and Writers Program grant.

Kenneth W. Brewer
Utah

The Persistence of Memory

Since 300 B.C. at Alexandria,
we have built houses for Mnemosyne,
hoping to remember who we are.

In this house, we save Ancestral Puebloan pottery,
Father Dominguez' maps, Navajo story baskets,
Ruess' woodcuts, shell brooches from Camp Topaz.

In this house, we see a pocket clock stopped
the moment one of 200 miners died in the blast
and the afterdamp gas of the Winter Quarters Mine.

We see the archived Probate of Brigham Young's Estate,
and in each wife's signature a story, different
as each touch to cheek, each kiss goodbye.

Under this dome of light,
between visions in glass and oil,
here is the home of memory.

Scarlet Penstemon

Bees can't see red
but hummingbirds can
so the scarlet penstemon
curls its lower lip,
picks its lover as certain
as Cleopatra picked Caesar.

In the southern Utah summer,
in the late afternoon
of long shadows, shimmering,
the scarlet penstemon pouts,
and, oh, sweet Jesus, to be
a broad-tailed hummingbird then.

Why Dogs Stopped Flying

Before humans,
dogs flew everywhere.
Their wings of silky fur
wrapped hollow bones.
Their tails wagged
like rudders through wind,
their stomachs bare
to the sullen earth.

Out of sorrow
for the first humans—
stumbling, crawling,
helpless and cold—
dogs folded their
great wings into paws
soft enough to walk
beside us forever.

They still weep for us,
pity our small noses,
our unfortunate eyes,
our dull teeth.
They lick our faces clean,
keep us warm at night.
Sometimes they remember flying
and bite our ugly hands.

Returning the Gaze

The good dog Gus and I
Stared into each other's eyes
as I spoke to him about
when I leave, and that I did
not mean to Cheyenne, he
will need to be Bobbie's best friend.

After saying that, I looked deeper
and realized my human weakness
to believe I needed to speak in words
to this superior being, to explain
what he already understood in
the silence of our eyes.

Kenneth W. Brewer is the author of numerous books of poetry, including *Why Dogs Stopped Flying* and *To Remember What Is Lost* from Utah State University Press, gave readings and conducted writing workshops throughout the western states. During his career, he was dedicated not only to the literary arts but also to music, theater, and the visual arts; he acted on the stage and also collaborated with other artists ranging from jazz guitarists to woodcut artists to printmakers. Famous throughout the state as a teacher of writing, he continued to teach workshops even after he retired from Utah State University after 32 years in the English Department. During his final year, he wrote eloquently and compassionately about his experience with pancreatic cancer. He and his cancer poems were featured in newspapers and on television programs regionally and nationally; they were released by Dream Garden Press in the collection *Whale Song: A Poet's Journey Into Cancer*. He lived in Cache Valley, Utah, with his wife, Roberta Stearman, and his good dog Gus. He died in office in March, 2006. He is greatly missed by Utah's literary community.

DAVID LEE
UTAH

Saturday Night Storm and Her Puppy is Frightened

(after Bobby Joe just called in from Junction
60 miles out on the last leg of a week-long haul)

The gods in the upper room
just flat racaucous tonight:
knocked a PBR off the counter
canclang on the bar rail, roll against the stool legs
beer seeps through the floorboards
thunder spreads across the rafters
ceiling bouncing as they dance
to the holy jukebox stormy weather pick hits
pool ball clack and waft of Bull Durham and joy weed
floating through the live oaks
living high while daddy's out on rain business
or wallowed up against big legged earth mama

the warm libation drips and drips
all across the hill country
and the dog shivers against the night sounds
screaming witches and caterwauls
singing along loud enough to peel wallpaper
Jupiter and Saturn torn away
from the milky way and moon
on the kid's bedroom walls
all the lunges the lightning
shoves into the warm sky
begs me to let him up in our bed
but he's pure shit out of luck

Go away baby dog
you're on your own this time
it's a storm a raging all both
out there and in here tonight
fast and pray however you do it
doggy style, work out your own
salvation with fear and trembling
your daddy will be home in an hour
I'm planning to tie a double knot
up in my own redemption righteously tight
I'm singing Come come ye saints
nookie's on the agenda this rainy night

Nocturne Sliver Moon Datura

—to Michael Donovan

In the tightest quiet
a sound of glistering.
A fragrance trapped within
the opening bud,
the breath of a night
without a yesterday or tomorrow.
The desert under
a piece of sharp light,
a shard of windstone
broken off the moon
hides its tangled dreams
inside the bone white blossom.

Slot Canyon

In the desert there is all and there is nothing.
God is there and man is not.—Balzac

Great smooth stanchions
vault like a slow gesture
across a corner of sleep

The mind's eye rises
to easy invitation
by the memory of sky

Twisted slickrock
tightens inward
gnarled roots tethered in sand

A moonflower huddles
in eternal shadow
against the nave wall

A blue collared lizard blinks
then closes its drowsy eyes
beneath a white blossom

One seamless furl
rock to sand to leaf
to body to white petaled next

As if the desert
turned itself inside out
to contain this moment

Century Plant

1
South wind moves
through a slash of cross timbered sandstone
and hoodoos like castaway burls
awaiting the pyre

under a waning quarter moon
snagged on a barb
in the horizon

empties itself
into the valley
of exhumed catacombs
channeling thin light
into the desert's exhausted wellspring

2
Cougarwind slinks
across the bajada
slices down a fault
and drops
into a gash of cañoncito

a serpentine cat's cradle
seeps away
like thought
into the clutch
of a Jungian death demon

3
Curled parchment
four-winged saltbush
rattles in the wind
as it searches
for a desiccated vision
to inflict on a dying pariah
an agave nearing the moment of death
in full twenty foot bloom
sacrifices its timelessness
to the moon's point of reference

this noneternal moment
of rising personal significance

the ultimate fragility

panicle of burst pods
rattle like arthritic knuckles
on a hallowed anchoress
counting prayer beads
between exequies

4
a martyr
gone to shelter
beneath a bloodshot sky

within a great fortress
of cactus and stone

death leers
over the bastions

the wind spirals

5
An owl's rusted voice
nailed by the moon
into a cross truss of sky

A white feather
curled upon wind drift sand

> *for Bill Holm*
> *1943-2009*

David Lee was Utah's first Poet Laureate (1997-2003). Retired from Southern Utah University, where he won every teaching award given by the Institution, including being named Professor of the Year on three occasions. Lee currently splits his time between Bandera, Texas, and Seaside, Oregon, where he is in intensive training to fulfill his goal of becoming a world class piddler.

KELLY CHERRY
VIRGINIA

Ithaca

I remember a hall of doors
opening and closing. Goldfish
nibbled grainy bits in a glass bowl,
and sunlight stained the walls and floor
like finger paint. I remember
the silence, thick and spongy as bread,
and sound cutting through it like a knife.
Oh, I remember my life then, how
my parents played their violins
half the night, rehearsing, while snow
piled on the sill outside the pane.
Mike was making a model plane;
the baby slept, sucking her thumb.
I used to come home from school late—
detained for misbehavior, or
lost in a reverie on State
Street: *I, Odysseus, having dared*
to hear the sirens' song, my ears
unstopped, have sailed to Ithaca,
where the past survives. Last of all,
I remember dressing for school;
it was still dark outside, but when
the sun rose, it melted the snow.
My galoshes had small brass clasps.

Fission

I
The atoms buzz like bees,
splendiferously. Trees
spring into leaf and light
kisses night good-bye.

II
Here's rain and grassblade!
Made for each other—
I seem to see you in shade
and sun, the trickiest weather.

III
A solitary fly
sews the sky around my head,
stitching with invisible thread.
Time is this needle's eye.

IV
You lie, you lie.
I unstopper my veins and drink
my heart dry.
Call me Alice. I shrink.

V
I split. I spin through space at full
tilt, keel, careen, smash, and mushroom
into smoke beside your oaken heart.
Death does us part.

My Marriage

(Genus: Lepidodendron)

It goes under like a spongy log,
soaking up silica.

I love these stony roots
planted in time, these stigmaria,

this scaly graduate
of the school of hard knocks,

these leaf-scarred rocks
like little diamonds.

And the rings! . . . the rings
and cells that show forth

clearly, fixed and candid
as the star in the north.

Giant dragonflies, corals,
the tiny bug-eyed trilobite

grace this paleosite
with shell and wing, cool,

amberstruck exoskeleton,
nice flash of improbability

felled and stuck, past
petrified in present, free

from possibility's hard and arbitrary
demands. Once, seed ferns swooned,

languid as the currents in a lost lagoon,
while warm winds swarmed over the damp earth

like locusts, and rain was manna.
I hold that time still.

Divorce keeps it real and intact,
like a fossil.

The Bride of Quietness

My husband, when he *was* my husband, possessed
electrifying energy, humor,
the vital heat of violent force compressed. . .
contraries in a controlling frame. Few more

creative and compelling men could fire
the clay I scarcely dared to call my soul.
Shapeless, lacking properties of higher
existence, it was perfect for the mold

he cast me in: classic receptacle,
a thing for use but full of elegance,
an ode to Greece, forever practical,
tellingly patterned with the hunt and dance.

My lines were lies; and yet he seemed to see
aesthetic validation in my form.
I asked him not to draw away from me.
He said he feared he might commit some harm—

some accidental, inadvertent hurt—
and shatter in an instant all the love
he'd poured out in the effort to convert
my ordinary mind to a work of

art. And how he shuddered if I assumed
a new position or a point of view!
As if I were a royal vase entombed
after the ancient style, and the issue

of my movement could only be a change
in where he stood, relative to his wife.
I must perdure inanimate and strange
and still, if he would justify his life.

For I was the object of his most profound
research, the crafty subject of his thesis,
and all I had to do to bring him down
was let my heart break into all those pieces

it ached to break into in any case.
Upon his graduation, when the guests
had gone, and night was settling on his face,
raising my voice above his dreams I confessed

that beauty held no truth for me, nor truth
beauty, but I was made as much of earth
as I had been, barbaric and uncouth,
enjoined to rhythm, shiftings, blood and birth,

and void of principle. He said he'd father
no children. I could hardly help knowing
that he'd be wrong to trust me any farther.
By sunrise it was clear he would be going

soon. Now from time to time I see him here
and there. The shoulders have gone slack, the eyes
conduct a lesser current and I fear
that when they catch me spying, it's no surprise

to him. He always found poetic justice
amusing, and he knows I wait my turn.
The artist dies; but what he wrought will last
forever, when I cradle his cold ashes in this urn.

Kelly Cherry is the author of twenty books of fiction (novels, short stories), poetry, and nonfiction (memoir, essay, criticism), eight chapbooks, and translations of two classical plays. Her most recently published titles are *The Woman Who*, a collection of short stories, *The Retreats of Thought: Poems* and *Girl in a Library: On Women Writers & the Writing Life*. She was the first recipient of the Hanes Poetry Prize given by the Fellowship of Southern Writers for a body of work. Other awards include fellowships from the National Endowment for the Arts and the Rockefeller Foundation, the Bradley Major Achievement (Lifetime) Award, a Distinguished Alumnus Award, three Wisconsin Arts Board fellowships and two New Work awards, an Arts America Speaker Award (The Philippines), and selection as a Wisconsin Notable Author. In summer, 2010 she was a visitor at the Institute for Advanced Study in Princeton while working on a book-length poem.

CAROLYN KREITER-FORONDA
VIRGINIA

Two Voices: Calla Lilies

After Diego Rivera's Desnudo con alcatraces

Kneeling on a petate mat,
The basket, deep enough,
an Indian woman sits upright,
supports our long, firm stems.
her unclothed frame scented.
We settle into clots of dirt.
Is it sandalwood? Mahogany?
Like absinthe, we intoxicate
I paint her broad shoulders:
the artist who shapes the woman's arms
    earthy dabs of nutmeg, hyacinth
with the mastery of sun
    so she can thrive like the flowers,
so she can embrace us.
    so she can feel the florets swell.
Her hands smelling of freesia,
    Soon, she will rise out of shadows
reach out to our trumpets blaring
    to gather bluets, yarrows.
as though she hears a mariachi horn,

What is happiness, if not this need?
feels our desire to return to marshes,
    See how she rests—a saint—holding
watery fields, shallow pools far from
    pearls tamed like fire?
the lover who approaches a street vendor—
    Now, maybe you understand who I am.
scissor snips ringing through the market,
    In the city, in the valleys,
fleshy tubes and arrow-shaped leaves
    I wander in search of legends
rolled into wrapping paper, sold for a few pesos,
    to begin anew. Oh, these calla lilies!
the blooms' swanlike hearts pounding.

Leaving the Mine

After Diego Rivera's Salida de la mina, *1923*

Again, you search me.
      With your cartridge belt
            clanging against your hip,

you are no better. You probe
      each miner until someone
            hands over the stolen silver,

which you'll steal yourself
      when no one's looking.
            I am nothing to you,

a poor worker longing
      for a few pesos. Bread
            the color of your shirt.

Beans lampblack. Corn
      sweetened by the sun-drenched
            skies I long for

in the tunnels of this open pit.
      I raise my arms into a granite
            sky, my sandaled feet

holding me straight up like a crucifix.
      Beneath your leather boots,
            my brother clings to a rope-

and-timber ladder, his face ashen,
      scarred by underground demons,
            whose eyes bulge with desire.

Hunched over, you frisk my sides.
        The stench of tobacco carries me
                back. My father had arrived

home late. "A boulder the size
        of this room," he said, "collapsed
                onto fistfuls of ore."

As someone dragged Papá
        through a narrow hole, he closed
                his eyes and dreamed

of gold and silver ready to mold
        into coins for market.
                Hoisted to the surface,

he barely felt the fingers
        of the light-skinned man
                run up and down his thighs.

Papá should have taken the ore,
        shaped the metals into swords,
                sharpened them until they slid

like a curse through the guard's ribs.
        He should have shown him
                the art of carving flesh.

Night of the Rich

After Diego Rivera's La orgía, 1928

". . . there is only one element more helpless
than the poor, and that is the rich."
            Clarence Darrow

I offer her a sip of champagne,
          which slides down her throat
                    like liquid gold, eyes glazed

over as if she's dreaming
          of easy dollars and a *casa grande*
                    she can keep. In a slinky dress

alabaster as moon, she leans
          toward me, hair pulled in a bun:
                    a decadent crown of jewels.

The room stifling with cigar smoke,
          I know what I'm doing is wrong,
                    but like spending a wad of cash,

I can't resist the urge to force
          myself on a *señorita* in heels.
                    Outside, the shouts of revolutionists

mount. I close my eyes, become
          a young bank teller longing
                    for more, the city racing by

like a frantic bird. It's come to this:
          money buys a young *inocente*.
                    I lure her into my den, teach her

the power of *los pesos duros*.

She dances before me. A sunflower
unfolds, her breath scented

with lavender. The magic's in the drink.
Her voice fluid as water, she lies down,
says I'm her salvation, then shows

off dainty hands, covering my limbs
with magnolia blossoms until I release
a sharp cry. We all scheme

before death's arm slithers
around our shoulders and relaxes
our grip on luxurious dreams.

Collage: My Dress Hangs There

*"I don't have the slightest ambition to be anybody. I don't give a damn
about airs."*
Frida Kahlo, Letter to Doctor Leo Eloesser, *March 15, 1941*

I can't bear another minute of these
                 Pretentious snobs,
gringachos putting on airs over cocktails.
                 the big shots crave liquor.
I hunger for Mexico's exotic cuisine,
                 I thirst for lime water,
for quesadillas, spun from squash blossoms.
                 a dessert of mango sorbet.
In Manhattan an arctic chill descends,
                 In a collage, I paste
Wall Street's Federal Hall looming dead-center.
                 a church, a stained-glass window,
While Diego kowtows to American progress,
                 serpentine $ around a cross,
I pay homage to socialites for their perfect
                 fuel pumps, smokestacks,
plumbing: lid propped wide-open on a toilet.
                 clouds grabbing the fumes,
Hats off to the sports hero, posing as a trophy,
                 a movie star, glamorous,
gold-lit on a pedestal. Hats off to the telephone,
                 aloft a faded dwelling,
wires winding through buildings like nooses.
                 the windows grim.
For the millions earned weekly,
                 On the inaugural site, I paste
hats off to the moneybags. Lined up, the masses
                 George Washington, stoic,
protest the city's waste, its spent greed spilling
                 patriotic reds weaving

from a garbage can. Hats off to the system
               throughout the city.
that gobbles up the poor like candy.
               I don't care to be somebody.
Against skyscrapers I hang my ruffled costume,
               I don't give a damn about airs.
dangling like an albatross. How like Lady Liberty
               Shrouded in fog,
to wave absently. How like her to keep her distance
               the harbor statue disappears,
from the lonely and forlorn.
               her eyes shut to a passing ship.

Paint Me Flying

It is certain they are going to amputate my right leg . . . .
I am very worried, but at the same time, it will be liberating.
                    From The Diary of Frida Kahlo, August 1953

Paint me flying through saffron skies:
              Feet—why do I want them?

a hummingbird, wavering like a supple leaf.
              Wings are enough.

Balanced on a sliver of dawn,
              I'll wear a wooden leg

I'll hover among trumpet vines.
              and dance on a dare—

Paint me curled up in a seamless knot:
              among honeysuckle, bee balm—

a hairless caterpillar on a pansy's back,
              slender as a flicker.

waving its gilded wand until a butterfly flits.
              I'll don leather boots,

Paint me reclining on a mandrake's tongue,
              cerise aflame,

stout as a root. Paint me ascending, a parrot
              adorned with bells.

from a basket of plums, luscious in a heap.
              If I have wings,

Píntame volando, a dragonfly, plaiting the air.
              what do I need feet for?

Two Voices: Deer Running

After Frida Kahlo's The Little Deer, *1946*

Beneath a coarse sky, I flee
through an enclosed glade,

> *Run toward the light,*
> *little deer. Catch hold of*

my limber frame: a young stag's
crowned with massive antlers.

> *brightness sizzling above*
> *the glazed, forest floor.*

Arrows gash my chest and flank.
Crimson trickles from wounds,

> *Raw sienna spools*
> *a well-worn path*

my pursuer crouched behind a tree,
the trunk's exposed roots swollen

> *in the distance. Birdsong*
> *pulses like waves bobbing*

like the flawed design of my human
form, stones in my soul.

> *crystal notes. Run toward*
> *the hymns, nimble deer.*

And you, Diego, place one leafy,
golden branch withering before me

Let loose your foe's nine arrows,
trembling in your hide.

as I prepare to die and resurrect
as growth: green bark,

Do not fear death. Your wounds,
their indelible marks will heal

green branches at the foot
of your shadow,

as I push away lightning
from the barren plot,

swallowed whole
by sun's unerring rays.

where your body collapses
in a spool of radiance.

Two Voices: Stone Worker

After Diego Rivera's Picapedrero, *1943*

Thick-built, solid, I am all man,
          Virile,
my woman says, rough-hewn
          a pillar
and durable as the bits
          of gray,
I hammer from this block
          crevassed
of coarse rock. The ground
          like magma,
swells with unwanted chunks,
          I hold still,
shattered by blows, every stroke
          counting
releasing a thud as I pound
          the chips
and lose myself in a dance,
          broken loose
my arm hurling downward,
          from my side
pulling back into air
          and tossed
with the force
          to the ground—
of each crushing thwack.
          flawed,
Late at night, I hear the echo
          he thinks,
of a mallet's smack.
          striking again,
The walls I build
          splintering

can't compare to the statues

    pieces

I shape in my mind: divine deities

    of my soul

from basalt, waiting.

    until there's

One day I will carry

    little more than

volcanic rocks home,

    fragments to

carve and burnish,

    break, yet

set free what is trapped

    my spirit soars

inside the crude blocks.

    as he smoothes, polishes,

In the quarries

    places me

I can hear

    on the wall's crest.

voices singing.

Carolyn Kreiter-Foronda served as Virginia's Poet Laureate from 2006-2008. She is also a painter, sculptor and educator. In 1969, she graduated from Mary Washington College (Mortar Board and Phi Beta Kappa) with a BA in English. She holds two masters degrees and a Ph.D. from George Mason University, where she received the university's first doctorate and a Virginia Educational Research Award for her dissertation. Her award-winning poems have been nominated for four Pushcart Prizes and appear in numerous magazines and journals, including *Nimrod, Hispanic Culture Review, Prairie Schooner, Poet Lore, Mid-American Review, Antioch Review, Passages North,* and *Anthology of Magazine Verse & Yearbook of American Poetry.* She has published five books of poetry, *Contrary Visions, Gathering Light, Death Comes Riding, Greatest Hits, River Country* and is the co-editor of two anthologies, *In a Certain Place* and *Four Virginia Poets Laureate.*

SAMUEL GREEN
WASHINGTON

Lady Slipper

This one is ten feet off the trail,
an inch from where I set down my saw,
the color of a girl's most earnest
blush, open, as she might open her lips
in mute surprise. Some call it
"Calypso," after the nymph who kept a man
seven years from his wife with the magic
of her body in bed, Greek for *hidden*.

Pick it, & the plant will not bloom
again. Dig it up, & it will die
away from where it was rooted.

Forgive me if all I bring you
is its name, & the brief story
of how it stands in a patch of moss
swept clean in a wash
of light no larger than a sole
into which we push with care
the small, perfectly fitting foot of love.

Home Town Park

written for the opening of the new children's playground,
Storvik Park, Anacortes

That crow, if there were wind,
might be a kite. Daisies are only white
until the mower comes again.

That child whining for a turn
on the slide could be yours,
or could be you, enough years gone.

That old woman who slid a stone
into her sweater pocket will take it out
& rub it with her thumb when she's alone.

That dry complaint is creaking swings.
A mother laughs & pushes.
Her daughter shouts & sings.

There, some boy counted the loose
change of love into a girl's hand, a ring
gathered & bent the light of stars onto grass.

There, a son collapsed on the damp seat
of a bench having said good-bye
at the funeral home across the street.

Here is where a gray dog decided not to bark.
He lies beside his gray master & listens
to the town grow quiet in the coming dark.

There's always more than one way in. Come. Stay
long enough to know what brought you here,
what you leave behind, what you take away.

Stroke

Where is the axe, says the ice in the trough, left in the field for the cows.
    Here, says the file on the bench in the shed, stuck in a hole by the vise.
Where is the cup with a chip in its rim, says the sink with its saucer & spoon.
    Here, says the kitchen linoleum square, in fragments the color of bone.
Where is the milk, says the pail on the porch, scalded, & shiny & worn.
    Here, say the bells of the shuffling herd, stalled at the door of the barn.
Where is the cream for the cinnamon cat, says the tuna can under the stairs.
    Here, says a shelf in the cold box, with the butter & leftover pears.
Where is the heat for the dinner, say the skillet & pans on the range.
    Here, say the split chunks of alder & fir, carefully dried & arranged.
Where is the ball made of leftover twine, says the unfinished rug on the stool.
    Here, says the awkward crochet hook made from an old-fashioned nail.
Where is the woman who lives in this house, says the work coat still hung on a chair.
    Here, says the wind through the grass of the field,
    here says the white on the waves past the bluff,
    here says the bird in the air.
Not here, says the cow, *not here*, says the cat, *not here*, say the boots by the door.
Not here, says the stove, *not here*, says the coat, *not here*, says the shape on the floor.

Calling the Old Dog In

for Jerry & Kathy

It's no good standing on the porch
& yelling. He's deaf
as a man with long years
in the engine room of a ship listening

for the sounds metal makes
before it fails, a faint break
in rhythm, something out of tune.
He is lying in the middle

of the road, staring east
across a field of pumpkins
ruined by the cold.
He can't hear ducks or geese

resting in the marsh talking one another
through the night in comfort
or complaint. Or coyotes
barking across the Valley.

Traffic is far away, only a whisper,
like blood through a vein.
Some dark scent, perhaps, tugs
his head back & forth in an old, old way.

If he hears anything, it is likely the light
beating in his chest, already diminishing,
though neither of us knows it.
He is sprawled in a black bed

of glittering frost,
so that I wonder if he's had to lie down
to keep from falling into the sea
of stars above him. When he turns

his head at my touch
his eyes fill with a small joy,
as though love is so easily given
even I might as well have a little,

as though, when he rises
& trots toward the house
& his bed,
I needn't follow after.

Cist, National Museum, Dublin

She is folded into a square
of stones the way a child might squeeze
herself into her mother's drawer
in a game of hide & seek, or the way
another might tuck herself under
a blanket too small for her, the night
cold & long. Her stillness is casual,
like a chair put away after summer,
or into a closet after church
coffee & cake. And yet nothing
is connected: each vertebrae is a pilgrim
who has given up & sprawled
in a long arc on the bank of a dry river;
the clever puzzle of her ribs is collapsed
like a basket left too long in the yard.
Each brown bone is light as a bird's least
intention. The stone bowl beside her head
is foolishly full of stale air. Absurd to think
we could fill it with anything meaningful—
the heavy coin of embarrassment, the paper
currency of prayer. Four thousand years confined
to her room. If we lifted the glass from her tomb,
slid away the cover, we could hear the slow
sound of atoms waving farewell.

Grandmother, Cleaning Rabbits

I shot this one by the upper pond of the farm
after watching the rings trout made rising
to flies, watching small birds pace the backs
of cows, hoping all the time she would run.

My grandmother told me they damaged her garden.

I think it was a way to make the killing
lighter. She never let me clean them, only asked
I bring them headless to her. I bring this one
to the fir block near the house, use the single-
bitted axe with the nick in the lower crescent
of the blade, smell the slow fire
in the smoke-house, salmon changing
to something sweet & dark. A fly turns
in a bead of blood on my boot. I tuck
the head in a hole beside the dusty globes
of ripened currants, talk quiet to the barn cat.

In her kitchen my grandmother whets the thin blade
of her Barlow, makes a series of quick, clever cuts, then tugs
off the skin like a child's sweater. This one was
pregnant. She pulls out a row of unborn rabbits
like the sleeve of a shirt with a series of knots.
The offal is dropped in a bucket. Each joint gives way
beneath her knife as though it wants
to come undone, as though she knows some secret
about how things fit together. I have killed
a hundred rabbits since I was eight.

This will be the last.

I am twenty, & about to go back
to the war that killed my cousin in *Kien Hoa*,
which is one more name she can't pronounce.

I haven't told her about the dead,
& she won't ask. She rolls the meat
in flour & pepper & salt, & lays it
in a skillet of oil that spits like a cat.
She cannot save a single boy who carries a gun.
All she can do is feed this one.

Tulip Field, McLean Road

If there were a single word
for the color of these tulips,
it would have to contain
the bright swirl of my mother's favorite
skirt. She square-danced in it for years, until
some inner joy faded faster than the fabric.
It would need to have the scarlet
of a single maple leaf
caught in a spider's web between
two trees in the orchard
my wife & I planted
together. And the splendor of an apple
polished on the wool of a Pendleton
shirt my grandfather left
a little wear in when he died.

I say *red* & want to hold it
with my tongue longer than teeth
& gums will let me—
skirt & *leaf*, *shirt* & *apple*—
& no lexicon to help me.

Samuel Green was born in Sedro-Woolley, Washington, and raised in the nearby fishing
and mill town of Anacortes. After four years in the military, including service in Antarcti-
ca and South Vietnam, he attended college under the Veterans Vocational Rehabilitation
Program, earning degrees from Highline Community College and Western Washington
University (B.A. & M.A.). A 35-year veteran of the Poetry-in-the-Schools program, he
has taught in literally hundreds of classrooms around Washington State. He has also
taught at Southern Utah University, Western Wyoming Community College, Colorado
College, and served eight winter terms as Distinguished Visiting Northwest Writer at
Seattle University, as well as eight summers in Ireland. Among his ten collections of

poems are *Vertebrae: Poems 1972-1994* (Eastern Washington University Press) and *The Grace of Necessity* (Carnegie-Mellon University Press), which won the 2008 Washington State Book Award for Poetry. He has lived for 27 years off the grid on remote Waldron Island off the Washington coast in a log house he built himself after living in a tent for three years. He is, with his wife, Sally, Co-Editor of the award-winning Brooding Heron Press, which produces fine, letterpressed volumes. In December, 2007, he was named by Governor Christine Gregoire to a two-year term as the first Poet Laureate for the State of Washington. In January of 2009, he was awarded a National Endowment for the Arts Fellowship in Poetry.

IRENE MCKINNEY
WEST VIRGINIA

At 24

At 24, I had written and read until my eyes were bloodshot,
spending nights and early mornings in a fervor
of page-filling while the baby slept.
I was writing to save my life as I knew it
could be. I was writing to inscribe my body
on a stone tablet, writing in defiance and silence.
Nothing could stop me, I kept saying No
to the paper, I kept saying you can't have me
to the Junior League, to the tiny streets, to impossible
jobs and prissy motherhood. I was certain
there was another way that didn't involve
slavery, another way to love and work than the
simian forms evolved so far. One morning I drank
eight cups of coffee and wrote four poems
and I didn't even care that my head was bursting
and I was lurching around while I scrubbed the bathroom.
Another time I left the children with my mother
and lay in bed all day reading a biography of Van Gogh
and groaning. What a life, what a life.
I thought about Toulouse-Lautrec, that little freak.
I was a freak myself, but only in private.
I stared at his bronzes and terra cottas and oranges
until they pulled the color nerves out of my chest.
That was a long time ago and now I know that
I knew nothing then, and if I had I wouldn't

have gone on. Dear Mr. President, I said, Dear Dean,
Dear Husband, Dear Our Father, Dear Tax Collector,
you don't know me. I don't know what I am,
but whatever it is, you can't have me.

Viridian Days

I was an ordinary woman, and so
I appeared eccentric, collecting gee-gaws
of porcelain and cobalt blue, mincing
deer-meat for the cat. I was unhooked

from matrimony, and so I rose up
like a hot-air balloon, and drifted
down eventually into the countryside,
not shevelled New England nor the

grandeur of the West, but disheveled
West Virginia, where the hills are flung
around like old green handkerchiefs
and the Chessie rumbles along, shaking

the smooth clean skin of the river.
If I wanted to glue magazine pictures
to an entire wall, or walk around nude,
I did so, having no standard to maintain

and no small children to be humiliated
by my defection. I spent years puttering
around in a green bathrobe, smelling of
coffee, perfume, sweat, incense, and

female effluvia. Why not. That was
my motto. I collected books like some
women collect green stamps, but I read
them all, down to the finest print,

the solid cubes of footnotes. Since no one
was there, nobody stopped me. Raspberry vines
slash at the Toyota's sides as I come in.
Flocks of starlings, grosbeaks, mourning doves

lift the air around the house. Fragments
of turkey bones the dog chewed on, a swarm
of ladybugs made into a red enameled necklace,
hulls of black sunflower seeds piled

on the porchboards. Locust, hickory, sweet gum
trees. Absolute silence stricken by crow calls.
Copper pans, eight strands of seed beads,
dolphin earrings. I climb over the fence

at the edge of the woods, back and forth
over it several times a day, gathering ferns,
then digging in the parsley, - shaggy, pungent, green.

Full Moon: Sitting Up Late at My Father's Bedside

What can I say. The moon looms in the nighttime sky
with brilliance, as it does. But we are going to touch it,

and then it will go away. The animals on earth
are breathing, but someone takes their hearts

and puts them into broken human bodies.
What can I say to those people? You took the heart

of a chimp: you found you could do it,
and you did? Secrets come out of the heart,

and nowhere else. We don't know how.
What can I say when my father is dying,

with his new eyes and his new heart.
His mind is like a flapping line of laundry,

clothing full of wind. How can I speak
about the babble of his speech? His saying

does not go from here to there, it's only here.
Out of the dog came five pups, slick wet packets,

each different. They grew at different rates.
Some slept, two leapt around all day.

What can I say about their secret selves,
their paws, their separate ways of walking?

What can be said about their natures, and
their flawed and perfect lives? I gave

them away. They have a new trajectory and
I'm still here. I think about them every day.

My father's manner is the same as it was
when he was sane. Senility's a secret, too.

It isn't vague to him. I see intensity in all
he misconstrues, - I think he misconstrues.

The night is brilliant, and the moon's too close.
It calls him out: to where, I cannot say.

Ready

I remember a Sunday with the smell of food drifting
out the door of the cavernous kitchen, and my serious
teenage sister and her girlfriends Jean and Marybelle
standing on the bank above the dirt road in their
white sandals ready to walk to the country church
a mile away, and ready to return to the fried
chicken, green beans and ham, and fresh bread
spread on the table. The sun was bright and
their clean cotton dresses swirled as they turned.
I was a witness to it, and I assure you that it's true.

I remembered this thirty years later as I got
up from the hospital bed, favoring my right side
where something else had been removed.
Pushing a cart that held practically all of my
vital fluids, I made my way down the hall
because I wanted to stand up, for no reason.
I had no future plans, and I would never
found a movement nor understand the
simplest equation; I would never chair the
Department of Importance. Nevertheless,
I was about to embark on a third life, having
used up the first two, as I would this one,
but I shoved the IV with its sugars and tubes
steadily ahead of me, passing a frail man in a hospital
gown pushing his cart from the other direction.
Because I was determined to pull this together,
hooking this lifeline into the next one.

Irene McKinney is the recipient of a National Endowment for the Arts Fellowship in Poetry and a West Virginia Commission on the Arts Fellowship in Poetry. She is the author of five books of poetry, including *The Girl with a Stone in Her Lap* (North Atlantic, 1976), *The Wasps at the Blue Hexagons* (Small Plot Press, 1984), *Quick Fire and Slove Fire* (North Atlantic, 1988), *Vivid Companion* (West Virginia University Press/ Vandalia), and *Six O'Clock Mine Report* (Univeristy of Pittsburgh Press, 1989). She is editor of *Backcountry: Contemporary Writing in West Viriginia*, and has held fellowships at McDowell Colony, Virginia Center for the Creative Arts, and Blue Mountain Center. She was appointed Poet Laureate of West Virginia in 1994. She has been writer-in-residence at Western Washington University at Bellingham, the University of California at Santa Cruz, and the University of New Mexico at Albuquerque, among others. She is Professor Emerita at West Virginia Wesleyan College. Her new book, *Unthinkable: Selected Poems*, is published by Red Hen Press. She does a monthly commentary for Public Radio, and her poems have been read on Garrison Keillor's *Writer's Almanac* five times, and on *Verse Daily's* website.

BRUCE DETHLEFSEN
WISCONSIN

The Hot Dog Man

she threatened to sell us to the hot dog man
I had my chance mom whispered
the hot dog man takes anything
he'd cart you off no questions asked

in summer my mother
having had it up to here
again with us three boys
would run away from home

we wouldn't notice for an hour or so
until we got hungry or thought oh no
this time she might be gone for good

she'd walk around the block a time or two
we saw her sitting on the corner curb
her legs stretched out across the sewer grate
holding her face in both her hands to cry

it was embarrassing
to have the neighbors see her sadding there

I was the one elected to collect her
say we're sorry ask forgiveness
tell her whatever it took
whatever we did we wouldn't do again
promise

I'd take her hand and bring her home
one of us would hug her
one would clean his room
I'd do the dishes

for the rest of the day
we put away our wooden swords
our wounding words
we gave her peace
we gave her quiet

and when tomorrow came
and we resumed the awful evil that boys do
I'd look around from time to time
to make sure she remained

we boys are grown
our mother's gone for good
yet no one knows what really goes
inside those hot dogs

so I look out for the man
who asks no questions
I listen for that jangle of his cart

Suicide Aside

suicide aside
try watching birds
regard them as they fly like salt to bread
spice up this crusty world

a giant spider web
their lines of flight
tie up and bind the world

they fly
birds jump up in the air and stay
you try it
flap your arms for all you're worth
no way   you're stuck
they're free to leave the world

the colors
lemon zest and lime and berry
sugar coffee cream
and all the rest
sublime delicious flavors how
our eyes drink in the world

and listen to them sing
the wind becomes a thing alive
with music whistles squawks and chirps
a melody of world

so tell me why you thought you'd rather die
check out   pluck all the feathers
close the lights

alright don't tell me
but please me
stick around a while
with me to watch the birds
see how they swirl and turn the world

Up in the Cupboard

there'll be a time you take down
a glass custard dish
when you remember
I made you tapioca once
and you cry
big dam busted cry

then you replace the custard dish
up in the cupboard
and shut the door

White Stallions

the children of the street
must see themselves
in the greasy puddles of the forenoon
in the sundown storefront windows
in the luster of the shoes they shine

must see themselves
in the reflection of a customer's sunglasses
in the tears of the old women
in the shadow of the bus

the children of the street
must see themselves
flying purple kites on sunny beaches
dining with the family after church
riding white stallions

the children of the street
must see themselves

(Quetzaltenango, Guatemala 1998)

Artists

(for Denise)

we chase the moon
too hard sometimes
and stumble in the stars

that sparkle always blinds us
we trip and tumble down
we suffocate in stardust
drown in floodlight

and still we recreate
we sing   we write
we dance   we paint
we one more time in space
ourselves remake

return   retune

gracefully we rise again
we're artists
grateful for another dreadful chance
to chase the moon

Bruce Dethlefsen was born in Kansas City, went to college in Wisconsin in 1966, and stayed for the rest of his life. He is the author of two chapbooks, *A Decent Reed* (Tamafyr Mountain Press, 1996), and *Something Near the Dance Floor* (Marsh River Editions, 2003); and one full-length poetry book, *Breather* (Fireweed Press, 2009). He has been appointed Wisconsin Poet Laureate for 2011 and 2012. A retired educator and public library director, Dethlefsen lives in Westfield, Wisconsin.

MARILYN L. TAYLOR
WISCONSIN

The Blue Water Buffalo

One in 250 Cambodians, or 40,000 people,
have lost a limb to a landmine.
—Newsfront, U.N. Development Programme Communications Office

On both sides of the screaming highway, the world
is made of emerald silk—sumptuous bolts of it,
stitched by threads of water into cushions
that shimmer and float on the Mekong's munificent glut.

In between them plods the ancient buffalo—dark blue
in the steamy distance, and legless
where the surface of the ditch dissects
the body from its waterlogged supports below

or it might be a woman, up to her thighs
in the lukewarm ooze, bending at the waist
with the plain grace of habit, delving for weeds
in water that receives her wrist and forearm

as she feels for the alien stalk, the foreign blade
beneath that greenest of green coverlets
where brittle pods in their corroding skins
now shift, waiting to salt the fields with horror.

Reading the Obituaries

Now the Barbaras have begun to die,
trailing their older sisters to the grave,
the Helens, Margies, Nans—who said goodbye
just days ago, it seems, taking their leave
a step or two behind the hooded girls
who bloomed and withered with the century—
the Dorotheas, Eleanors and Pearls
now swaying on the edge of memory.
Soon, soon, the scythe will sweep for Jeanne
and Angela, Patricia and Diane—
pause, and return for Karen and Christine
while Susan spends a sleepless night again.
   Ah, Debra, how can you be growing old?
   Jennifer, Michelle, your hands are cold.

The Geniuses Among Us

They take us by surprise, these tall perennials
that jut like hollyhocks above the canopy
of all the rest of us—bright testimonials
to the scale of human possibility.
They come to bloom for every generation,
blazing with extraordinary notions
from the taproots of imagination—
dazzling us with incandescent visions.
And soon, the things we never thought would happen
start to happen: the solid fences
of reality begin to soften,
crumbling into fables and romances—
and we turn away from where we've been
to a new place, where light is pouring in.

The Lovers at Eighty

Fluted light from the window finds her
sleepless in the double bed, her eyes

measuring the chevron angle his knees make
under the coverlet. She is trying to recall

the last time they made love. It must have been
in shadows like these, the morning his hands

took their final tour along her shoulders and down
over the pearls of her vertebrae

to the cool dunes of her hips, his fingers
executing solemn little figures

of farewell. Strange—it's not so much
the long engagement as the disengagement

of their bodies that fills the hollow
curve of memory behind her eyes—

how the moist, lovestrung delicacy
with which they let each other go

had made a sound like taffeta
while decades flowed across them like a veil.

On Learning, Late in Life, that Your Mother Was a Jew

Methuselah something. Somethingsomething Ezekiel.
—Albert Goldbarth

So that explains it, you say to yourself.
And for one split second, you confront
the mirror like a Gestapo operative—
narrow-eyed, looking for the telltale hint,

the giveaway (jawline, profile, eyebrow)—
something visible that could account
for this, the veritable key
to your life story and its denouement.

It seems the script that you were handed
long ago, with all its blue-eyed implications,
can now be seen as something less than candid—
a laundry list of whoppers and omissions.

It's time for something else to float
back in from theology's deep end: the strains,
perhaps, of *A-don o-lam,* drowning out
the peals of *Jesus the Conqueror Reigns,*

inundating the lily and the rose,
stifling the saints (whose dogged piety
never did come close, God knows,
to causing many ripples of anxiety)

and you're waiting for the revelation
on its way this minute, probably—
the grand prelude to your divine conversion,
backlit with ritual and pageantry.

But nothing happens. Not a thing. No song,
no shofar, no compelling Shabbat call
to prayer— no signal that your heart belongs
to David rather than your old familiar, Paul.

Where does a faithless virgin go from here,
after being compromised by two
competing testimonies to thin air—
when both of them are absolutely true?

Why Don't You

Shut up? Shut up, shut up, shut up. Okay?
You're not my lucky star, you are a damn
black hole. I do not love you, Sam-I-am.
Get lost. Scram. Beat it. Go away.
Clear out your retrosexual groceries—
that loaf of bread, the jug of wine—right now;
and as for your adoring little *thou* ,
just watch her kick you in the fantasies.

I get the sense you're painfully aware
that you're a sorry-ass. The Big Dumpee.
How sad. Let me extend my sympathy
by offering you a simple little prayer:
May your next cocktail be a Molotov,
and everything that you hold dear fall off.

Summer Sapphics

Maybe things are better than we imagine
if a rubber inner-tube still can send us
drifting down a sinuous, tree-draped river
        like the Wisconsin—

far removed from spores of *touristococcus.*
As we bob half-in and half-out of water
with our legs like tentacles, dangling limply
        under the surface

we are like invertebrate creatures, floating
on a cosmic droplet—a caravan of
giant-sized amoebas, without a clear-cut
        sense of direction.

It's as if we've started evolving backwards:
mammal, reptile, polliwog, protozoon—
toward that dark primordial soup we seem so
        eager to get to.

Funny, how warm water will whisper secrets
in its native language to every cell— yet
we, the aggregation, have just begun to
        fathom the gestures.

Marilyn L. Taylor was appointed Poet Laureate of the state of Wisconsin in 2009. She taught for many years at the University of Wisconsin-Milwaukee for the Department of English and the Honors College. The most recent of her six collections of poetry, titled *Going Wrong,* was published by Parallel Press in 2009. Taylor's award-winning poems have appeared in many anthologies and journals, including *The American Scholar, Poetry, Smartish Pace, Measure,* and *Mezzo Cammin.* She is a Contributing Editor for *THE WRITER* magazine, where her articles on craft appear bi-monthly.

DAVID
ROMTVEDT
WYOMING

Western Aid

We worked in the East African hill country
running a parasite dipping tank. Local farmers
brought their cows and goats twice a week
and the animals were led into an ever narrowing chute
until they were forced to walk single file
to the lip of a concrete tank filled with pesticide.
They balked and bellowed, and tried to turn.
Their feet slipped out from under them
on the oozing carpet of urine and excrement
left by those who'd gone ahead.

Finally, they fell into the pesticide laden water
and swam for their lives. At the far side of the tank
the bottom sloped up and the terrified animals
stumbled back onto land where they shook
and ran then stopped to lick themselves.

One morning an army patrol appeared.
I say army as if things were that clear.
The soldiers had removed the mirrors
from the front fenders of their Jeep
and, on the vertical steel supports,
had mounted the heads of captured rebels
they were fond of calling communists.

Vous n'en avez pas? Ambiguous,
the question might have pertained
to medicines, gasoline, canned milk,
or rebels disguised as starving farmers.
"Nous ne cachons rien," my co-worker said.
We are hiding nothing then pointed at the heads
and added, "C'est pas juste." It's not right.

The Jeep driver stepped forward
and poked the barrel of his rifle
into her chest. I heard the quick
inhalation as he flipped the weapon
and then, swinging it like a machete
to clear a path, knocked her down.
When she didn't rise, he moved
to strike her again. A second soldier
held him back and they left,
heads wobbling on their mounts.

Illegal Alien

When I was drafted to fight in Vietnam,
my father, who was in the Army Air Corps
during World War II and twice shot out of the sky,
who spent a year in hospital undergoing plastic surgery
and attempted suicide, told me, "It doesn't matter
if your country is right or wrong, when you are called
to fight, you go." In my Arizona neighborhood, this
was the view. Refusing was to be a coward,
a chicken shit, a commie, and a faggot.

Afraid, I told my roommate who was Canadian.
He told his father, who called me and said,
"You're not a coward for refusing to become a killer."
then offered me a job. And so I began my new life
in British Columbia, an illegal alien on a landscape
garden crew. I mowed lawns, dug in mulch,
planted bushes, fertilized flowers, trimmed trees,
and drank beer. Each day I was paid in cash.

When the war ended, I came home and now
I'm a respectable American reading about the fence
being built along the southern border of the nation—
Texas, New Mexico, Arizona, California,
a fence from sea to shining sea to keep out Mexicans
and Guatemalans, Salvadorans and Colombians,
to keep out everyone, o sea la gente humilde,
la gente sin otros recursos. Even the shadows
will find no access to move across the ground.

These days I drive long distances to work
and return late to the sage grasslands
and pine forest, to the creek, the tumble of water
I can hear from my bedroom window,
the dark mountains rising near my house,
far from any border.

Sometimes in the night when I can't sleep,
I turn on the radio and listen to mysteries
from the Golden Age of Broadcasting,
to the exhortations of evangelical Christians,
to the Omaha grain market reports, and
to the political commentators shouting
down their guests. When it's late
and the air is still, I sometimes hear
a faint voice in French from Vancouver,
Et maintenant, the announcer says,
pour la région du Delta, le météo.
The weather report then the cheery
wish that I have a good evening—
nous vous souhaitons une bonne nuit—
and the sign off, Ici Radio Canada.
I turn off the radio and remember the rain,
the sparkling green lawns and blooming flowers
in the city where I was an illegal alien.

Accident

My father rises from the asphalt
and turns to me, his look of alarm
revealing the pain he's soon to feel.

I should explain—he was working on a loading dock
and a tractor trailer fell, the hitch landing on his arms
and breaking the bones into dozens of pieces.

With the Workman's Comp money, he bought me
a piano accordion. "Good easy work." He said. "Keep
your ass out of a factory or off a Goddamn loading dock."

But I couldn't imagine a life saved
by the piano accordion and wondered why
he wanted me to be as much unlike him as possible.

For a year his arms were encased in heavy casts
held up with metal armatures, his hands suspended
far from his body, useless as windows in a coffin.

At mealtime I lifted the fork or spoon to his open mouth,
his eyes drilling into mine. "I gave my arms for you."
He said. Between bites—"I gave my arms."

I was nervous enough. He'd hit me plenty before
the accident or the accordion. What if he turned his head
and I missed, the food dribbling down his chin?

And one day it happened. Not that I missed,
only that in the middle of lunch he lunged at me,
knocking us both out of our chairs and onto the floor.

It's funny how memory, even painful,
remains a pleasure and I return to my father
rising, casts and all, as if he might fly, then falling.

The midday sun hovers in the bright kitchen. My father's bent arms wrapped in plaster make him look like an angel with petrified wings, the blur of white swinging toward me.

Impounded

I slept in the jail, not for a crime exactly
unless you consider parking violations
criminal acts. It was the beginning
of a blizzard. The mechanical arms
had dropped across the Interstate
like the wooden bars on the turnpike
between Opelousas and Basile,
the rain doomed path
snaking across the Cajun Prairie.

And there was Antibon Legbo,
third cousin to the hoodoo voodoo loas of Haiti,
remnant dancing bones of assorted Nigerian Gods
covered in red mud, dripping Legbo leering
at every jolie jeune fille teenage girl
trying to get home before the caked hem
of her dress drags her down,
Legbo groaning and lifting the bar,
waving the girls by like Joel Gray
as the troubled emcee at the cabaret
whose back door opens to the land of the dead,
white powdered face and black lipstick,
singing Wilkommen, Bienvenu, Welcome.

Once I saw Legbo turn away and let
two indentured servants slip by,
escaping New Orleans as if it were hell.
Two white men. You get what I mean?
What could I do but drive back to town,
park the car, and get a bite to eat?
You drive on a blizzard closed interstate
in Wyoming, the cops'll haul your ass in
as soon as look at you, or look at your ass,
whatever, they'll haul you in. The snow
was screaming down from Lodge Grass

and Lame Deer and nobody cared
if it was Crow snow or Northern Cheyenne.
I could barely make out the flash of red
and green on the traffic signals much less
the amber or the No Parking signs
along Main Street like it mattered,
all of six cars cheek to jowl
with the sidewalk. When I came out
of the café, disheartened enough
by the chicken fried steak to wonder
if maybe I should have risked the fine
for driving on a closed highway,
my car was gone.

It's best not to look Antibon Legbo
in the eye, the red shine of blood
in the white. Best to look down
and ask politely to pass, say,
"Antibon Legbo, ouvrez barrière
pour mo passer." Lift the bar
so I can go by. Maybe say it twice—
ouvrez barrière pour mo passer.
Don't look up then either. Just
keep talking—"Quand mo mo passer
mon mercis tous loas yé." If he lets
you by, thank every spirit left
in this snow infested mud covered world.
Mercis tous loas yé. Keep your eyes down.
You don't have to see the bar go up—
no oil since medieval days
so the hinges creak as it rises.

Antibon Legbo himself shivers
to hear the screech and says,
"Tout le monde dans la fièvre,
tout le monde dans le feu,
grand hibou pour mon chapeau."

Everybody burning up with fever,
everybody thrown into the fire,
Legbo wearing a snake for his overcoat
and an owl for his hat, a snowy owl
with its white feathers burned gray.

The point is they hauled the car away
and impounded it and it was after hours
and me, middle class and fully prepared
with credit cards and ATM access,
well, none of that mattered cause
the lot where they store the cars
had an eight foot fence around it
and concertina wire at the top
and a chain as thick as Legbo's snake
and a lock as big as a ham.

Every hotel in town was full
so the police, as kindly as men
and women can be when they wear
revolvers and sticks on their pants,
offered to let me stay in the jail.
No additional charge, they joked,
for a victim of the storm, the same
storm that comes every winter
and the same victim turning up
day after day, far from Louisiana
with another barrier blocking the way.

David Romtvedt, born in Portland, Oregon and raised in southern Arizona, is a graduate of Reed College and the Iowa Writers' Workshop, he has worked as a cab and truck driver, an assembly line worker in a ski pole factory, a field hand in grapes, oranges, cantaloupe, and blueberries, as a bookstore clerk, and now, as a half-time professor at the University of Wyoming. It's surprising. He is a recipient of the Pushcart Prize, NEA fellowships from the literature and international programs, the Wyoming Literature fellowship, and the Wyoming Governor's Arts Award. His book *A Flower Whose Name I Do Not Know* was selected for the National Poetry Series. His other books of poetry include *Moon, How Many Horses, Certainty,* and *Some Church.* With the Fireants, he plays dance music of the Americas. The Fireants' most recent cd is *It's Hot (About Three Weeks a Year).*

PERMISSIONS

All poetry has been printed with full permission of each poet.

Peggy Shumaker: "Long Before We Got There, Long After We're Gone" first published in *Copper Nickel*, then in *Gnawed Bones*. "In Praise, Ephemera" first published in *Collaborative Visions: The Poetic Dialogues Project*, then in *Gnawed Bones*. "Chatanika" first published in *The American Poetry Review*, then in *Gnawed Bones*. "Gnawed Bones" first published in *International Journal of Healthcare and Humanities*, then in *Gnawed Bones*. "Mother Tongue" first published in *Weber Studies*, then in *Gnawed Bones*.

David Mason: "Foghorn" and "A Bit of Skin" first published in *Poetry*, "Fathers and Sons" first published in *The New Yorker*, "Home Care" first published in *The Times Literary Supplement*, "Marco Polo at the Old Hotel" first published in *Prairie Schooner*.

Dick Allen: "An AIDS Alphabet" first appeared in *Connecticut Review*, "Poetry Editors at Dawn" appeared first in *Nassau Review*, "Bravo" and "Poetry in Memory of the Big Bopper" first appeared in *Smartish Pace*, "Sea" first appeared in *Gettysburg Review*.

JoAnn Balingit: "Speaking of Snow" first published in *Pearl*, and appears in *Your Heart and How It Works* (Spire Press, 2009); "Your Heart and How It Works" published in *Diagram, Diagram.2*, and *Your Heart and How It Works* (Spire Press, 2009); "Julian's Lullaby" published in *Your Heart and How It Works* (Spire Press, 2009); "The Blue-Spotted Salamander" first published in *Kweli Journal;* "History Textook, America" first published in *Best New Poets, 2007;* "Song of a River" published in *Your Heart and How It Works*.

Kevin Stein: "Autumnal" first published in *Poetry*.

Norbert Krapf: "The Day John Lennon" and "Someone Who Misses New Orleans" appeared on the CD with Monika Herzig, *Imagine: Indiana in Music and Words* (Acme Records, 2007).

Mary Swander: *Crazy Eddy on the Judgment Day* is a section of Mary Swander's book-length poem *The Girls on the Roof*. The book tells the tale of a mother and daughter stuck on top of Crazy Eddy's Café for three days on the banks of the Mississippi River during the 1993 flood. There, they discover that they have both had an affair with the same man. Crazy Eddy is a little person, the deceased owner of the café, whose coffin floats downstream to New Orleans by the rush of the water.

Marvin Bell: "This Library" was commissioned by the Iowa City Library Board for the opening of the expanded Iowa City library in 2004. It is mounted on the wall of the entrance hall in the form of a bronze plaque. "Writers n a Café" was commissioned in 2008 by Christopher Merrill to accompany the petition of Iowa City to UNESCO to be designated a Creative City of Literature. It was printed as a broadside by Empyrean Press. "The Case for the Arts and Humanities" was commissioned by Humanities Iowa in celebration of the State of Iowa's "Year of Arts, Culture and Recreation" and the University of Iowa's "Year of the Arts and Humanities," July, 2004, to July, 2005.

Caryn Mirriam-Goldberg: All poems reprinted from *Landed* (Mammoth Publications, 2010).

Betsy Sholl: "Belmullet" first published in *Rhubarb*, "Lullaby in Blue" from *Rough Cradle* (Alice James Books, 2009).

W.E. Butts: "Radio Time" first published in *Saranac Review*, "Odds Against Tomorrow" and "The

Gift of Unwanted Knowledge" first published in the February, 2010 issue of the online journal ConnotatonPress.com.

David Allan Evans: "For the Woman Who Cleans My Teeth" first published in *North American Review*, "Cartoon Universals" first published in *South Dakota Review*, "Saturday Morning" first appeared in *Elkhorn Review*, "Bus Depot Reunion" first published in *Shenandoah*.

Kenneth W. Brewer: The Estate of Kenneth W. Brewer gives full permission to print these poems.

Samuel Green: "Grandmother, Cleaning Rabbits" first published in *Alaska Quarterly Review*.

Bruce Dethlefsen: "Hot Dog Man", "Suicide Aside" and "Up in the Cupboard" first published in *Breather*, Fireweed Press. "White Stallions" first published in *Something Near the Dance Floor*, Marsh River Editions. "Artists" first published in *Recovering the Self, a Journal of Hope and Healing*.

Marilyn L. Taylor: "The Blue Water Buffalo" first published in *Emily Dickinson Awards Anthology* (Universities West Press), "Reading the Obituaries" first published in *The Formalist*. "The Geniuses Among Us" first published in *Poetry*. "The Lovers at Eighty" first published in *Indiana Review*. "On Learning, Late In Life, That Your Mother Was a Jew" first published in *GSU Review*. "Why Don't You" first published in *The Seven Very Liberal Arts* (Aralia Press, 2007).

Irene McKinney: All poems are from *Unthinkable: Selected Poems 1976-2004*. (Red Hen Press, 2009). Reprinted by permission of the publisher.

Robert Dana: Peg Dana gives full permission to print these poems.

Ice Cube Books began publishing in 1993 to focus on how to live with the natural world and to better understand how people can best live together in the communities they share and inhabit. Since this time, we've been recognized by a number of well-known writers, including Gary Snyder, Gene Logsdon, Wes Jackson, Patricia Hampl, Greg Brown, Jim Harrison, Annie Dillard, Ken Burns, Kathleen Norris, Janisse Ray, Alison Deming, Richard Rhodes, Michael Pollan, and Barry Lopez. We've published a number of well-known authors as well, including Mary Swander, Jim Heynen, Mary Pipher, Bill Holm, Connie Mutel, John T. Price, Carol Bly, Marvin Bell, Debra Marquart, Ted Kooser, Stephanie Mills, Bill McKibben, and Paul Gruchow. As well, we have won several publishing awards over the last seventeen years. Check out our books at our web site, with booksellers, or at museum shops, then discover why we strive to "hear the other side."

Ice Cube Press (est. 1993)
205 N Front Street
North Liberty, Iowa 52317-9302
steve@icecubepress.com
www.icecubepress.com
319-558-7609

fe fi fo fum, this here
ryhme is just for fun
with a hug, und ein kiss
to Fenna Marie-ah &
Laura Lee-ah-lo!

Gestapo

THE STORY BEHIND THE NAZIS' MACHINE OF TERROR

LUCAS SAUL

ARCTURUS

ARCTURUS

This edition published in 2016 by Arcturus Publishing Limited
26/27 Bickels Yard, 151–153 Bermondsey Street,
London SE1 3HA

ISBN: 978-1-78599-220-9
DA004672UK

Printed in China

CONTENTS

INTRODUCTION
BIRTH OF A MONSTER

In the films, they are the men in black leather trench coats, knocking on doors in the middle of the night and arresting anyone who dares to threaten the Third Reich. But who, exactly, were the Gestapo? How did they fit into the Nazis' oppressive regime, and why did they become so powerful, so effective and so feared?

The true picture is inevitably more complicated than the myth. The men of the Gestapo, though often accountable only to themselves and their immediate superiors, did not work in isolation. They shared a single chain of command with their sister organization, the *Sicherheitsdienst*, or SD. The SD was the intelligence agency of the *Schutzstaffel*, or SS, Hitler's protection squadron. The SS and the Gestapo are frequently confused, which is hardly surprising given that they worked in close co-operation throughout the war. The SS swore its allegiance to Hitler and the Reich, whereas the Gestapo was, ostensibly, the secret state police for Germany. To confuse matters further, there was also the *Kriminalpolizei* ('Kripo'), which handled purely criminal matters in Germany. Like the Gestapo, they were answerable to the Reich Security Main Office (*Reichssicherheitshauptamt*, or RSHA). The Gestapo and Kripo were collectively known as the *Sicherheitspolizei* (Security Police) or 'Sipo'.

To some extent the distinctions between these different organizations are artificial: the chief investigators at the Nuremberg trials concluded that applicants for positions in the Gestapo, SD and Kripo received similar training and co-operated so closely as to often be indistinguishable from one another. All were concerned with combating perceived 'enemies of the Reich' and, as the war progressed, they all operated far beyond anything that could be called the rule of law. In broad-brush terms, the SD could be considered to be an information-gathering agency and the Gestapo the executive agency of the police. The Gestapo's targets were political and ideological enemies of the Reich, while purely criminal activity was left for the Kripo to handle.

The monster that the Gestapo became was born on 26 April 1933, when the new Minister of the Interior for Prussia, Hermann Göring, was charged with creating an effective political police force. On 30 November 1933, Göring issued a decree stating that the new force would be answerable only to him, and to the Reich. All other police authorities would be subordinate to it. A further decree on 8 March 1934 separated the regional state police offices from their district governments. To complete the job of forming a nationwide extra-judicial organization, a decree on 10 February 1936 declared that orders of the Secret State Police were no longer subject to the review of the administrative courts. The new, all-powerful force was now also tasked with investigating crimes against the Nazi Party as well as against the German state.

On 1 October 1936 this new force received a new name: the *Geheime Staatspolizei*, or Gestapo for short. The name means 'Secret State Police'. In fact, the Gestapo served the Nazi Party and the leadership. Göring relinquished control of the force in order to take charge of the Luftwaffe (air force), at which point Heinrich Himmler became the overall Chief of the German Police. The first Chief of the Security Police (and SD) was Reinhard Heydrich. The different police and intelligence forces were later centralized under the Reich Security Main Office (RSHA).

Bureaucracy at the Heart of the Gestapo

One of Göring and Himmler's first tasks had been to imbue the political police force that they inherited – which was subject to judicial review and staffed by criminal investigators concerned with protecting the German state rather than any political party – with a Nazi ideology. Through Heydrich, they espoused the view that since the Nazi Party represented the German people, defending the interests of the party was the

Reinhard Heydrich

Described by Hitler as 'the man with the iron heart', Reinhard Tristan Eugen Heydrich was chief of the Reich Security Main Office, which included the Gestapo, and founder of the *Sicherheitsdienst* (or SD, the intelligence agency of the SS). Born in 1904, he was handed control of the Gestapo by Heinrich Himmler in 1934. One of Heydrich's first operations was the 'Night of the Long Knives', when some 200 members of the rival para-military *Sturmabteilung* (SA) force, including its leader Ernst Röhm, were executed.

Heydrich set about organizing the Gestapo into a national and international instrument of terror. He established a system of colour-coded index cards for keeping information and monitoring the movements of perceived enemies of the Nazi state. He also instigated the so-called 'Night and Fog' disappearances of 'persons endangering German security'. Through such actions, the words 'Gestapo' and 'terror' would become synonymous.

In 1942 Heydrich chaired the infamous Wannsee Conference, which formalized plans for the 'Final Solution' or Holocaust. Shortly afterwards, he was assassinated by a team of British-trained Czech and Slovak soldiers. He was buried with full military honours, though Hitler railed in private that Heydrich had been 'stupid and idiotic' for driving around in an unarmoured open-top car. At least 1,300 people were massacred by the Gestapo in retaliation for Heydrich's murder.

same as defending the interests of the people. The Gestapo's key legal counsel, Werner Best, described the organization as a 'doctor to the German body', keeping a watchful eye on any 'symptoms' that might lead to the nation becoming 'sick'. It was a stroke of genius, allowing the Nazis to imply that the life or death of the German people was in the hands of the Gestapo. The political police were no longer to be viewed as investigators of crimes but as protectors of the nation's well-being.

Initially, the spine of the Gestapo was recruited from the Prussian political police, and had a modest size of around 1,000 employees. Regional Gestapo offices tended to be located in dense urban areas or at key strategic border zones. There were 64 such offices at the outbreak of the war. The number increased as the Reich expanded into new territories, but there was also a drive to centralize authority, so many smaller regional offices were merged together. For this reason the total number of Gestapo offices remained in the dozens rather than the hundreds, even at the height of the Reich.

In terms of personnel, the organization grew rapidly throughout the 1930s: there were an estimated 6,500 Gestapo officers across the Reich by 1937. The outbreak of war brought a new urgency to the expansion process and the number of officers swelled to 15,000 by late

1941. The sheer size of the organization necessitated a radical restructuring, and Himmler used the opportunity to further strengthen the ties between the Gestapo and the SS by bringing them together in one building. Hence the RSHA opened in September 1939.

There were six (from 1941 it became seven) separate offices at the RSHA: Personnel (I), Administration (II), German Lands (III), Combating Opponents (IV), Fighting Crime (V), Foreign Intelligence (VI) and Ideological Research (VII). The first two departments were the bureaucratic heart of the organization, responsible for the day-to-day running of all other departments. Office V was the headquarters of the Criminal Police, while Offices III, VI and VII evolved from former SD agencies.

Office IV was dominated by Gestapo personnel. It had a reputation for dynamism and flexibility, which meant that its exact areas of influence were not easily defined. As the war progressed, Office IV absorbed former SD offices and extended its reach into almost any area it considered important to the survival of the Reich. Heinrich 'Gestapo' Müller was trusted by Himmler and Heydrich to 'get the job done', no matter what it involved. As a result, when the chaos of war enveloped Germany and its police forces, an increasing amount of responsibility was handed to the Gestapo.

Heinrich ('Gestapo') Müller

Known as 'Gestapo Müller' to distinguish him from another SS general of the same name, Heinrich Müller was born in 1900 to working-class Catholic parents in Munich, Bavaria. He was awarded the Iron Cross for his service as a pilot during the First World War, and went on to become the head of the Munich Political Police Department during the Weimar Republic. He was initially hostile to the Nazi Party, describing Hitler as 'an immigrant unemployed house-painter', but his diligent work nonetheless brought him to the attention of Reinhard Heydrich, chief of the Reich Security Main Office. Müller was a workaholic who knew how to follow orders – an ideal puppet for the Nazi leaders. In time, his eagerness to impress his superiors led to him becoming reviled as one of the chief architects of the Gestapo's worst crimes.

Müller joined the SS in 1934, and by 1936 had risen to become the Operations Chief of the Gestapo. Throughout the Second World War he helped oversee the transportation of Jews and other 'undesirables' to the Nazi concentration camps. He was Adolf Eichmann's boss and intimately involved in the detailed planning of what became the 'Final Solution'. In addition, Müller was responsible for co-ordinating much of the espionage and counter-espionage activities of the Gestapo. He successfully infiltrated the 'Red Orchestra' network of Soviet spies, and ordered the execution of over 200 people alleged to have been involved in the plot to assassinate Hitler in July 1944.

Müller remained confident of a Nazi victory right up until the very end of the war, at which point he disappeared from Hitler's bunker and was never seen again. A later CIA report concluded that he was probably killed in Berlin shortly after the war, but there is no conclusive proof of this. He remains the most senior Nazi figure never to have been captured or confirmed as dead.

The damaged Reich Security Main Office, Prinz-Albrecht-Strasse, Berlin in 1945.

Throughout its history, the internal organization of Office IV changed frequently, as the demands placed upon it shifted. For the majority of the time, however, it consisted of six groups, usually referred to by letters of the alphabet. Group A handled Political Opposition, B Religious Dissent, C Protective Custody & Press, D Occupied Zones, E Counter-intelligence and F Foreigners. These groups were themselves further subdivided into six sections (Group IV B section 4, for example, handled Jewish matters and was headed by Adolf Eichmann).

Such a bureaucratic structure required a large team of civil servants and administrative staff. Indeed, the majority of Gestapo employees were not fanatical Nazis inspired by

Himmler's ideological training, but everyday German citizens attempting to provide for their families. Many were also driven by a genuine belief in protecting the German state from the corrupting influence of communism. In the early stages of the Gestapo's history, the chief focus was on the political enemies of the Nazi Party and so employees with experience of anti-communist activities were actively sought. Veteran criminal-police officers of the Weimar Republic were also recruited into the Gestapo in large numbers, and many welcomed the fact that they could operate with limited judicial oversight because it allowed them to get their jobs done more easily.

Intermingled with such veteran police officers were ambitious young legal administrators who bought into the Nazi ideology and made sure their superiors were aware of their loyalty to the cause. This 'new blood' that flowed into the Gestapo had no first-hand experience of war, and generally came from well-educated middle-class backgrounds. Many had studied law at university, and were entering the workplace for the first time. Remarkably, however, there was relatively little tension between the very different types of employees working for the Gestapo. This unity was one of the great strengths of the organization, and one of the key reasons for its astonishing success.

CHAPTER ONE
THE EARLY YEARS

The focus of this book from here onwards is not on the Nazi bureaucracy that lay behind the Secret State Police, but on the brutal actions of that force. For, in the words of its first chief Reinhard Heydrich, the Gestapo:

... are still adorned with the furtive and whispered secrecy of a political detective story. In a mixture of fear and shuddering – and yet at home with a certain feeling of security because of their presence – brutality, inhumanity bordering on the sadistic, and ruthlessness are attributed abroad to the men of this profession.

A taste of things to come

The Gestapo's main focus in the early years of its history was the destruction of its political enemies. Communists topped the list, but Hitler also feared that some of those within his own party had grown too powerful, and he wanted them eliminated. The veneer of judicial process was maintained by the establishment of the 'People's Court', which opened on 1 July 1934. Hitler was frustrated by the judicial system bequeathed to him and wanted a 'kangaroo court' to do his bidding. Most Gestapo prisoners found themselves in the dock of the People's Court, where show-trials were held to convince the German people that due process was being followed.

Even this early in its history, the Gestapo had a strong presence in the concentration camps that would later come to epitomize the horror of the Nazi regime. The Gestapo had an office at Dachau, where detailed records of prisoners were kept along with the transcripts of interrogations. Registrations, identifications, admissions and releases were all overseen by Gestapo chiefs. Their underlings were generally SS men; the Gestapo chiefs were themselves nominally subordinate to the camp commandants.

The Gestapo also advised on camp security, both in the concentration camps and in the prisoner-of-war camps that soon sprang up across the Third Reich. And they ran their own 'work education camps'. These detention centres were initially used to punish 'shirking' workers for short periods of time, but later all manner of minor crimes could result in offenders being sent to them for 're-education'.

It was inevitable that such treatment would sound a warning bell, causing discontentment and anger in many and leading to dissent.

The Reichstag Fire

In 1933, just four weeks after Adolf Hitler had been sworn in as Chancellor of Germany, the historic German parliament building the Reichstag was deliberately burnt down. This was a propaganda gift for the Nazi Party,

The Reichstag building during the devastating fire of 1933.

which had long warned of the danger of a communist insurrection. Indeed, many historians dispute the official explanation that a young Dutch communist called Marinus van der Lubbe plotted the arson attack on his own. Herman Göring was said to have publicly boasted of having planned the attack as a 'false flag' operation to whip up hysterical fear in the German population.

Certainly the effect of the fire was to grant the Nazi Party unprecedented power, as Hitler immediately forced through the so-called Reichstag Fire Decree, which suspended many of the key civil liberties in Germany. Thousands of communists were rounded up and imprisoned, and countless more were prevented from voting in the hastily arranged fresh elections, which saw the Nazis increase their majority of the vote and consolidate their new-found power. The fear of a communist plot succeeded in pushing the population to the extreme right, and by suppressing their main rivals, the Social Democratic Party, the Nazis were able to secure the two-thirds majority required to pass the Enabling Act. This gave Hitler the power to rule by decree. Democracy was at an end, and the dictator Adolf Hitler was now free to march the country to war.

Five communists were tried for the attack on the Reichstag, but only van der Lubbe was found guilty. Hitler was furious and promptly ordered the establishment of the People's Court (*Volksgerichtshof*), which would be under his direct control. His Minister of the Interior, Herman Göring, re-ordered the police force into a paramilitary group of loyal Nazis, and on 26 April 1933 a decree was issued to officially create the Secret Police Office.

It was to become the most notorious secret police force in history.

Night of the Long Knives

Although the Enabling Act had granted Hitler absolute power over the German people, he still feared that his position was vulnerable. The rise of the Nazi Party had been predicated on forming alliances with those who did not share Hitler's vision for the future of Germany, and internal dissent now represented the greatest threat to the dictator.

Two figures in particular were at the top of Hitler's hit list for elimination. Gregor Strasser led the left-wing ('Strasserist') wing of the Nazi Party, which pursued an anti-capitalist agenda of social reform. Ernst Röhm was head of the *Sturmabteilung*, also known as the SA, or 'Brownshirts'. This paramilitary force had been vital in facilitating Hitler's rise to power but it had now grown so powerful and out of control that it threatened his own military units. In addition, the short-tempered

Röhm had referred to Hitler as 'the ridiculous corporal' when ordered to acknowledge the subordination of the SA to the *Reichswehr* (or 'Reich Defence', the forerunner of the German armed forces or *Wehrmacht*). The crunch point came when German president Paul von Hindenburg threatened to impose martial law if Hitler failed to control the almost daily street battles between the Brownshirts and the communists. In late June 1934, Hitler decided to eliminate all his opponents in one fell swoop. To carry out the purge he turned to his newly formed secret police force, the Gestapo, and the SS.

The codeword 'Hummingbird' was used to send the death squads into action. The list of targets had been drawn up by Heinrich Himmler and Reinhard Heydrich, with Hermann Göring and top Gestapo official Willi Lehmann adding the names of 'undesirables' outside of the SA. Lehmann would personally take part in the murderous rampage that followed. He himself would later fall victim to summary execution on the orders of Himmler, after he was discovered to be a Soviet double agent. In the early hours of 30 June, however, Hitler was concerned with eliminating threats from within the SA, and when he arrived at the Hanselbauer Hotel in Bad Wiessee he took Ernst Röhm and the other leaders based there totally by surprise. Most were arrested, though SA

Hermann Göring

Born in 1893, and an ace fighter pilot in the First World War, Göring was a leading early member of the Nazi Party and founder of the Gestapo. He was shot in the leg while taking part in Hitler's failed military coup (the 'Beer Hall Putsch') in 1923. After being treated with morphine he became addicted to the drug for the rest of his life. Hitler named him Interior Minister of Prussia when he first came to power, giving Göring command of the largest police force in Germany. Göring promptly filled the force with committed Nazi Party members and merged the political and intelligence departments together to form the Gestapo. Originally he planned to name the force the *Geheime Polizei Amt*, ('Secret Police Office'), but the German initials GPA were too reminiscent of the Soviet secret police force, the GPU (*Gosudarstvennoye Politicheskoye Upravlenie*, or 'State Political Directorate').

It was Göring's idea to extend the fledgling force's authority throughout Germany, which he did after dismissing the Gestapo's original commander, Rudolf Diels, and taking over himself in 1934. Soon after, he relinquished control to Heinrich Himmler, and went on to become commander-in-chief of the Luftwaffe. In 1941 he became Hitler's official designated successor and deputy in all of his offices, though he was stripped of this illustrious title shortly before Hitler's suicide in 1945.

He was sentenced to death at the Nuremberg trials in 1946, but committed suicide by ingesting cyanide.

leader Edmund Heines was shot on the spot after being found in bed with an 18-year-old male troop leader.

Hitler then addressed a crowd of supporters outside his headquarters in Munich, describing his actions as a firm response to a treacherous plot to overthrow him. It was the trigger for Phase 2 of the operation, in which Gestapo death squads kicked in the doors of their unsuspecting victims and executed them. The Gestapo later furnished Hitler with a list of those they had managed to find and kill: it contained 77 names.

Vice-Chancellor Franz von Papen's inner circle were key targets. Papen had criticized Hitler in a speech at the University of Marburg two weeks earlier, and the writer of that speech was one of the first to be gunned down by the Gestapo. Edgar Julius Jung was shot in the cellar of the Gestapo headquarters then dumped in a ditch near the town of Oranienburg, just outside Berlin. Papen's secretary, Herbert von Bose, was shot at his desk in the Vice-Chancellery building itself, supposedly while resisting arrest. Another close associate of Papen, Erich Klausener, was also killed at his desk at the Ministry of Transport, and Papen himself was arrested and forced to resign. It is widely believed that Papen was due to be murdered but was saved by Göring, who believed that Papen might be more useful to the Nazis alive than dead. He was sent to Austria to be the puppet German ambassador there, preparing the way for the later annexation of that country.

Hitler's predecessor as Chancellor, Kurt von Schleicher, also received a visit from the Gestapo. He was murdered in his own home, along with his wife. His close associate Ferdinand von Bredow was tied to a chair and shot five times. Prominent former Nazi Gregor Strasser was similarly slaughtered as Hitler settled old scores with his rivals. Strasser was shot once from behind, and left to bleed to death on the floor of his prison cell, a process that reportedly took almost an hour.

It was not just high-ranking political and military figures who were murdered by the Gestapo on the Night of the Long Knives, however. Some reports suggest that in total up to 1,000 people were killed, and the most recent study names 89 certain victims. The list includes lawyers, doctors, civil servants, journalists and even a music critic. Hitler's most dangerous rival, Ernst Röhm, was handed a revolver and invited to commit suicide. When he declined to do so, he was shot in the chest at point-blank range.

By the end of the Night of the Long Knives, thanks to the ruthless efficiency of the Gestapo and SS, Hitler had total control over Germany.

Expansion and purge – at all cost

Having eliminated the political and military threats to his 'Thousand Year Reich', Hitler was now faced with the new threat of a financial meltdown in Germany. The price of the country's rapid re-armament was high, and in 1935 Germany was engulfed by an economic crisis. Hitler had prioritized importing raw materials over importing food, and as a result the queues outside shops grew longer and longer. Inflation spiralled, currency reserves collapsed and the Nazi regime's popularity sank. Over half the German population was living below the poverty line by 1935 and the Gestapo was struggling to cope with the growing dissent. Hitler desperately needed a foreign-policy triumph to distract attention away from such domestic problems.

On 7 March 1936, he ordered German troops into the demilitarized Rhineland. It was a flagrant breach of Articles 42 and 43 of the Treaty of Versailles, and Articles 1 and 2 of the Treaty of Locarno, which sought to preserve the territory as a buffer-zone between Germany and France. Hitler took the chance that France and Britain would not send troops to resist the remilitarization. The risk paid off, and German troops were welcomed as heroes when they entered Cologne for the first time since the end of the First World War.

Hitler called a referendum on the action on 29 March,

which the Gestapo helped to police. Anyone refusing to vote 'yes' was subject to intimidation and denunciation. The official turnout was close to 99 per cent, and the percentage voting in favour was similarly high.

Hitler was emboldened, and his popularity soared, but the fundamental problem of supply shortages remained. The German navy, air force and army all reported that they could not build their military capabilities without access to steel and other raw materials. Hitler called a conference on 5 November 1937 in order to outline his plan. A summary of the meeting, known as the Hossbach Memorandum, set out for the first time the expansionist policy that would soon plunge Europe into the Second World War. Germany would solve its supply problems, Hitler decided, by invading Austria and Czechoslovakia.

Himmler responded to the plan by accelerating the assimilation of the state's secret police with the SS – a dream he had long shared with Heydrich. In February 1938 Himmler decreed that the training guidelines for the Gestapo and SD should be identical. With armed conflict now inevitable, it was deemed necessary for military and state police intelligence officers to work side by side. From June 1938, all members of the security police who joined the SS were also automatically made members of the SD. The Gestapo, the SS and the SD were thus not merely separate departments that co-operated closely with one another: their guru Himmler ensured that they were all indoctrinated with the same fanatical ideology.

The Nazi policy of military expansion helped cure the issue of massive unemployment but soon created the new problem of labour shortages. To combat this, increased numbers of foreign workers were allowed into the country – many of them from Poland, where agricultural workers in particular were keen for employment. By 1938, there were almost 100,000 such Polish workers in Germany.

Discrimination against them was rife, as Poles were considered by many to be clumsy and stupid. Poles were paid less than German workers and allowed or even encouraged to work 14-hour days as opposed to the German maximum of eight hours. As a result, civil disorder between Polish workers and the local population was commonplace.

Race relations were of interest to the Gestapo as national unity was the stated key aim of the Nazi Party. Anything that undermined the sense of a single German people was considered a threat to the Reich. Foreign workers were either to be 'Germanized' or kept under strict control. There was a real fear that Poles would import communism or leftist beliefs from the east, and the Gestapo was constantly on guard for any signs of sedition.

Another concern was 'racial mixing' between Germans and Poles, and in particular between German women and Polish men. The idea of half-German and half-Polish offspring was abhorrent to the Nazis, and the Gestapo encouraged neighbours to denounce any such relationships. Women were often seized and had their hair shaved off while Gestapo officers stood by and protected those who perpetrated such acts. Though physical injury was frowned upon at this time, humiliation was not only tolerated but actively encouraged. After the outbreak of war, a Polish man convicted of sexual relations with a German woman was liable to be executed. Young Polish women who had sex with German men were treated more leniently, for the simple reason that it was incredibly common: German bosses were in a position of great power over their employees, who knew that refusing any sexual advances would lead to them losing their jobs.

Above all, the Gestapo was determined to ensure that the foreign workers remained leaderless and disorganized. They arrested or hounded any figure who appeared to threaten this goal. Or, indeed, anyone who might interfere with the larger aims of expansion and racial purity.

Anschluss

'Not as tyrants have we come, but as liberators.' This was Hitler's declaration, as German troops crossed the border into Austria on 12 March 1938.

By the time Hitler's motorcade had passed through his birthplace of Braunau, the Gestapo was already hard at work. Austrian Nazis had spent months compiling a list of 'enemies of the state', and Himmler led an advance party of SS and Gestapo officers into the Third Reich's first occupied territory ahead of the troops. The objective was to crush any resistance before it could organize; prominent anti-Nazis such as the Mayor of Vienna Richard Schmitz were rounded up and sent to Dachau concentration camp in Bavaria. Union leaders and left-wing politicians topped the wanted list, helping to ensure that when Austrians were asked to vote on whether to become part of the far-right Third Reich the over-whelming majority placed their mark in the large 'yes' circle on the ballot paper rather than daring to mark the much smaller 'no' circle.

The Gestapo soon commandeered the Hotel Metropole in Vienna as its headquarters, and in time it grew to become larger than its equivalent in Berlin, employing more than 900 staff. Countless numbers of unfortunate prisoners were taken to its soundproofed cells for inter-rogation, torture and execution during the Second World War. Many were chained backwards to the bars in their cells with their toes barely touching the floor. All were chained hand and foot during Allied bombing raids, while the Gestapo personnel cowered in the relative safety of the basement or the city's extensive catacombs. Several bombs hit the building as Vienna was pummelled towards the end of the war and the remains of the hotel were torn down to eradicate a landmark associated with terror and brutality. Today, a plaque at the site reads:

Here stood the House of the Gestapo. To those who believed in Austria it was hell. To many it was the gates to death. It sank into ruins just like the 'Thousand Year Reich'. But Austria was resurrected and with her our dead, the immortal victims.

Kristallnacht

After the annexation of Austria, the Nazi German government began to focus its attention on the question of how best to purge itself of its sizeable Jewish population. Hitler was determined to garner popularity by scapegoating the Jews for all that had gone wrong with German society. In addition, he wanted to seize Jewish property and businesses in order to shore up the precarious finances of his fledgling Reich.

His most trusted henchmen, the members of the Gestapo, were charged with driving as many Jews out of Germany and Austria as possible. They rounded up and deported some 12,000 Polish Jews across the border to Poland, giving them one night in which to pack a

Furnishings and ritual objects from the synagogue are burned in the town square, Mosbach, southern Germany, 10 November 1938.

single suitcase. Many of those forcibly removed by the Gestapo were refused entry by Polish border guards. Thousands became trapped in a makeshift refugee camp between the borders of Poland and Germany. Among them were Sendel and Riva Grynszpan, who sent a note to their son Herschel in Paris, pleading with him to help. Herschel Grynszpan responded by entering the German embassy in Paris and shooting dead a German diplomat, Ernst vom Rath.

Hitler retaliated by introducing a slew of anti-Jewish legislation, and authorizing Joseph Goebbels to make a speech which made clear that any 'spontaneous demonstrations' the German people wished to make would not be hampered. The message was received loud and clear: it was open season on Jews in the Reich. On the night of 9 November 1938, the German dictator unleashed his secret police in an act of state-sponsored terrorism that later became known as 'Crystal Night' or *Kristallnacht*. The name derives from the countless windows that were smashed during the rampage that the Gestapo co-ordinated. Shards of glass littered streets across Germany and Austria as Jewish-owned stores, homes and synagogues were attacked by angry mobs. In Vienna alone, 95 synagogues were burned – across the German Reich the figure was over 1,000. More than 7,000 Jewish businesses were damaged or destroyed. Tombstones were uprooted, sacred texts burned and statues defaced.

Many Jewish residents were also assaulted: although the official death toll was 91, several modern historians put the figure in the hundreds. In addition, some 30,000 Jews were rounded up by the Gestapo and incarcerated in concentration camps. The Nazi-employed mobs went about their brutal work while the police stood by watching, under strict instructions to protect only non-Jewish residents and foreigners. In the days after *Kristallnacht*, Jewish residents were forced to clear up the mess made by the mob, and many were obliged to scrub steps while crowds of non-Jews jeered and hurled abuse.

The attacks were widely reported by the numerous foreign correspondents based in Germany and Austria, and the first-hand accounts of the mayhem sent shock waves across Europe. It was considered a new low for a regime that the world had come to view with growing unease. Very soon, however, that unease would turn to horror. The Gestapo had only just begun.

CHAPTER TWO
THE OUTBREAK OF WAR

Terror unleashed

The Nazis' expansionist plans continued, most significantly when German forces invaded Poland in September 1939. This resulted in Britain and France declaring war on Germany. From the Gestapo's perspective, it also brought about the new challenge of operating in foreign territories that were under military occupation. Himmler hastened the integration between the security police and the German military machine. The Reich Security Main Office (RSHA) was founded on 27 September 1939, bringing the security police and SD under the same roof for the first time. Heydrich was the natural choice as its first head. The Nazi Party's own intelligence service now shared a physical space with an official state service, consolidating Himmler's power over both.

After the invasion of Poland, some 300,000 prisoners of war would be used as slave labour, and the Gestapo's attitude to foreign workers would harden into utter pitilessness. Before the outbreak of war, however, the Gestapo maintained at least the veneer of working within the judicial system when dealing with non-Jews.

The Gleiwitz Incident

The town of Gleiwitz in Upper Silesia had been fiercely contested by Germany and Poland between the wars, before a League of Nations ruling determined it should

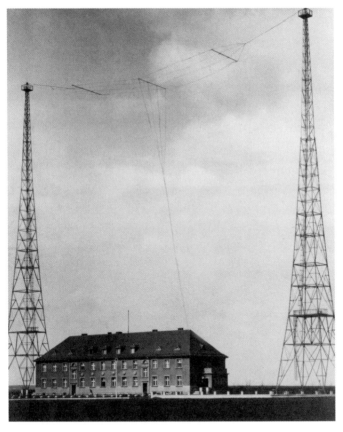

The radio station at Gleiwitz before it was attacked.

officially remain part of Germany. On 31 August 1939 it became the scene of a Gestapo 'false flag' operation that led to the start of the Second World War. The Nazis required a pretext for invading Poland, and utilized Gleiwitz's history of conflict to persuade the German people that the Poles intended to seize the territory by force.

The plan was hatched by Reinhard Heydrich and Heinrich Müller, the chief of the Gestapo. A small force of Gestapo agents dressed in Polish army uniforms were transported to the Gleiwitz radio station, where they broadcast a brief anti-German message in Polish. They then murdered a 43-year-old local man called Franciszek Honiok – a German who was known to be sympathetic to the Poles. He had been arrested by the Gestapo the previous day and dressed in clothing appropriate for a Polish saboteur. His corpse, complete with fresh gunshot wounds, was paraded as evidence of the fact that Poles had attacked Gleiwitz, and that one of their number had been killed by German troops.

German forces, already massed on the border with Poland, invaded the next day from the north, south and west. Hitler's great gamble was that the other European nations would not resist him militarily despite the invasion. It was a gamble that failed. Two days after the first tanks rolled across the Polish border, the United

Kingdom and France, both of whom had signed pacts with Poland, declared war on Germany.

Neither of the Allied countries was remotely ready to take on the might of the German military machine, which Hitler had so carefully prepared for the coming war. The Gestapo, meanwhile, was by now the most technologically advanced and experienced secret police force in the world. By 1939 they had the ability to monitor wireless communications and telephones. The mail service was also in its pay, and was able to steam open and reseal a suspect's mail so well that it was practically undetectable. When the Gestapo asked the mail service to monitor an individual or organization's mail, the teamwork was so efficient that the mail was delayed by just a couple of hours. The contents of any letter could be copied and sent to the local Gestapo office before the letter had even reached the intended recipient.

The secret police already had an iron grip upon the population of the Third Reich. In the coming years, as the war spread, that grip of terror would extend to cover most of Western Europe.

The Testimony of Anton Pacholegg

A great deal about the arrest of Dr Anton Pacholegg, on 2 August 1939, is shrouded in mystery. We know that he was picked up by the Gestapo on that date, and that he had been under surveillance for some time. We also know that the Gestapo believed his name to be Anton Guttenberg, and that Pacholegg used the name von Guttenberg from time to time too. Pacholegg himself later claimed that he was a patent lawyer who was picked up by the Gestapo on the Swiss border after meeting a 'business partner'. He believed the entire meeting was a ruse concocted by the Gestapo to capture him. The Gestapo files suggest that Pacholegg was accused of being a currency smuggler, but elsewhere he is referred to as a spy, and accused of committing high treason. Pacholegg stated that the Gestapo believed he was working for 'English intelligence', but that his interrogators could find no evidence to back this up.

We know nothing of what happened to Pacholegg immediately after his arrest: the next time we hear of him it is three years later, and he is languishing in the Nazi concentration camp at Dachau. He was presumably sent there in 1942 after serving a sentence handed down at trial. The Gestapo frequently picked up those who had served such sentences as soon as they were released, and sent them to the 'protective custody' of the concentration camps.

Pacholegg's story is of interest to historians because he would later testify at the Nuremberg trials and offer insight into one of the more macabre aspects of the Gestapo's operations: human medical experiments at

Dachau concentration camp. Pacholegg became the assistant to one of the most twisted SS men in history, Dr Sigmund Rascher. A close personal friend of Gestapo leader Heinrich Himmler, Rascher requested permission to experiment on those condemned to die at Dachau. Himmler incorporated the programme of human experimentation into his SS *Ahnenerbe* ('Ancestors' Heritage') institution, which was ostensibly founded to research the cultural history of the Aryan race.

The experiments at Dachau were performed by the *Ahnenerbe* offshoot 'The Institute for Military Scientific Research', presided over by Wolfram Sievers. Rascher performed the majority of the hands-on experiments, which investigated the effects of low pressure and intense cold – both subjects considered to be of potential use to the Luftwaffe. Allied aircraft were reaching heights of 12,000 m (40,000 ft) and German fighter pilots were required to follow them. At such heights gas bubbles can form in the blood vessels, resulting in potentially fatal embolisms.

It was Gestapo officers who selected which inmates would prove suitable for Rascher's sadistic experiments, which nobody outside of the SS was allowed to witness. Pacholegg later told the military tribunal at Nuremberg what he saw 'first-hand' at Dachau. There is some dispute over whether he could, in fact, have seen with his own eyes the things he later related, but it is beyond doubt that he worked very closely with Rascher and that experiments of the kind he described did indeed take place. Pacholegg stated:

I have personally seen, through the observation window of the chamber, when a prisoner inside would stand a vacuum until his lungs ruptured. Some experiments gave men such pressure in their heads that they would go mad and pull out their hair in an effort to relieve the pressure. They would tear their heads and faces with their fingers and nails in an attempt to maim themselves in their madness. They would beat the walls with their hands and head and scream in an effort to relieve pressure on their eardrums. These cases of extremes of vacuums generally ended in the death of the subject.

At least 80 victims were killed by Rascher alone at Dachau, either in low-pressure experiments or through being exposed to freezing temperatures. He also experimented with Polygal, a substance made from beets and apple pectin, to see whether it could coagulate the blood after a gunshot wound. Subjects were given a Polygal tablet, and shot through the neck or chest, or their limbs were amputated without anaesthetic. It was Pacholegg who helped give rise to one of the most infamous claims about the Nazi concentration camps, namely that the skin of dead prisoners was turned into lampshades, gloves, pocketbooks and other items after they had been

Heinrich Himmler

One of the most powerful men in Nazi Germany, Himmler was *Reichsführer* of the *Schutzstaffel* (SS) and later Chief of German Police and Minister of the Interior. He oversaw all internal and external police and security forces, including the Gestapo. It was Himmler who selected Reinhard Heydrich to head up the secret police and instructed him on how it would operate.

Born in 1900, Himmler was in a reserve battalion during the First World War and never saw action. He studied agronomy in Munich and while there met Ernst Röhm, an early member of the Nazi Party and co-founder of the paramilitary *Sturmabteilung* (SA). Himmler joined the Nazi Party in August 1923 after failing in his ambition to pursue a military career in the German army. He was involved in the failed 'Beer Hall Putsch' three months later but escaped prosecution due to insufficient evidence against him. Shortly afterwards he moved in with his parents, abandoned his Catholic faith and became ever more involved in Nazi ideology, occultism and mythology. He joined the SS and toured the country delivering speeches on behalf of Hitler and the National Socialist German Workers' Party (NSDAP).

In September 1927, Himmler outlined to Hitler a radical plan to transform the SS from a small 'personal protection' unit into an elite private army loyal to the

Nazis rather than to Germany. By January 1929 he was head of the new force and had established himself as one of Hitler's most trusted deputies. When the Nazis came to power in 1933, Himmler's SS had grown from 290 men into a force of in excess of 52,000. He was placed in charge of the country's police forces state by state until only Göring's Prussian force lay outside his control. In 1934 Göring ceded control of that force too, leaving Himmler with complete authority over the Reich's policing. Himmler placed Reinhard Heydrich in control of the secret state police, the Gestapo.

Throughout the war, Himmler was occupied with heading the SS, organizing the creation and running of concentration camps, and overseeing Heydrich's command of the Gestapo. In late 1944, with the war entering its final phase, Hitler appointed Himmler commander-in-chief of Army Group Upper Rhine (*Oberrhein*). Himmler's subsequent failure as a military commander led to him having a nervous breakdown, which destroyed Hitler's faith in him. Himmler entered into secret peace negotiations with the Allies, which resulted in him being stripped of all military ranks by a furious Hitler. After Germany's defeat, Himmler was arrested by the British while trying to escape, posing as 'Sergeant Heinrich Hitzinger'. He admitted his real identity under interrogation but committed suicide by biting on a cyanide capsule before he could be tried for war crimes.

killed. He claimed to have seen Mrs Rascher with a handbag made from human skin.

The Dachau experiments were known to be entirely contrary to international law, but Rascher's close relationship with Himmler ensured they were kept secret, and the Gestapo supplied a steady stream of prisoners to allow them to continue. Things unravelled for Rascher in March of 1944, however, when he himself became a prisoner of the Gestapo. It transpired that Rascher's large SS family of four children was not all it seemed: he and his wife had abducted the children and passed them off as their own. Himmler had used the Rascher family as a model example of Aryan breeding and was furious at being deceived. Rascher was thrown into a concentration camp at Buchenwald, and then transferred to the scene of his gruesome crimes, Dachau, when the Allied troops closed in. He was executed there by firing squad just three days before American troops liberated the camp.

Institute director Wolfram Sievers was sentenced to death on 20 August 1947 for crimes against humanity, and hanged on 2 June 1948, at Landsberg prison in Bavaria. Anton Pacholegg escaped from Dachau but was recaptured by the Gestapo. He was finally liberated in 1945, when he gave his crucial testimony to the Americans. Thereafter, he changed his name several times and moved every few years for the rest of his life, often giving conflicting stories regarding his background. This has led some to conclude that the Gestapo was right first time about Pacholegg, and that he was indeed somehow associated with the intelligence services. His story about the horrors of Dachau was corroborated by several other witnesses, however.

Throughout the war, at all of the Nazi concentration camps, the Gestapo worked hand in glove with the SS 'Death's Head Units' to guard prisoners and select those who lived or died. At Dachau, the fate of those selected to die was arguably the most horrific of all the camps in the Reich.

Johann Elser: a Long Ordeal

On 8 November 1939, a German factory worker called Johann Georg Elser planted a bomb in a beer hall in Munich, the Bürgerbräukeller. It was placed inside a speaker's rostrum due to be used by Adolf Hitler for his annual speech on the anniversary of the failed 1923 Nazi coup (the 'Beer Hall Putsch').

However, Hitler arrived earlier than scheduled and cut his speech from the customary two hours down to a single hour. He left the building at 9.07 pm, just 13 minutes before the bomb exploded. Seven members of the audience who had stayed behind were killed, and the building itself was badly damaged. The task of finding and interrogating the perpetrator fell to the Gestapo. By 11 pm the same evening, they had their man in custody at the border town of Konstanz. The next morning, Elser was transferred to Munich Gestapo headquarters.

Franz Josef Huber, head of the Gestapo in Vienna, was called in to assist in the investigation. He ordered Elser to bare his knees, which were revealed to be badly bruised as a result of all the work he had done planting the bomb in the rostrum. Now confident they had the right suspect, the Gestapo officers, led by Himmler, tortured Elser mercilessly in order to extract a confession. One eyewitness spoke of Elser groaning and bleeding profusely from multiple wounds after being beaten for hours. He finally signed a written confession on 15 November, though it was almost certainly a forgery as by then he was in no physical condition to write anything.

Despite this, Elser's ordeal was far from over. He was transferred to the Berlin Gestapo headquarters, where his mother, sister, ex-girlfriend and brother-in-law were interrogated in his presence. All maintained their innocence, and Elser continued to insist that he had acted alone, despite a further five days of agonizing torture during which the Gestapo demanded he admit to being part of a wider plot. In the end it hardly mattered: Hitler claimed that Elser was working in cahoots with the British Intelligence Service despite the official Gestapo report reluctantly concluding he was a 'lone wolf' attacker.

Elser was kept at the Berlin Gestapo headquarters until early in 1941 and was subjected to every manner of novel torture that the Gestapo could develop. He was fed salty herrings and deprived of liquids; subjected to intense heat; hypnotized and injected with methamphetamines. The only thing he revealed was how he had crafted the bomb: a design so intricate and effective that the Gestapo adopted it into their field manuals. Elser was transferred to a concentration camp and spent the rest of the war there, before being executed in April 1945 on the direct orders of Hitler. His execution was covered up and his death was blamed on an Allied air raid.

Policing far and wide

For Germany, 1940 was an extraordinary year, and the staggering success of its military machine brought the Gestapo a host of new problems to deal with. The Germans invaded and occupied Norway, Denmark, the Netherlands, Belgium, Luxembourg and France. Their ally Italy also invaded Greece. These vast new territories now had to be policed and all resistance within them crushed. The Gestapo had nowhere near enough resources to manage the task on its own. Instead, it relied on a network of informants and collaborators to feed through information about the Resistance movements of each occupied territory.

Torture and intimidation were the chief methods of 'turning' prisoners into informants. The Gestapo often threatened to arrest a suspect's entire family if they did not co-operate. Payment and favourable treatment was also used to persuade the civilian population to inform on their fellow citizens. One of the most notorious traitors of the war, Stella Kübler, was reputedly paid 300 reichsmarks for each Jew that she betrayed, for example. Nicknamed 'Blonde Poison' because of her striking good looks, Kübler gave the Gestapo information on between 600 and 3,000 Jews posing as non-Jews in Berlin. As a Jew herself, she would have been fully aware of the fate that awaited those she betrayed: indeed her own family perished at the hands of the Nazi regime.

The Gestapo also encouraged 'denunciations' from the civilian populations it controlled. Every day, citizens were told that it was their duty to inform the Gestapo of any suspicious activity they observed, or information they received. Many denounced their neighbours or work colleagues for petty or selfish reasons, hoping to ingratiate themselves with the powerful state police. Even when no information of real value was obtained by such denunciations, they helped to cultivate a state of fear and oppression that kept the population from openly discussing their hatred of the Nazis.

Hitler's hopes for a short and decisive war were

thwarted by the RAF in the skies above Britain in the summer of 1940. Losing the 'Battle of Britain' meant that Germany could not invade England as Hitler had originally intended. Morale in Germany remained high, though. The German people, and the Gestapo, were not anticipating a long and bloody conflict.

There were many, however, who would do everything in their power to make things as difficult as possible for the Nazis.

Jan Karski's Capture and Escape

At the outbreak of war, the Polish Armed Forces were hopelessly out-gunned, and without the anticipated military aid from Britain and France, defeat was inevitable. The Nazis duly took control of the country and the Polish Resistance moved underground. One of its most significant members was Jan Karski, who would later bring to the world's attention for the first time the horrors of the concentration camps and the Holocaust. In November of 1940, however, he was working as a courier between Poland and the Polish government-in-exile in Angers, France. On one such courier mission he was captured by the Gestapo while in possession of photographs of sensitive documents.

Karski's first-hand testimony of his treatment by the Gestapo was chilling, and served as a warning for all future underground operatives during the war. He

Jan Karski, captured and tortured by the Gestapo in 1940.

recounted that he was tied to a chair with Gestapo agents to his front and rear. One asked questions, which he was expected to answer without the slightest delay. Whenever he failed to do so he was struck on the jaw from behind, or beaten with piping. Even pausing to recollect details would result in fresh blows. The Gestapo knocked out all of his teeth and broke his jaw and several of his ribs. Eventually he could take it no more and slit his own wrists with a blade he had concealed in his shoe.

Karski was too valuable as an informant for the Gestapo to allow him to die, however. He was taken to a prison hospital and guarded around the clock. Despite this, the Polish Resistance managed to smuggle in a cyanide capsule for him to take if he was ever returned to the hands of his torturers. The capsule was brought in by a Resistance member dressed as a nun. She later helped Karski to escape by jumping from a second-floor window, after which he was spirited away by a group of Resistance fighters.

Due to the Gestapo's brutal reputation, anyone who was freed from their captivity was subjected to a three-month 'quarantine' period in a Resistance safe house to ensure they had not been 'turned' into a double agent. Karski's wounds healed during this period and he was able to return to Poland later in the war in order to document the horrors of the Holocaust. He also provided details of how the Gestapo handled prisoners, and to avoid such horrific treatment most Resistance members elected to carry cyanide pills on their missions throughout the rest of the war.

Battling the red army

Hitler's decision to invade the Soviet Union in 1941 fundamentally changed the focus of the war, and drew huge numbers of German troops eastwards. In their wake followed the Gestapo, and it was during this period

An Einsatzgruppe D soldier about to shoot a prisoner
kneeling in front of a mass grave in Vinnitsa, Ukrainian SSR,
Soviet Union, in 1942.

that many of their most heinous crimes took place. Although the *Einsatzgruppen* ('task force') death squads that operated throughout the occupied Soviet lands were nominally an SS creation, Gestapo officers worked hand-in-glove with them. The scale of the slaughter for which they were responsible is truly breathtaking, and the number of bloody incidents too numerous to list. At Babi Yar ravine in Ukraine over 33,000 people were murdered in a single operation, between 29 and 30 September 1941. Around 25,000 more were killed on two separate days at the Rumbula Forest in Latvia later the same year. This was slaughter on a scale never seen before, and though the Gestapo men were not the ones pulling the triggers they oversaw many of the most inhumane bloodbaths.

Initially the invasion of Stalin's vast homeland was a great success for Hitler, and the German forces were jubilant. By the end of the year, however, the fierce Russian winter and even fiercer Red Army resistance had slowed and then halted the German advance.

In December of 1941 Japan attacked the American naval base at Pearl Harbor, Hawaii. The United States entered the war as an ally of Britain and the Soviet Union. The Gestapo now had to adapt to the new reality of 'total war', and it was to become even more ruthless in its dealings with those who worked against it.

Maria Bruskina: a Warning to Others

On 22 June 1941, Hitler had broken his non-aggression pact with Stalin and invaded the Soviet Union. Initial progress during 'Operation Barbarossa' had been swift, with the Nazis taking vast swathes of territory in the east as they drove towards Moscow. The Soviets, caught by surprise, had appeared to be in disarray.

However, the Germans had grossly underestimated the Red Army's strength, and in the following months the invasion stalled. Hitler decided to change tack and attempt to capture the industrial centres and oil fields

Maria 'Masha' Bruskina with fellow partisans shortly before her execution in Minsk, Belarus, on 26 October 1941. A placard hung around her neck reads, in German and Russian: 'We are partisans and have shot at German troops'.

of the Caucasus in the south rather than shedding more blood seizing the Russian capital. Resistance fighters began to organize themselves within the captured territories in Belarus, Lithuania and Latvia, making them much more difficult for the Germans to hold. The Gestapo, as ever, was sent in behind the troops to terrorize the local populations and ensure that German domination of these territories continued.

One member of the Soviet Resistance handed over to the Gestapo was Maria 'Masha' Bruskina. Born into a Jewish family, she was forced to live in the Minsk ghetto in Belarus after the German army rolled into the city in July of 1941. The 17-year-old had volunteered to work as a nurse at the hospital at the Polytechnic Institute, tending to wounded members of the Red Army. In addition to this work she also helped soldiers to escape, by smuggling civilian clothing and false identity papers into the hospital. A Nazi collaborator reported what she was doing and on 14 October 1941 she was arrested by the Gestapo.

Interrogation provided no useful details regarding the Minsk underground Resistance, and so Maria was handed back to the 707th Infantry Division in order to be publicly hanged without trial. Images of her being paraded through the streets with two other members of the Resistance became famous worldwide. A placard was hung around Maria's neck stating that she was a member of the Resistance who had shot at German soldiers. Her body was left hanging for three days as a warning to others who might dare to resist the occupation. Only later when the body was cleaned did anyone learn that Masha's blonde hair was dyed as a disguise, and she remained an 'unknown partisan' until 2009 when her name was added to a memorial plaque at the execution site.

Bruskina's execution was unusual in that it was meticulously photographed and widely distributed. The Nazis soon realized that this had the opposite effect to the one they had hoped for: rather than being terrorized, those who saw the photographs instead became enraged and ever more determined to resist the occupation. Because of this, the vast majority of future executions took place in secret. The Gestapo continued to publicly execute prisoners en masse, however. Four weeks before the invasion of the Soviet Union, Himmler had created special *Einsatzgruppen* (Einsatz Groups or task forces) charged with eliminating Jews, partisans and communists, each unit headed by a member of the Gestapo or senior SD officer. The groups had complements of 400–500 men, subdivided into smaller units of *Einsatzkommandos*, who in turn were further subdivided into *Sonderkommandos* and *Teilkommandos*. Although attached to army units that determined where they worked, they took their directives directly from the RSHA in Berlin.

In the first four months of the occupation of the Soviet Union, the *Einsatzgruppen* killed hundreds of thousands of Jews, communists and members of the Resistance. The vast majority were lined up in front of deep ditches and shot in the back of the head or neck. One report writer complained bitterly about the fact that the Gestapo was hampered in its work by a lack of staff and poor working conditions:

In view of the enormous distances, the bad condition of the roads, the shortage of vehicles and petrol, and the small forces of Security Police and SD, it needs the utmost effort to be able to carry out shootings in the country. Nevertheless 41,000 Jews have been shot up to now.

'Night and Fog' Decree

'*Nacht und Nebel*' (or 'Night and Fog') was the codename given to a decree of 7 December 1941, issued by Adolf Hitler and signed by Field Marshall Wilhelm Keitel, Chief of the German Armed Forces High Command. The name stemmed from a phrase coined by Germany's celebrated writer Johann Wolfgang von Goethe, who used the term to describe clandestine operations.

The directive stated that persons captured in occupied

territories were to be brought to Germany in secret for trial by special courts, thus circumventing all international conventions governing the treatment of prisoners. Relatives and loved ones of the prisoners were given no details about the fate of the captive and were therefore left unsure where they had disappeared to, what their sentence might be, or even whether they were dead or alive. Hitler believed that the conventional systems of military and civilian justice were too cumbersome to deal effectively with resistance and sabotage activities. He therefore instructed the Gestapo to utilize 'Night and Fog' tactics to expedite interrogation, torture and execution. The decree letter specifically mentioned that the policy was designed with 'efficient intimidation' in mind, and it became one of the most feared tactics deployed by Hitler's terror police.

In practice, 'Night and Fog' was most widely used in German-occupied Western Europe, and especially common in Nazi-occupied France. After capture and interrogation by the Gestapo, 'Night and Fog' prisoners faced special kangaroo courts (*Sondergerichte*), which handed down lengthy prison sentences or, more commonly, death sentences. Those who escaped death were sent to concentration camps where they wore uniforms marked with the letters 'NN' to signify that they were '*Nacht und Nebel*' prisoners. The death rate among such prisoners was even higher than that for standard concentration camp detainees.

Later on in the war, as the Nazis' situation became increasingly desperate in the face of ever more effective resistance, Hitler issued the 'Terror and Sabotage' decree. This expanded even further on the provisions of the 'Night and Fog' decree and more often than not resulted in summary executions for all violent acts perpetrated by non-German citizens in the occupied territories. For the Gestapo it was, essentially, a 'licence to kill'.

CHAPTER THREE

RESISTANCE, RESISTANCE, RESISTANCE

The entry of the United States into the war heightened the threat to Germany and stiffened the resolve of the Nazi regime. All remaining legal or moral restraints were removed from the Gestapo. The 'Night and Fog' decree that the Gestapo now followed made the organization synonymous with midnight raids during which suspects simply disappeared without trace. Meanwhile, the grim operation of the Holocaust was accelerated. By this stage a ruthlessly efficient death machine had been engineered that was capable of killing thousands of people a day.

The Resistance movements across Europe were buoyed by the news that a powerful new ally had entered the war on their side, however. And British troops drove Rommel's forces out of North Africa, while the German advance through Russia was halted just short of Moscow. Closer to home, the Gestapo was rocked by the assassination of its leader, Reinhard Heydrich. The loss of such a charismatic head was a bitter blow for the organization, and many Gestapo officers must have felt, for the first time, that victory in the war was not assured.

The Telavåg Tragedy

Remaining neutral in the war did not spare Norway from Hitler's attention: the Scandinavian country was too strategically important to him for that. Indeed, the British had plans of their own to invade, in order to open a second front against the Germans away from France, before Hitler gave the order for his troops to cross the border on 9 April 1940. The largely unprepared Norwegians were defeated relatively swiftly, and the country would remain occupied until the capitulation of German forces in Europe in May 1945. The long occupation gave birth to widespread resistance and as a result a large contingent of Gestapo officers was stationed in Norway's major towns and cities. These Gestapo units would commit some of the most infamous crimes of the war, and in 1942 one such war crime occurred in the small Norwegian village of Telavåg.

Telavåg is located on the island of Sotra, around 39 km (24 miles) south-west of Bergen. With direct sea links to Great Britain, it was of great strategic interest to British Intelligence and to the Norwegian Resistance. The British Special Operations Executive (SOE) trained and organized Norwegian volunteers to conduct intelligence and sabotage operations under the leadership of liaison officer Captain Martin Linge. The attacks launched by Linge's Norwegian Independent

Company 1 (NOR.I.C.1) were staggeringly effective and included the operation to sabotage the heavy-water plant at Telemark. The damage caused to the Vemork Hydroelectric Plant inhibited the Nazis' development of nuclear weapons.

Linge himself was killed in 1941 during a raid on the island of Vågsøy ('Operation Archery'), but the band of special forces he established continued to be known as the *Lingekompaniet* or Linge's Company in his honour. Members of this force were at the very top of the Gestapo's most-wanted list, and when they learned that a secret smuggling route was operating out of Telavåg they were quick to investigate. The safe house harbouring them belonged to 63-year-old fisherman Lauritz Telle and his son Lars, who organized secret boat trips between Telavåg and the Shetland Islands in Britain. Fishing boats were the only vessels allowed to sail by the Germans and the crossing took some 30 hours. Telle's boats were secretly retrofitted with anti-aircraft guns, and ferried vital supplies, and Resistance fighters, back and forth between Britain and Norway. The route was known colloquially as the 'Shetland Bus'.

On 23 April, the first Gestapo agent entered Telavåg, disguised as a travelling Bible salesman, to collect information. Later, further agents in disguise arranged a 'boat trip' with Lauritz and Lars. They gave false names and addresses but established that the Telles were indeed engaged in suspicious activities, and so on 26 April the Gestapo returned, this time in the dead of night and in full uniform. The four Gestapo officers were heavily armed and had surprise on their side, but they grossly underestimated the level of resistance they would encounter. Staying with Lauritz and Lars that night were two of Linge's highly trained special forces soldiers. Arne Meldal Værum and Emil Gustav Hvaal were all too aware of the Gestapo's reputation, and were prepared to die rather than fall into the hands of the terror police. A furious gun battle developed between the Gestapo and Linge's men, during which two senior Gestapo officers were killed. Arne Værum (codenamed 'Penguin') was also killed, but Emil Hvaal (codenamed 'Anchor') managed to escape – albeit with nine separate gunshot wounds.

The surviving Gestapo officers retreated back to Bergen, where news of the incident reached the head Nazi commissioner in Norway, Josef Terboven. He immediately decided to travel to Telavåg to personally oversee the collective punishment of the village. It would be brutal, and utterly unjust, targeting every single inhabitant of Telavåg.

Lauritz Talle was taken, along with his wife and youngest child, to Gestapo headquarters in Bergen and tortured. His eldest son Lars was taken to a concentration camp near Oslo, along with 18 other men believed by the Gestapo to have been involved in the 'Shetland Bus' operation. All other men from Telavåg between the ages of 16 and 60 were sent to the Sachsenhausen concentration camp outside Berlin. They were marked for especially severe treatment and 31 of them died in the camp. The women and children were taken to a prisoners' camp a few hours from Bergen. Commissioner Terboven then ordered the total destruction of Telavåg, and that its name be removed from all maps. Every home was rigged with dynamite and blown to pieces. The village was so utterly obliterated that not even the wells remained.

Gerhard Flesch

A fanatical Nazi whose last words before a firing squad were '*Heil Hitler*!', Gerhard Flesch headed the Gestapo in Norway. In this role he executed countless members of the Norwegian Resistance, often without trial. He was notorious for torturing captives in order to extract information from them, and was also chief of the Falstad concentration camp near Trondheim. He fled from there after the war (with a gold bar in his luggage), but was caught and tried for war crimes in 1946. His guilt, and the resultant death sentence, were never in doubt and he was executed in 1948.

Emil Hvaal was captured and transported to a concentration camp to be executed. His wife Kamilla was allowed to visit him in hospital before his transportation. Her parting words to him were '*Vær Norsk*', which translate as 'Be Norwegian'.

The Daring Assassination of Reinhard Heydrich

One million reichsmarks was a vast sum of money in 1942, and in the end it was too tempting an offer for

Rows of murdered civilians from the village of Lidice near Prague, Czechoslovakia, June 1942.

Karel Čurda to resist. The Nazis offered the reward in return for information that would lead to the arrest of those responsible for the most audacious and high-profile assassination of the Second World War, that of Reinhard Heydrich, the head of the Gestapo, which took place in the Czechoslovak capital, Prague. Čurda, a Czech, was a member of the sabotage group 'Out Distance' and was facing intensive interrogation by Gestapo officers, who believed he was involved in the Heydrich assassination plot. He elected to betray his underground comrades and pocket the cash rather than face brutal torture at the hands of his Gestapo handlers. Indeed, under his new identity of 'Karl Jerhot' he became a valuable Gestapo spy for the rest of the war, after which he was captured and hanged for treason.

Čurda was the break the Gestapo were desperate for in their investigation into Heydrich's murder. The pressure from Hitler to find and punish those responsible was intense. At the time of his assassination, Heydrich was not only head of the Gestapo but also chief of the Reich Security Main Office and Protector of Bohemia and Moravia. The slaying of such a high-ranking Nazi official sent shock waves through Germany. Until 1942 the occupied Czech lands had offered little in the way of visible resistance to the Nazis and had produced valuable military material for the Third Reich. The

'Whip and Sugar' policy instigated by Heydrich, in which rations were increased to dissuade resistance, with the threat of them being reduced in the event of trouble, seemed to be working. Heydrich had arrested some 5,000 anti-Nazi partisans and so many of them ended up on the scaffold that he was nicknamed the 'Hangman'.

'Operation Anthropoid', as the assassination was codenamed, had been organized by the British Special Operations Executive with the approval of the Czechoslovak government-in-exile. It was designed for maximum effect in terms of boosting morale and inspiring further resistance across occupied Nazi Europe. Jozef Gabčík and Jan Kubiš were airlifted from the United Kingdom into Czechoslovakia, along with seven soldiers from Czechoslovakia's army-in-exile. On 27 May 1942, they waited at a tram stop near a tight curve on a road in Prague, known to be on Heydrich's daily commute from his home in Panenské Břežany to Prague Castle. As Heydrich's open-topped Mercedes 320 Convertible B reached the spot, Gabčík stepped out in front of it and opened fire with his British Sten sub-machine gun. Nothing happened. The gun jammed. Heydrich, fatally, ordered his driver to stop the car rather than speeding away.

Kubiš grabbed a grenade from his briefcase and hurled

it at the car. The highly sensitive impact fuse prepared by the British SOE caused the grenade to explode as soon as it struck the rear wheel and bumper of the car. The car, unlike most official Nazi vehicles, was not armour-plated. Shrapnel tore through Heydrich's body, but he managed to draw his pistol and trade fire with the assassins. As they fled, Heydrich and his driver pursued them, until Heydrich was forced to stagger back to the car, bleeding heavily. His driver continued to chase Gabčík until two revolver rounds to his leg forced him to let the assassin go. Gabčík and Kubiš escaped largely unhurt, but were convinced their attack had failed. In fact, however, Heydrich's shrapnel wounds were severe and his driver had suffered serious gunshot injuries to the leg.

Despite excellent medical treatment, Heydrich died of his wounds on 4 June. It was probably horsehair from the car's upholstery that festered in his wound to cause a fatal infection. He lay in state for two days before his coffin, draped in swastika flags, was taken on a tour past famous Nazi landmarks on its way to Berlin's Invaliden cemetery. By then a state of emergency had been declared in Czechoslovakia and the huge reward for information had been offered. Hitler ordered the Gestapo to 'wade in blood' throughout Bohemia in order to capture the culprits, and the secret police needed no further encouragement. Hitler's original plan was the simple mass murder of thousands of Czech civilians, but the area was vital to the Reich's industrial output and wiser heads suggested the labour force was too important to lose.

Then came the arrest and betrayal of Karel Čurda. Before paying him the bounty, the Gestapo made sure to extract from him the name of every associate he knew in Czechoslovakia. It was a disaster for the partisans. Already hundreds of suspects had been arrested throughout the country, and now the Gestapo had a long list of names and addresses of confirmed conspirators. Those they had already arrested who were not on that list were usually executed or transported to concentration camps anyway: the Gestapo simply went after anyone they considered 'suspicious'. This included eight men and seven women from the Horak families in Lidice, a favourite drop-point for Resistance paratroopers. They were arrested on 28 May, and the inhabitants of Lidice doubtless imagined that the Gestapo would leave the village alone after that. They were tragically mistaken.

On the evening of 9 June, the Gestapo returned with reinforcements. This time, the entire village was sealed off and Gestapo officers went from house to house, ordering everyone out into the street in their nightclothes. As they watched, their homes were torn apart by Gestapo officers looking for anything incriminating. In total almost 200 men were marched out of the village to the farm owned by the Horak family. There, they were lined up, and mattresses were placed against the walls to prevent ricochets. As Nazi film cameras rolled, in groups of five or ten, all of the men were shot. In addition, 52 women were killed, and all other inhabitants of the village were transported to a concentration camp. The buildings of Lidice were soaked with petrol and then burnt to the ground. Bulldozers and dynamite were used to destroy the remaining walls and uproot trees. It is said that even a stream that once flowed through the village was diverted.

Jewish prisoners were bussed in from a concentration camp to dig a mass grave for the executed men. The children of Lidice fared hardly any better than the adults: the vast majority were handed over to the Gestapo office in Łódź, Poland, from where they were taken to Chelmno concentration camp and gassed. Others died in the brutally austere German orphanages. Of the 101 who were taken away from their homes, just 17 made it back alive to Lidice.

None of those living in Lidice had anything to do with 'Operation Anthropoid'. However, the Gestapo's investigation revealed that several inhabitants from the village of Ležáky did help the assassins. A radio set was secretly hidden there. On 24 June, every man and woman in the village was shot. In total, 33 were executed, with a further 13 children taken away, and the village itself was levelled.

The two assailants themselves hid in safe houses before taking refuge in Karel Boromejsky church in Prague. When Karel Čurda betrayed his comrades to the Gestapo, the net closed in almost immediately. A raid on the home of the Moravec family in Žižkov occurred on 17 June. Marie Moravec and her son Ata were key members of the Resistance, and Marie chose to bite upon a cyanide capsule rather than face a Gestapo interrogation. Her son Ata was tortured, made drunk on brandy and then shown his mother's severed head in a fish tank in order to get him to talk. It was the Gestapo's threat to kill his entirely innocent father that finally persuaded him to give his tormentors the information they wanted.

Though the Gestapo was desperate to take the two assassins alive, ultimately Gabčík and Kubiš chose to fight to the death. A two-hour gun battle at the church ended with Kubiš dying from his wounds and Gabčík committing suicide, along with three other partisans.

In total the number killed by the Gestapo in revenge for the assassination of their leader is estimated at around 1,300.

The Oslo Mosquito Raid

When the British learned that the Nazi-appointed fascist Norwegian leader Vidkun Quisling had organized a rally for 25 September 1942, they decided to launch a raid on that date in order to boost the morale of the Resistance. The most loathed symbol of Nazi power was the Gestapo headquarters, based at the Victoria Terrasse building in Oslo. The Royal Air Force used the raid to announce to the British public a new aeroplane: the de Havilland Mosquito. It was a fast fighter-bomber that would subsequently take part in some of the RAF's most famous raids and garner the nickname the 'Wooden Wonder'.

Four Mosquitoes took part in the attack, which involved a round trip of some 1,800 km (1,100 miles). One was shot down by the Luftwaffe's Focke-Wulf Fw 190 fighters, but the other three returned safely and at least four bombs smashed through the Gestapo headquarters. Three of them penetrated the building and exited through the rear wall before exploding. The fourth failed to detonate. The Gestapo building was thus damaged rather than destroyed as intended, and several surrounding civilian residences bore the brunt of the damage. The Norwegian government-in-exile, which had not been informed of the raid in advance, protested when news of 80 civilian deaths reached them.

Gestapo operations in Norway were, however, badly disrupted by the attack, and it further weakened the position of Quisling, whose star was already in the descendent in Hitler's eyes. Fascists attending Quisling's rally had to run for their lives as the Mosquitoes hurtled across the skies of Oslo as low as 13 m (40 ft). The British and Norwegian public received a major boost to morale as a result of such a high-profile raid: 'Nazis Stung by Mosquitoes' read the headline on the front page of *The Times*.

The Gestapo retained an iron grip on the population for the remainder of the war, despite fierce resistance from bands of Norwegian underground fighters. The success of the Gestapo in Norway was due in no small part to active collaboration from certain well-connected locals. These undercover collaborators posed as anti-Nazi civilians and engaged others in conversation on buses and in cafés. Any signs of sedition were reported back to their Gestapo superiors. One of the most active Gestapo units was *Sonderabteilung Lola*, led by ex-Norwegian army truck driver Henry Rinnan. He infiltrated various Resistance groups and personally tortured and murdered those he later arrested. It is believed more than 80 people died at the hands of *Sonderabteilung Lola*.

Rinnan was executed after the war, along with another

notorious collaborator and Gestapo agent, Siegfried Fehmer. Fehmer was infamous for setting his pet German shepherd dog on his prisoners. He was captured after the war when British Military Police posted a round-the-clock watch on the dog, banking on the fact that Fehmer would attempt to collect it before fleeing. He did so, and was put in front of a firing squad on 16 March 1948.

The Red Orchestra Spy Ring

'The Red Orchestra' (*Die Rote Kapelle*) was one of the most successful spy rings of the Second World War, operating throughout Nazi-occupied Western Europe and in the very heart of Hitler's Third Reich, Berlin. Although ostensibly a Soviet-run operation, its agents included Poles, Frenchmen and women, Germans and Brits. The Nazis were aware that such a ring was operating as early as June 1941, as several intercepted radio messages appeared to share the same call signs and ciphers. The Germans termed enemy radio operators 'pianists', after the Soviet term 'musicians', which is where the name 'Red Orchestra' stemmed from. However, it took until December 1942 for the Gestapo to finally track down its key members. When they did smash the ring, their response was typically brutal.

Leopold Trepper was the heart of the operation. A

Leopold Trepper, organizer of the Red Orchestra spy ring, photographed in 1974.

Soviet military intelligence service officer, he established a small espionage ring in 1939 in Brussels, posing as the proprietor of a firm selling raincoats. Following the fall of Belgium, he moved to Paris in May 1940 and set up further 'cover firms' there. Gradually Trepper's spy ring expanded, and at the time of its discovery the Red Orchestra was comprised of three main branches: the Trepper network in France, Belgium and Holland, the 'Schulze-Boysen' network in Berlin and the 'Lucy Ring' operating out of neutral Switzerland. Harro Schulze-Boysen was an intelligence officer assigned to the German Air Ministry and thus had access to extraordinarily sensitive information that, when leaked, caused significant damage to Nazi operations. The Lucy Ring included Lieutenant General Fritz Theile, a senior *Wehrmacht* communications branch officer, and Colonel Rudolf Christoph Freiherr von Gersdorff, an Army Group intelligence officer on the Eastern Front. The Nazis could hardly fail to notice that top-secret information kept falling into enemy hands, and they made finding the source of the leaks a top priority for the Gestapo.

The agents of the Red Orchestra, however, were highly skilled and extremely diligent in covering their tracks. Teams of radio trackers who scoured the streets of Berlin every night looking to pin down the source of the spies' transmissions were thwarted time and time again. The 'pianists' who transmitted via secret receivers constantly changed their locations, call-signs and broadcast wavelengths.

Things began to unravel for the Red Orchestra in spring 1942, when the Gestapo arrested over 600 people in Germany, France and Belgium. Many were innocent but some were major figures within the espionage network. The Gestapo's brutal torture techniques (known officially as 'intensified interrogation') broke the resistance of some, and they began to talk. One lead led inexorably to another, and eventually Trepper himself was arrested on 5 December 1942 in Paris. He agreed to become a double agent for the Germans and began to transmit disinformation under the close scrutiny of his handlers. However, Trepper managed to escape in September 1943 and survived the war after being sheltered by the French Resistance. It is widely believed that he was able to tip off the Soviets by deliberately broadcasting mistakes in the messages he sent under duress.

The vast majority of the Red Orchestra did not share Trepper's happy ending. Suzanne Spaak, one of Trepper's most important agents, was executed at Fresnes Prison, south of Paris, just 13 days before the liberation of the French capital after years of torture and mistreatment. Mildred Harnack, a lecturer before the war and crucial member of the Schulze-Boysen network during it, was given a sentence of six years' hard labour. Hitler, enraged in the wake of the German defeat at Stalingrad, ordered a retrial and this time she received the same sentence as her husband Arvid: death. Harro Schulze-Boysen himself was executed in December 1942, along with his wife and co-conspirator Libertas.

In total, more than 50 of the group's members were murdered. During the period in which it operated, however, the Red Orchestra did huge damage to the Nazi war effort. By the time it was discovered and destroyed by the Gestapo, the tide of the war had turned against the Nazis. An increasingly paranoid Adolf Hitler would blame all of his woes on betrayal, and turn ever more frequently to his trusted secret police to liquidate the traitors. The Gestapo's reign of terror had yet to reach its peak.

'Operation Freshman'

By late 1942, the German atomic weapons programme was believed to be on the brink of successfully creating a nuclear reactor. One of the key problems they still had to overcome was creating enough deuterium-enriched 'heavy water' to allow a reactor to operate. The heavy water was produced at the Vemork Hydroelectrical plant in Telemark, Norway. British commandos were dispatched to destroy it on 19 November 1942. It was the first British attack to utilize gliders, and from the outset things went disastrously wrong. Both of the gliders used in the assault crash-landed, resulting in the deaths of 15 servicemen. All of the remaining commandos were left injured and far from help, and were soon arrested by the Gestapo.

Adolf Hitler had issued his infamous 'Commando Order' a month earlier, which stated that all commando troops were to be killed immediately upon capture. Three of the four surviving crew from the first glider were tortured by the Gestapo before being murdered by having air injected into their bloodstreams. The fourth was shot in the back of the head the following day. The surviving crew from the second glider fared no better. Five uninjured men were sent to Grini concentration camp where they were held until January 1943. Gestapo agents then marched them out into woods and shot them. The remaining survivors were shot within a few hours of being captured.

The Gestapo flooded the area with armed officers and arrested over 21 local people for questioning. However, the team of Norwegian saboteurs with whom the British had been due to rendezvous managed to slip away. They would return to the same target later in the war, with far greater success.

CHAPTER FOUR
THE GROWING CHALLENGE

On 2 February 1943, news of the surrender of the German 6th Army at Stalingrad sent shock waves through the German Reich, and shattered the myth of German military invincibility. The Gestapo had benefited from the same aura of omnipotence, and now found its authority being openly challenged by the German population for the first time. Less than a month after the Stalingrad surrender, the Gestapo began a massive operation to round up the almost 9,000 Jews in Berlin who were spouses in or children of 'mixed marriages'. Designated 'exempted Jews', they had been spared deportation to concentration or forced-labour camps thus far. On 27 February 1943, almost 2,000 of them were transported to the Jewish community building at Rosenstrasse 2–4.

As word of the operation spread, something extraordinary began to happen: the spouses, siblings and friends of those captured by the Gestapo gathered on the streets outside the building. Mostly women, they refused to leave until given assurances that their loved ones were not going to be deported. A crowd of 200 stood in the freezing temperatures and openly defied repeated orders to disperse. It was an unparalleled protest and soon made headline news across the world. Never before had the German people protested on behalf of Jews, and the Gestapo simply did not know how to react.

In the end, all but 25 of the 2,000 prisoners were released – though the vast majority were quietly re-arrested once the protest had died down. The German authorities were worried that the German public's morale was collapsing and they feared public unrest if they cracked down too hard on their own citizens. The British RAF and US Eighth Air Force began round-the-clock bombing of German cities later the same year, further damaging morale. Allied forces landed in Sicily, and Italy soon surrendered, drawing German forces south to defend Rome in place of the Italian army.

Until this point the Gestapo had concerned itself mainly with foreign spies and Resistance fighters. From 1943 onwards they also had to deal with an increasing level of resistance to the war from within the Reich itself.

The White Rose Movement

The year 1943 began badly for the Germans on the Eastern Front, with a massive counter-attack by the Soviets at Stalingrad on 10 January. The Germans were forced to surrender on 2 February, the first major defeat for a German army at the hands of the supposedly genetically inferior Red Army. By now some of the German public were aware of the mass execution of Jews in concentration camps, with the British Foreign Secretary having pledged in the House of Commons to bring those responsible to justice. A stream of Germans who had witnessed the horrors of the war on the Eastern Front flooded back to the Fatherland. Many of them now realized the madness and brutality of the Nazi regime and dedicated themselves to destroying it. In the summer of 1942, several students from the University of Munich formed themselves into a Resistance group called the 'White Rose Movement'.

The movement was non-violent and targeted the German intelligentsia, mailing leaflets directly to those in a position of power or influence and leaving pamphlets in public places for the general public to find. Most were written by Alexander Schmorell, an Eastern Orthodox Christian who had both German and Russian ancestry. Schmorell had served as a combat medical assistant in the Russian campaign and was one of the founders of the White Rose, alongside fellow University of Munich alumnus Hans Scholl and another medical student, Willi Graf. In January 1943 the group produced 9,000 anti-Nazi leaflets using a hand-operated duplicating machine and a network of couriers operating in cities throughout Germany. This print run, exhorting the German people to support the Resistance and warning them that defeat was inevitable, caused a sensation. The search for the source of the propaganda became the Gestapo's top priority.

The scrawling of the slogans 'Freedom' and 'Down with Hitler!' on the walls of Munich University buildings gave the Gestapo the first clue that students of the institution might be involved. But it was when Hans Scholl went further and personally left leaflets in the lecture rooms of the university that things began to unravel for the White Rose. A maintenance man at the university observed Hans and his sister Sophie hurling leaflets from a top-floor window, and reported them to the authorities. They were interrogated by Robert Mohr, the head of the Gestapo special commission established to search for the White Rose agitators. After initially claiming to be innocent, both siblings admitted their involvement on being presented with incontrovertible evidence. However, they continued to insist they were the only ones involved in the production of the leaflets. The two, along with co-conspirator Christoph Probst, were charged with treason.

What followed was a Nazi show-trial during which prosecutor Roland Freisler, the Gestapo's favourite judge, berated the conspirators for their ingratitude towards the Fatherland. The sentences were never in doubt, and all three were duly ordered to be beheaded. In a particularly ruthless gesture, the executions were carried out the very same day. In due course a total of seven members of the White Rose group were executed, and more than a dozen more were imprisoned. Alexander Schmorell was sent to the guillotine after a second show-trial, alongside fellow White Rose member Kurt Huber. Willi Graf was beheaded on 12 October 1943 after six months' imprisonment and torture by Gestapo

The 'Manifesto of the Students of Munich' and accompanying explanation. Thousands of copies of this pamphlet were dropped over Germany by the British Royal Air Force in 1943.

interrogators. He revealed no information of value. Hundreds of suspected supporters and sympathizers were arrested and interrogated by the Gestapo, some for simply being in possession of White Rose leaflets. The final leaflet produced by the White Rose was smuggled out of Germany and reprinted by the British as the propaganda leaflet 'Manifesto of the Students of Munich'. Millions of copies of the manifesto were dropped over Germany by Allied bombers, and today the group are regarded in Germany as national heroes.

Roland Freisler

Freisler was the judge appointed by the Nazis to preside over the 'People's Court', where many 'political crimes' prosecuted by the Gestapo were heard. It was essentially a kangaroo court, and no defendant brought before Freisler could expect a fair trial. Famous for shouting abuse at those brought before him, Freisler happily handed down death sentences for any crimes that he considered harmed the ability of the Nazi regime to protect itself. He was killed in 1945 when American bombers scored a direct hit on the courtroom while Freisler was presiding there.

Sophie Scholl went to the guillotine with the following words:

Such a fine, sunny day, and I have to go, but what does my death matter, if through us, thousands of people are awakened and stirred to action?

The Return of Dietrich Bonhoeffer

Though the Gestapo generally targeted political dissidents and artistic 'degenerates', it also had a department responsible for arresting 'religious opponents'. One of this department's most famous victims was arrested in 1943. Dietrich Bonhoeffer was picked up by the Gestapo's 'IV B' department, which dealt with regional policy, alongside 'IV A', which handled subjects hostile to the state, including 'religious opponents'. He was initially imprisoned at Tegel military prison in Berlin. A well-known and popular Lutheran pastor, he was an outspoken critic of the Nazi regime and its policy of genocide against the Jews. He was also a prominent member of the *Abwehr*, the German military intelligence organization that was a hotbed of anti-Hitler sentiment during the war.

Bonhoeffer had been under surveillance by the Gestapo since 1941, when he was forbidden to publish any further writings or make radio broadcasts that were critical of Hitler. Bonhoeffer had warned of the dangers of the Nazi regime ever since its rise to power

Dietrich Bonhoeffer, German theologian, arrested by the Gestapo in 1943.

in 1933, and in one message urged the church not to 'bandage the victims under the wheel, but jam the spoke in the wheel itself'. He resisted the Nazification of the German Evangelical Church and asserted the supremacy of Christ over the Führer as head of the church. In autumn 1933, Bonhoeffer left Germany for England and then Switzerland; he returned to Germany in 1935. The church he had helped to found (the 'Confessing Church') was shut down by the Gestapo in 1937, and 27 pastors associated with Bonhoeffer were arrested. Despite this, Bonhoeffer continued to offer services in East German villages, continually moving and lodging with sympathetic friends. In 1938, the Gestapo officially banned him from Berlin, and the following year Bonhoeffer left for the safety of America. Once there, however, he soon came to the conclusion:

I will have no right to participate in the reconstruction of Christian life in Germany after the war if I do not share the trials of this time with my people.

Returning to Germany now that war had broken out was incredibly risky, but Bonhoeffer believed he had to follow his conscience. From the moment he arrived back he was harassed by Gestapo officers and ordered to report to them regularly. Despite their constant attention, Bonhoeffer became a courier for the German Resistance, travelling across Europe under the cover of being an *Abwehr* intelligence officer. Almost inevitably, given the Gestapo's long-held mistrust of him, he was arrested, interrogated and imprisoned in April 1943.

Bonhoeffer was detained for 18 months, ostensibly awaiting trial, though in reality it suited the Gestapo simply to shut him away where he could do little harm. Many of his prison guards were sympathetic to him and one even offered to help him escape, but Bonhoeffer refused on the grounds that the Gestapo would then target his family instead. Everything changed in 1944, when the failed plot to assassinate Adolf Hitler on 20 July led to a massive Gestapo investigation into the *Abwehr*. Bonhoeffer was discovered to have been involved in the *Abwehr*'s anti-Nazi conspiracy and he was immediately transferred to the Gestapo's high-security prison at the Reich Security Main Office. After interrogation there, he was transported in secret to Flossenbürg concentration camp.

On 4 April 1945, Hitler read the diaries of the head of the *Abwehr*, Admiral Wilhelm Canaris. Enraged by their treacherous contents, he ordered the immediate execution of all those involved in the *Abwehr* conspiracy, including Bonhoeffer. He was hanged just two weeks before United States forces liberated the concentration camp. Many other *Abwehr* members and Resistance fighters were hanged alongside him, as the Gestapo liquidated as many witnesses to their own barbarity as possible before the Allied forces closed in.

Jean Moulin: The Man Who Knew Everything

France had one of the best-organized Resistance movements of the war, the military wing of which was the *Armée Secrète* ('Secret Army') led by General Charles Delestraint. They were given significant support from the British just across the Channel, who provided arms, training and intelligence throughout the Nazi occupation. The threat of the French Resistance was so great that one of the Gestapo's most infamous leaders was

French Resistance member Jean Moulin, circa 1940.

stationed in Vichy France to counter it. Klaus Barbie, the 'Butcher of Lyon', would play a key role in one of the most infamous arrests of the war, that of French national hero Jean Moulin in 1943.

The story really began with the arrest in Paris of Delestraint, though many believe that another arrest prior to this actually led to the Resistance being betrayed. It is alleged that a Resistance member by the name of René Hardy was captured and tortured by Barbie, and it was he who gave them Delestraint's name. Regardless of who betrayed Delestraint, his arrest sent shock waves through the underground Resistance. It was a major coup for Barbie's Gestapo men and a terrible blow to the anti-Nazi forces led by Moulin. The young one-time *préfet* (state representative) had been chosen by France's leader-in-exile Charles de Gaulle to unify the piecemeal Resistance in occupied France and had discharged his mission brilliantly to date. He had already been arrested once by the Germans in 1940, and shortly afterwards attempted to commit suicide by slitting his throat. Ever since that unsuccessful attempt he had worn a trademark scarf around his throat to cover the scar. He was, in June 1943, one of the most-wanted men in Nazi-occupied France.

Moulin hastily organized a conference of key Resistance leaders in a doctor's house in Caluire, a suburb of the city of Lyon. His great genius lay in holding

89

together the disparate forces of the Resistance, and he was desperate that all of the main factions should agree upon a successor to Delestraint. René Hardy was one of those in attendance, and is frequently cited as the man who betrayed the meeting's location to the Gestapo. Some, however, claim that Hardy was simply careless and the Gestapo tailed him to the meeting. Others suggest that Moulin was betrayed by rogue communists. What is not in dispute is that the Gestapo raided the house and arrested several high-ranking members of the Resistance, including its head, Jean Moulin. Hardy escaped the raid, which fuelled suspicions that he had been 'turned' by the Gestapo after his earlier arrest.

Part of the reason that we know what happened next is due to the twisted mind of Moulin's principal tormentor, Klaus Barbie. When he had finished torturing Moulin he placed his battered half-dead body on display as a warning to the other suspects. If they refused to talk, he told them, this is what would become of them. Moulin was laid out on a chaise longue in Barbie's office like a gruesome, living museum exhibit of Nazi brutality. Aware that the man they had captured was the head of the French Resistance and could thus name all senior figures involved in the conspiracy, Barbie personally tortured Moulin for three straight weeks. Hot needles were shoved under his fingernails, and his fingers were forced between the hinges of a door, which was slammed shut repeatedly until Moulin's knuckles broke. Handcuffs were tightened with screws until they tore through his flesh and broke the bones beneath. He was routinely whipped and beaten, until the skin hung from his flesh in strips. His face was so badly beaten that even his friends could barely recognize him.

Too badly injured even to talk any more, Moulin was given a piece of paper by Barbie and ordered to write down the names of his co-conspirators. He responded by drawing a mocking caricature of his torturer. Eventually, after more remorseless torture, the head of the French Resistance slipped into a coma. He had not revealed a single detail of use to the Gestapo. Barbie ordered him to be taken to Berlin, via Paris. Moulin died en route – either from his injuries, or from suicide. As a result of his refusal to betray his colleagues, the French Resistance survived as an effective organization and would later play a crucial role in preventing the Nazis from re-inforcing their positions on D-Day. The Allies successfully gained a foothold on the beaches of northern France, and from there marched all the way to Berlin. The importance of Moulin's heroic silence cannot be overstated.

Moulin's sister later summed up his story with the following words:

Klaus Barbie

Nikolaus 'Klaus' Barbie, the infamous 'Butcher of Lyon', personally tortured suspected members of the French Resistance while working for the Gestapo in France. He was born in 1913 in Godesberg, now part of Bonn. He originally wanted to study theology but became actively involved in the Nazi Party after being drafted into its labour service while he was temporarily unemployed. He rose through the ranks of the security service of the *Schutzstaffel* (SS) and the *Sicherheitsdienst* (SD), and was posted to Amsterdam after the German conquest of the Netherlands.

In November 1942 Barbie was sent to Lyon to head the local Gestapo at the Hôtel Terminus. The name Barbie and the Gestapo's French address would become synonymous with many of the cruellest and most sadistic of the Gestapo's war crimes. Historians estimate that Barbie was involved in the deaths of up to 14,000 people. One witness described her father being beaten, skinned alive and then plunged head-first into a bucket of ammonia. In return, the Nazi regime awarded Barbie the 'First Class Iron Cross with Swords' for his work in quelling the French Resistance.

After the war, the French sentenced Barbie to death *in absentia*, but by then he was working as an agent for the United States, who helped him flee to Bolivia. There he worked for a number of Bolivian dictators and

senior generals, and drew a salary from the West German intelligence agency, the BND. He was also alleged to have played a major role in the assassination of Che Guevara in 1967.

He was finally extradited to France in 1984, and sentenced to life imprisonment in 1987. He died of cancer in a Lyon prison four years later.

His part was played, and his ordeal began. Jeered at, savagely beaten, his head bleeding, his internal organs ruptured, he attained the limits of human suffering without betraying a single secret; he who knew everything.

The Polish 'War Within a War'

Resistance organizations elsewhere in Europe were of secondary importance to the overall Allied war effort, with one exception: Poland. The Polish Underground State, and its armed wing, the Home Army (*Armia Krajowa*), were crucial suppliers of intelligence to the British, and their efforts in sabotaging and harassing German forces in the East were vital to the Soviets. Several German divisions were tied down in fighting the Polish threat, and the Allies were alerted to the threats of the V-1 and V-2 flying bombs and rockets by the Poles. Perhaps inevitably, then, the Gestapo's presence in Poland was significant, and anyone suspected of being a member of the Polish Underground could expect no mercy at its hands.

In retaliation for the brutal tactics of the Gestapo, the Polish Underground tracked down and assassinated known collaborators and agents of the Gestapo. One of the most prominent of these was the actor and stage performer Igo Sym. Before the war he had acted alongside major stars such as Marlene Dietrich. When the war broke out he settled in Warsaw, where he became one of the most high-profile figures to embrace the occupying Nazi regime. In late 1939 he became a Gestapo agent, and helped set a trap that caught several prominent members of the Polish Resistance. The Underground took their revenge in 1941, when they assassinated Sym at his Warsaw apartment, posing as delivery men.

The Gestapo's response was a 'Palmiry Massacre'. Throughout the war, these mass executions in the Kampinos Forest near the village of Palmiry, north-west of Warsaw, were used to intimidate the local population and dissuade them from helping the Resistance. It is believed that between 1939 and July 1941 some 1,700 Poles were taken into the forest glades and shot. The majority were Jews and what the Germans considered the Polish 'intelligentsia'.

Often, when the Gestapo wanted to track down a particularly high-value target, they would take hostages from the general population and threaten to murder them unless the target they sought was brought to them. The *łapanka* (round-up) of random civilians was a favourite terror tactic of the Gestapo across Europe, but was especially prevalent in Poland – and in Warsaw in particular. This is what happened in the case of the assassination of Igo Sym. A total of 21 prisoners, including two professors from the University of Warsaw, were shot when no one came forward with the names of the assassins. It was, in truth, nothing out of the ordinary by the Gestapo's standards: between 1942 and 1944, the number of victims executed was estimated to be around 400 per day. Some 37,000 were killed during the war at the local Gestapo-run Pawiak prison alone.

The struggle between the Gestapo and the Polish Underground State had thus become a 'war within a war' in Warsaw by 1943. Both sides considered it a battle to the death. The commander of the Polish Home Army, Stefan Rowecki, was the Gestapo's most high-value target of all. A legendary Polish general who had fought the Nazis ever since they first invaded, he inspired fanatical loyalty and organized his Underground army into a ruthlessly efficient force of resistance. Unbeknownst to Rowecki, however, the Gestapo had infiltrated his organization with double agents of its own.

Ludwik Kalkstein is perhaps the most notorious Polish traitor of all time, betraying his fellow countrymen not only to the occupying Nazis during the Second World War, but to the occupying Soviet forces after the end of the war too. Turned by the Gestapo after intensive interrogation in 1942, Kalkstein led them to Rowecki, who was immediately arrested and turned over to the Gestapo's most senior interrogators. Himmler himself was involved in questioning Rowecki, and when he

departed he ordered progress reports on Rowecki's ques-
tioning to be delivered to him every evening. The Nazis
had by now suffered serious defeats at the hands of the
Red Army and were desperate to try to persuade the
Polish Resistance to side with them against the commu-
nists. They believed that if they could turn Rowecki over
to their cause then his influence would win over the rest
of the Polish Resistance. For this reason, Rowecki
escaped the kind of brutal torture suffered by Jean
Moulin and countless other Gestapo prisoners.

Despite intensive questioning lasting many weeks,
and offers of hugely favourable treatment if he changed
sides, Rowecki refused to either collaborate with the
Germans or provide them with any information. He was
eventually taken to Sachsenhausen concentration camp
while the senior Nazi leadership decided how best to
deal with him. The answer came after the Warsaw
Uprising in August 1944, when Polish Jews revolted with
the assistance of the Polish Home Army. In reprisal,
Rowecki was executed, on the direct orders of Himmler.

Rowecki's arrest and subsequent death was a hammer
blow for the Polish Resistance, but things were to get
worse. The commander of the National Armed Forces
(NSZ) was also captured by the Gestapo in the same period.
Colonel Ignacy Oziewicz had been negotiating with the
leaders of the Home Army in order to form a coalition

between the two Resistance forces. He was sent to Auschwitz but managed to survive the war. Just a couple of weeks after the arrest of these two senior Resistance figures, the prime minister of the Polish government-in-exile, General Władysław Sikorski, was also killed. A plane carrying Sikorski crashed shortly after take-off from the British-controlled territory of Gibraltar. Officially ruled an accident by investigators, many conspiracy theories have suggested he was murdered, either by Polish rivals or by the British or Soviets. Whatever the truth, the Polish Resistance had lost three of its most senior figures within the space of a month, and the Gestapo had restored its iron grip on the Polish population.

Destruction of the Prosper Network

The British Special Operations Executive's largest Resistance network in occupied France was the 'Physician-Prosper' (or simply 'Prosper') network. It was set up in 1942 and headed by Francis Suttill, a London barrister with a British father and French mother. Suttill succeeded in establishing a large and highly effective group of anti-Nazi partisans, and throughout the early part of 1943 arms and agents flowed into France from Britain at a prodigious rate. As the group grew in influence, however, the risks of its discovery grew too. On 12 June 1943 an arms drop went badly wrong when a

Noor Inayat Khan, code-named 'Madeleine', captured by the Gestapo in 1943.

container exploded, and a local collaborator reported the event to the Gestapo. The area was flooded with over 500 Gestapo and SS men, who conducted house-to-house searches and arrested anyone they suspected of aiding the arms drop. Despite this, the British elected to parachute a further two SOE agents into the area just eight days later.

The SOE operative sent to meet the parachutists was Yvonne Rudelatt, the first female SOE agent parachuted into occupied France in the Second World War. An interior decorator from Kensington, London, Rudelatt was recruited while working as manageress of a London hotel at which many senior members of the SOE stayed. The SOE were keen to use women as agents as they were less likely to draw the suspicion of the Gestapo than men of military age out of uniform. Rudelatt quickly became vital to the SOE network in France and played a key role in several of the Resistance's most significant, and dangerous, operations. On 20 June 1943 she was tasked with picking up SOE agents Frank Pickersgill and John McAlister. The Germans were waiting for them. As the agents sped away from the drop-point, their car was showered with bullets and Rudelatt was struck twice. The bullet that lodged in her brain was too dangerous to remove, but her injuries were not life-threatening. She revealed nothing during her interrogation and was transported to Ravensbrück concentration camp. She died of typhus there shortly after the camp was liberated. At the time of her death she was still using her cover-name of Jacqueline Gautier and was buried in a mass-grave without being identified as an SOE agent.

A further wave of arrests and interrogations followed in

the wake of the capture of the SOE agents, however, and the information gleaned from them led the Gestapo to Francis Suttill. He was arrested, along with other key members of the Prosper network such as Andrée Borrel and Gilbert Norman. All were interrogated and Suttill was singled out for especially severe torture at the Gestapo headquarters at 84 Avenue Foch. After several days of brutal punishments he was transferred to Sachsenhausen concentration camp near Berlin where he was held in solitary confinement until his execution in March 1945.

Some writers have claimed that Suttill agreed to provide the Germans with information, while others maintain it was Gilbert Norman who cracked. Whatever the truth, hundreds of local agents were arrested over the next three months, of whom 80 were either executed immediately or died in concentration camps later. The Gestapo executed many captured agents as Allied forces moved through occupied Europe in 1945, and Norman and Borrel were among their victims. The Prosper network was shattered by the Gestapo's activities, with those agents who remained at large no longer sure which of their colleagues had been 'turned' by the threat of brutal torture. Communication back to Britain became incredibly difficult, and those receiving messages from the Prosper network were unsure if the agents transmitting were loyal or operating under instruction from Gestapo handlers.

Into this chaotic and highly dangerous situation was parachuted one of the SOE's most celebrated agents, Noor Inayat Khan, code-named 'Madeleine'. With most other radio operators captured or compromised, her work sending reliable messages back to Britain became vital. It allowed the British and French to begin to rebuild the Prosper network, which would prove crucial in the run-up to D-Day and the Allied advance through Normandy. Khan continued to broadcast despite the intense scrutiny of the Gestapo, who were well aware that a rogue wireless operator remained at large. She was eventually betrayed in October 1943, allegedly by a fellow female Resistance agent who was jealous of her relationship with a man in whom she shared an interest.

Khan was arrested by the Gestapo and a search of her home revealed a set of copies of her secret signals. This was entirely against her training and would prove disastrous in the coming months, as it allowed the Gestapo to send bogus messages to Britain and entrap further agents. They would face the same interrogation, torture, imprisonment and murder that was the hallmark of the Gestapo.

Khan was sent to Pforzheim prison in Germany in November 1943, where she was kept in chains in solitary confinement. Considered an especially unco-operative and dangerous prisoner, she gave no information and twice tried to escape from the Gestapo. On 12 September 1944 she was transferred to Dachau camp, where she was shot. Some reports suggest she was raped before her execution. Her remains were immediately taken to the camp crematorium. Britain awarded her the George Cross posthumously, and France honoured her with the Croix de Guerre.

In total there were 470 agents in the French section of the British SOE, 39 of them women. A total of 15 of these women were captured by the Gestapo, and 12 of those did not live to tell the tale. That means almost a third of female agents paid for their activities with their lives. By way of contrast, the figure for male agents was 18 per cent. This led some to suggest that female agents were deliberately 'sacrificed' by their handlers, in order to allow the Gestapo to get their hands on British wireless sets. The conspiracy suggests that the British used these sets to feed back erroneous messages about the location of the D-Day landings.

It is true that the campaign of deception launched by the Allies to convince the Nazis that they would land in Calais rather than Normandy was vast and full of intrigue. However, the overwhelming majority of the female agents undoubtedly contributed to the vital sabotage work that the Resistance did in order to ensure that the landings themselves succeeded. The high mortality rate they suffered as a consequence is almost certainly the result of the callousness of the Gestapo rather than an act of abandonment by the British Intelligence Services.

CHAPTER FIVE

PLOTS AND SUBPLOTS

By 1944, the Gestapo had over 30,000 employees. The Kripo had over 12,000 and the SD a little over 6,000. Despite the large number of staff, however, the police and intelligence services were permanently stretched. Men were desperately needed at the Eastern Front, which was by now absorbing vast numbers of soldiers as Hitler fought a bloody battle to the death with Stalin. In the west, Allied troops took Rome and then landed in Normandy to open a second front in the war. By August Paris was liberated and by October the Nazis had been driven out of Athens too. German forces launched a massive counter-attack in Belgium: it would later become known as the 'Battle of the Bulge'. Though it slowed the Allied advance, it failed to reverse it.

The war, then, was going badly for the Germans on all fronts. The Gestapo responded by now unleashing the same pitiless tactics it had used in the occupied territories upon the German Reich itself. Germans who had long since realized the futility of the war were cast as traitors to their country. Those identified as enemies of the state were subjected to a bloodthirsty frenzy of torture and execution. The Nazi regime, and the Gestapo in particular, was fighting for survival.

Stalag Luft III: Escape and Recapture

The site of the Luft III prison camp in Sagan, 160 km (100 miles) south-east of Berlin, was specially selected by the Luftwaffe for its most secure facility as it was considered near impossible to tunnel out of. The sandy soil in the area made any tunnels dug highly prone to collapse, and the sand was easy to detect, being bright yellow in marked contrast to the grey, dusty surface soil. The camp's remote location meant there was nowhere to tunnel to anyway. Or so it seemed.

The prison camp was guarded by Luftwaffe personnel, and was thus very different in character from those run by the Gestapo. While the guards were by no means the

Stalag Luft III, scene of 'The Great Escape', circa 1944.

cream of the German air force, they were fellow airmen who had a healthy respect for the Allied air force prisoners they watched over. Meagre food rations were sometimes an issue but other than that the prisoners were well treated. Despite this, however, many considered it their duty to try and escape and return to the frontline, and so an elaborate mass-escape plan was hatched. It consisted of the building of three separate tunnels, nicknamed 'Tom', 'Dick' and 'Harry'. As each of the prison barracks was elevated above ground as a security precaution, the tunnels were dug through stoves that were mounted on brick plinths.

It was a massive undertaking: each tunnel was dug at a depth of 9 m (30 ft) and when completed was 100 m (335 ft) long. The depth was necessary to avoid the microphones the Germans had buried in order to detect any digging noise. An extension to the camp covered Dick's planned exit point so it was abandoned and used to store the sand from the other tunnels and the equipment the escapers would need. Prior to this, prisoners nicknamed 'penguins' stuffed the sand down their trousers and distributed it around the prison yard as they walked on their breaks. The Germans eventually got wise to the practice and Tom was discovered, leaving only Harry as an escape option. The escape was originally planned for the summer, but the Gestapo visited the camp in early

1944 and advised increased security, so the date of the break-out was brought forward. The pilots would make their break for freedom as soon as Harry was finished.

That date was Friday, 24 March 1944. A moonless night increased the escapers' chances of evading detection. It had been hoped that hundreds would be able to make it out, but major problems with the plan soon emerged. The freezing March temperatures meant the tunnel's escape hatch had iced shut, and it took an hour and a half to force it open. Worse still, the tunnel was too short. The plan was for it to open in a nearby forest, but the actual exit was close to a sentry point. It left those emerging from the tunnel with a significant distance to cross in the open before reaching the forest. With snow on the ground, they would be highly visible.

Despite these problems – plus an air-raid alarm and a partial tunnel collapse – 76 airmen made it through the tunnel to freedom before the 77th was spotted, at 4.55 am on 25 March. An immediate inspection of the prison revealed that 4,000 bed boards had been broken up to provide supports for the tunnel. Countless articles of cutlery, bedding and furniture had also been utilized by the prisoners. Hundreds of metres of electric cabling, left unattended by German workers, had been stolen for use in the escape. The workers concerned were rounded up and shot by the Gestapo for failing to report the loss.

The incident was a grave embarrassment to the Nazi regime, and the Gestapo was determined to track down all of those who had escaped. According to the Geneva Convention, the maximum punishment allowable for escaped prisoners was 28 days in solitary confinement, but an incensed Hitler declared that all those who had escaped should be shot upon recapture. Eventually he was talked down by Göring and other senior Nazi figures, who pointed out that many German airmen were in the hands of the British and may be murdered in a tit-for-tat reprisal. Still, Hitler maintained that 50 of those who had escaped must be executed and immediately cremated as an example to the others. A national alert was ordered and Hitler's directive was teleprinted to Gestapo HQ by Himmler. A list of 50 names was then drawn up to satisfy their leader's order.

The Allied airmen were, quite literally, running for their lives. The thick snow in Sagan slowed their progress, and in the pitch-dark night many struggled to find the entrance to the local railway station, which was positioned in an unusual place, recessed under the train platforms. As a result, most of the escapers could not board night trains as planned. Many foreign workers used the trains, and the airmen had hoped to blend in with them. Instead they had to catch the first morning trains or slog their way out of Sagan on foot.

This combination of misfortunes for the Allied airmen made the Germans' task in capturing them considerably easier. In usual circumstances, escaped prisoners would be handed over to civilian police in order to be returned to their prison camp. The prisoners of Stalag Luft III, however, were all handed over directly to the Gestapo.

Of the 76 who emerged from the tunnel and fled into the night, just three managed to make it to safety and freedom. One by one the others were caught in the vast net that the Nazi regime had thrown across the area: 100,000 men were assigned to check the identities of every single person they encountered. Of those 73 recaptured, 17 were returned to Sagan, with another four being sent to Sachsenhausen concentration camp and two more to the infamous Colditz Castle.

The other 50 all suffered near-identical fates at the hands of the Gestapo. They were driven to remote locations, having been told they were being transferred to a distant camp. En route the Gestapo car would stop and the prisoners would be offered the opportunity to relieve themselves. As they turned their backs to do so they were shot in the back of the head. The Gestapo reports for each execution claimed the prisoners were shot while trying to escape. Half of those killed were British. Squadron Leader Roger Bushell – nicknamed 'Big X' and the man who originally conceived the 'Great

Escape' – was shot by Gestapo official Emil Schulz just outside Saarbrücken, Germany.

In due course the hunters would become the hunted: Allied forces placed the Gestapo executioners of the Stalag Luft III prisoners at the top of their wanted list after Germany lost the war. Foreign minister Anthony Eden had denounced the murders as a war crime and told the British Parliament:

His Majesty's Government must record their solemn protest against these cold-blooded acts of butchery.... They will never cease in their efforts to collect the evidence to identify all those responsible.... When the war is over, they will be brought to exemplary justice.

The Special Investigation Branch of the Royal Air Force Police hunted the perpetrators after the war with personal zeal – the only time a war crime was investigated by a single branch of any nation's military. They spent over three years chasing down leads and eventually identified 72 men who they believed were involved in the murders. A total of 21 Gestapo officers were duly executed after standing trial, with another 17 imprisoned. Of the rest, 11 committed suicide, six were killed during the war, five were arrested but charges were not brought, three were acquitted, one got a plea-bargain and one sought refuge in communist East Germany. Just seven remained untraced, though several of those were probably killed in the war.

The Ardeatine Massacre

On 3 September 1943, the Italians surrendered uncondi-
tionally to the invading Allied troops, and Hitler lost a key
European ally. The Germans rushed to reinforce their posi-
tions in Italy and quickly took control of Rome, imposing
Germany military law in the city. Fascist leader Benito
Mussolini was freed from prison and re-installed as a
puppet leader, to the consternation of many Italians who
had long since grown sick of war. The Italian Resistance
began to attack the occupying German and Fascist Italian
forces, and in retribution the Gestapo launched a series of
punitive raids against those thought to be responsible. In
January 1944, the Allies made a surprise landing at Anzio,
just 48 km (30 miles) from Rome, and an emboldened
Resistance redoubled its attacks. One of their more spec-
tacular successes was an operation launched on 23 March
1944 against a column of German soldiers marching
through the narrow street of Via Rasella in Rome.

A partisan disguised as a street cleaner pushed a rubbish
cart packed with TNT into the street, and 40 seconds later
it exploded, killing 28 soldiers and two civilians. Sixteen
partisans then traded fire with the Germans before melting
away into the back streets of Rome. The same evening,
senior German Secret Police officials decided that they
would retaliate by killing ten Italian civilians for every
German killed. As the death toll of the attack reached 33,

the Gestapo sifted through all available prisoners to decide which of them would be executed. When they discovered only four of those in their custody had been sentenced to death, they made up the numbers from others convicted of relatively minor crimes, and from Jews. The Gestapo, and their Nazi superiors, were concerned only with filling the huge quota that had been determined.

Doctors, lawyers, shopkeepers, artists and teenage boys were among those selected for murder. Some had simply had the misfortune to have been named as anti-Nazi by the Gestapo's vast network of informers. Perhaps the most famous victim of the massacre, however, was a key figure in the Italian Resistance and one of its most celebrated national heroes today. Colonel Giuseppe Montezemolo was the leader of the FRMC ('Clandestine Military Front of the Resistance') and had been in continual radio contact with the Italian government-in-exile until his arrest by the Gestapo on 25 January 1944. Like so many Gestapo victims before him, he had been brutally tortured in an attempt to glean further information on the Resistance's activities. Despite having his nails and teeth pulled out, he told them nothing. Another victim was General Simone Simoni, a 64-year-old war hero who endured being tortured with a blowtorch but refused to betray his Resistance comrades.

Due to a counting error, a total of 335 victims were

brought to the execution site, five more than the Gestapo's own barbaric mathematics had called for. The victims were taken in trucks to the Ardeatine caves on the rural outskirts of the city. With their hands tied behind their backs, they were led into the caves in groups of five and ordered to kneel down. The commanding officer had brought cases of brandy for his troops, to calm the nerves of men unused to cold-blooded murder. Each prisoner was killed with a single bullet to the back of the head. The cave was soon full of bodies, and those executed last had to kneel on the bodies of their fellow victims before being shot themselves. With 330 already dead, it was discovered that five extra prisoners had been brought to the scene. After a brief discussion, the men were shot anyway – to prevent any witnesses to the massacre reporting the location of the crime scene.

The bodies were placed in piles around a metre high and covered in rocks. German military engineers then set explosives to blast the cave rock and seal the entrance. Most of the relatives were told nothing about the fate of the prisoners. Those who were informed were given terse letters indicating only that their loved one was dead. The bodies lay undiscovered in the caves for over a year, until the Allies liberated Rome on 4 June 1944. Then a tip-off led investigators to the scene and the rubble was painstakingly removed in order to give the dead a proper burial.

Violette Szabo: Bravery and Defiance

Violette Szabo joined the British Special Operations Executive following the death of her highly decorated husband Étienne, who was killed in action during the Second Battle of El Alamein on 24 October 1942. Just a couple of months earlier, Violette had given birth to their first child, and she was inconsolable at the loss of the newborn's father. As she was French-born and fluent in both English and French, she was assigned to F-Section and trained as a field agent to work in Occupied France. She performed poorly in some aspects of training, and had to return home after spraining an ankle on her first parachute jump, but eventually passed through the SOE's 'finishing school' at Beaulieu in Hampshire. Like many female SOE agents, she enrolled with the First Aid Nursing Yeomanry (FANY) in order to disguise her connection with the Special Forces. Her cover story while in France was that she was a commercial secretary called Corinne Reine Leroy. She was parachuted into Cherbourg in Occupied France on 5 April 1944.

Standing just 1.6 m (5 ft 3 in) tall, she was nicknamed La Petite Anglaise, but it was her secondary nickname, 'Louise', that became her codename. Szabo and her SOE colleague Philippe Liewer (working under the cover name of 'Major Charles Staunton') were tasked with finding out what had happened to the 'Salesman'

Violette Szabo, captured by the Gestapo in 1944.

Resistance network, which had operated in Rouen and the northern coast of France. The network, co-founded by Liewer, was known to have been disrupted by wide-scale Gestapo arrests and the British were desperate to rebuild it before the critical Normandy landings in June. The Rouen area was considered too dangerous for Liewer to operate in as the Gestapo had his name and physical description, and so Szabo took a train to Paris and then on to Rouen alone. The mission was incredibly dangerous, and Szabo made her last will and testament before departing for France.

For the next few weeks she travelled extensively through the Rouen area, teeming as it was with German soldiers and Gestapo officers. Though she spoke perfect French, she did so with a thick Cockney accent and so had to be careful to keep her conversations with officials brief. Her physical beauty meant that she often drew the unwanted attention of strangers, and of German servicemen in particular.

Despite the danger and the difficulty, Szabo managed to reach all of the areas of interest to the British and ascertain which members of the Salesman network had fallen into the hands of the Gestapo. The information she provided on the state of the Resistance was of the utmost importance to the war effort, and in addition she managed to identify German munitions factories that would later become key targets for Allied bombers. Szabo discovered that the Salesman network had been decimated, with most of its key members having become victims of the Gestapo's 'Night and Fog' tactic and spirited away to Germany. She re-established a new network of Resistance agents and returned safely to Britain on 30 April 1944.

SOE was hugely impressed with Szabo's work, increased her salary and gave her a couple of weeks to rest and recuperate. With D-Day looming, however, she was soon pressed back into service. The network 'Salesman 2' was to be established in Haute Vienne and would concentrate on the strategic sabotage of railway lines and other infrastructure targets, to prevent the Germans being able to reinforce northern France once the Allied invasion began. Szabo was reunited with Liewer, who would head up the new network, with Violette acting as courier. They flew out to France on 7 June but were forced to turn back after the expected reception committee failed to show. On their return journey to England they flew over the vast invading fleet of Allied ships heading to the beaches of Normandy.

The next day the SOE agents successfully parachuted into France, which buzzed with the news of D-Day. The panicked Germans raced to shore up their defences and placed roadblocks on numerous roads into and out of the area. Szabo's mission was to contact the leader of another Resistance network ('Digger') in order to co-ordinate attacks on the German forces. She requested, and was given, a submachine gun in order to defend herself. The request was unusual as anyone carrying arms would undoubtedly be arrested if stopped by the Germans. Perhaps Szabo had already decided that events had moved beyond the stage of subterfuge and into the realms of open warfare.

The car she was travelling in with Jacques Dufour and Jean Bariaud, two other members of the Resistance, was stopped at a roadblock near the village of Salon-la-Tour. With Dufour and Szabo both heavily armed, allowing themselves to be stopped would result in their inevitable arrest. They elected to try and blast their way to freedom. Dufour brought the car to a halt and the three passengers leapt out, with Szabo and Dufour laying down withering machine-gun fire to cover their escape.

Bariaud, who was unarmed, managed to make a successful break for freedom in the ensuing mayhem. In time he would make contact with the rest of the Salesman network and warn them of the fate of his comrades. Szabo and Dufour broke away in the other direction, leaping a gate and running across a cornfield as German armoured cars swarmed to the scene of the gun battle. As the fugitives approached the relative safety of a forest, Szabo fell heavily and badly twisted her ankle. She refused Dufour's offer of help and insisted on covering his escape as best she could. For the next half an hour Szabo pinned down the massed German forces pursuing her, killing a German corporal and wounding several other soldiers.

Dufour used the time granted to him by Szabo's defensive fire well, and hid in the barn of a local Resistance sympathizer. One account suggests Szabo herself was taken to the same barn for interrogation after finally running out of ammunition. What is certain is that once disarmed she was taken into custody and gave her questioners the name of 'Vicky Taylor'. She was interrogated for four days at Gestapo headquarters in Limoges. When Dufour learned of her fate he organized a daring mission to rescue her. The plan was to attack the two guards who escorted her each day from Limoges prison to the Gestapo headquarters around half a mile away. Unfortunately, before the plan could be put into action, Szabo was moved to Fresnes prison in Paris, and from there to the infamous Gestapo HQ at 84 Avenue Foch.

The Gestapo by now knew the true identity of 'Vicky Taylor' and her links to the Special Operations Executive. She was interrogated relentlessly over the course of the next few days, and some assert that torture was also used on her. There is no conclusive evidence that she was physically harmed, but the pressure placed upon her to betray her comrades was doubtless intense. Despite this, Szabo gave the Gestapo no useful information. She carved her name in the wall of cell 45 to let others know she had been there, but aside from that we know nothing of her time at Avenue Foch. With the Allies pushing through Normandy towards Paris, it was decided that all prisoners of particular significance be evacuated back to Germany.

On 8 August Szabo was shackled at the ankles to another SOE agent, Denise Bloch, and placed on a train for the first part of the journey. Ironically the train narrowly avoided being hit by an Allied air raid en route. When her German guards leapt from the train in panic, Szabo took the opportunity to crawl along the floor of the train distributing water to her fellow prisoners, who were packed together in searing heat. Several later testified that her calmness, generosity and bravery were inspirational to them. With transportation badly disrupted due to the very sabotage she was in France to facilitate, her journey to Ravensbrück concentration camp took 18 days.

Most female SOE agents ended up at Ravensbrück, and Szabo suffered the same brutal conditions as the other prisoners. Ravensbrück's reputation was terrifying, with murder, torture and medical experimentation commonplace. Often made to work in freezing conditions, with only subsistence rations to draw energy from, the mortality rate among inmates was extremely high. Just three British SOE agents made it out of Ravensbrück alive, and Szabo was not among them.

Some time late in January or early February of 1945,

Szabo was summoned from her cell, along with her fellow agents Denise Bloch and Lilian Rolfe. By this time, Szabo was the only one of the three who could walk unaided. The three women were taken to a courtyard known to the prisoners as 'execution alley' and ordered to kneel. They held hands as each was shot in the back of the neck by a Gestapo officer. Immediately after their executions, they were stripped and cremated. Violette Szabo was 23 years old. When her death became known, she was awarded a posthumous George Cross by the British, and the Croix de Guerre by France.

July 20 and 'Operation Thunderstorm'

In part, the Gestapo grew from Hitler's fear that he would one day be betrayed by his own countrymen, and this concern was far from being a paranoid delusion. Ever since the Nazis' rise to power, certain parts of the German military machine had been secretly plotting to get rid of him. The resistance centred on the military intelligence organization the *Abwehr*. Many of the plotters were senior German armed-forces personnel who believed that the Fatherland would be destroyed if Hitler continued to pursue the war. They believed that if the fanatical leader was removed, Germany would be able to secure favourable peace terms with the Allies.

By the summer of 1944 it was clear to most Germans

Claus von Stauffenberg, the leader of 'Operation Valkyrie'.

that the war could no longer be won, and the only question remaining was whether the coming defeat would be total, or negotiated. Above all, those involved in the plot feared an invasion of Germany by the Soviet Union. A peace deal with the British and United States was considered infinitely preferable to that, and both allies had made clear that no deal would be done as long as Hitler was in power.

Though the plot is often termed 'Operation Valkyrie', that name in fact referred to the coup planned for the wake of Hitler's assassination. After Hitler's death, the plotters would occupy and take control of Germany's key ministries to prevent a breakdown in law and order or a counter-strike by the Nazis. For this plan to swing into action, of course, required the leader himself to be slain. This task fell to Lieutenant Colonel Claus Schenk Graf von Stauffenberg. He had been badly wounded in the North African campaign and was considered a war hero of impeccable standing. The Gestapo was incredibly suspicious of the more senior members of the *Abwehr*, and Stauffenberg was considered to stand a greater chance of getting close to Hitler. On 1 July 1944, Stauffenberg was appointed chief of staff to General Friedrich Fromm at the Reserve Army headquarters on Bendlerstrasse in central Berlin. This position enabled him to attend Hitler's military conferences. By the summer of 1944 the conspirators became aware that the Gestapo was closing in on them. It was now or never.

On 20 July 1944 the conspirators struck. At Hitler's *Wolfsschanze* ('Wolf's Lair') retreat in the Masurian woods of East Prussia, Stauffenberg brought a bomb to a military conference. The device was hidden in a briefcase, and primed by Stauffenberg in the bathroom of Field Marshal Wilhelm Keitel's office shortly before the conference began. Upon entering the conference room, Stauffenberg placed the briefcase under the table at which Hitler and 20 other senior Nazis were sitting. A few moments later, Stauffenberg excused himself from the meeting to make a telephone call. Ten minutes after Stauffenberg left the room, at around 12.45, the bomb detonated.

The conference room was devastated. However, the blast was deflected away from Hitler because the briefcase had been moved in Stauffenberg's absence. Placed behind a thick table leg, it killed four people in the room but left Hitler with only minor leg injuries and a perforated eardrum. Stauffenberg had originally intended to leave not one but two devices: had he done so, or had the first bomb not been moved, the plan would almost certainly have succeeded. Indeed, Stauffenberg, as he raced away from the complex towards Berlin, believed he had killed the Führer and that all was going to plan.

On one of the last planes to leave the area before aircraft were grounded, Stauffenberg had no way of contacting his fellow conspirators, nor did they have any way to contact him.

'Operation Valkyrie' now began to swing into action, but the conspirators were confused by conflicting messages about whether Hitler was dead or alive. The commander in chief of the Home Army responsible for implementing Valkyrie was 'Generaloberst' Friedrich Fromm, and he refused to do so without proof positive that Hitler was dead. Aware of the conspiracy, Fromm wanted to back whichever side was most likely to triumph, and he knew that if Hitler had indeed survived then any action against the Nazis at this point would be suicidal for him.

When Stauffenberg arrived, he exaggerated his story to claim that he had personally seen Hitler's body being taken from the conference room, and confessed to Fromm that he was the one who had placed the bomb. Instead of issuing the order to commence 'Operation Valkyrie', Fromm instead tried to arrest Stauffenberg, at which point Fromm himself was detained by two other conspirators who drew their pistols on him. Stauffenberg and fellow plotter General Friedrich Olbricht then tried to ring around to enact 'Operation Valkyrie' and spread the message that Hitler was indeed dead.

Attempts to wrest power from the Nazis floundered

once Himmler took personal control of the situation. He made it clear to all that Hitler remained in charge and that any disloyalty would be dealt with ruthlessly. By 7 pm Hitler had recovered enough to make phone calls to key personnel himself. The Bendlerblock building, home to the *Abwehr* and the meeting point for the conspirators, was surrounded. Stauffenberg was injured during the fighting that broke out; several other key plotters elected to commit suicide rather than face arrest.

Shortly after midnight, General Fromm was released from his armed detainment and he promptly ordered that Stauffenberg and the other plotters be arrested. Impromptu courts martial were held and Stauffenberg, Olbricht and two other officers were executed – probably to prevent them revealing the identities of others (including Fromm himself) involved in the plot. Many of the conspirators scrambled to distance themselves from those who had been directly involved in the day's events now that it was clear the plot had failed. It was in their interests to silence Stauffenberg before he could incriminate them.

They were right to be worried. A furious Hitler ordered Himmler to unleash the full power of the Gestapo in investigating the plot. He wanted every last link of the conspiracy tracked down and ruthlessly punished. The Gestapo operation that followed was one of the largest and most brutal that they ever embarked upon. In the coming days, weeks and months some 7,000 people were arrested, and the best estimate for the total executed is 4,980. Many had nothing whatsoever to do with the plot, but the Gestapo now had licence to settle any outstanding scores. On 23 August 1944, the investigation into the failed 20 July plot morphed into a wider purge of all those who might threaten the Reich's survival. 'Operation Thunderstorm' gave the Gestapo carte blanche to arrest and eliminate just about anyone they chose to. They leapt at the opportunity enthusiastically, in an environment of near-hysteria.

The first arrests, of those who organized the plot, resulted in show-trials and subsequent executions designed to be as demeaning and brutal as possible. Eight of those convicted (Robert Bernardis, Albrecht von Hagen, Paul von Hase, Erich Hoepner, Friedrich Karl Klausing, Helmuth Stieff, Erwin von Witzleben and Peter Graf Yorck von Wartenburg) were stripped naked and hanged with piano wire rather than rope. Their bodies were then hung on meathooks as the film cameras rolled. The footage was sent to Hitler, who replied with approval and urged the Gestapo on to root out each and every other conspirator.

Most of the thousands arrested were simply packed off to concentration camps and held without charge or trial. The bewildered 'enemies of the Reich' were often taken under 'Night and Fog' conditions, leaving their desperate families bereft of any information about their whereabouts. The Allies were by now close, pushing through Maastricht and Luxembourg, ever closer to the German border. For those opposed to the Nazi regime, liberation seemed tantalizingly near, yet many of those who most loathed Hitler were in the hands of his dreaded secret police.

The Gestapo's persecution of those associated with left-wing political views also intensified during the operation, as the unions had played a key role in the conspiracy. Their main representative, Wilhelm Leuschner, was interrogated and eventually executed for supporting the planned coup. His last word was 'Unity!' – but in the face of the Nazi terror police it was all too often 'every man for himself'. Known communists already being held in concentration camps were taken before firing squads and executed, in reprisal for the part their comrades had played in the conspiracy.

Anyone believed to be closely involved in the plot was treated with the utmost brutality by their Gestapo interrogators. Horrific torture caused many of them to crack, and gradually the names of all of the conspirators and sympathizers became known. Across Germany and those territories still occupied by German forces, wave after wave of arrests followed, producing further information, which led in turn to a further expansion of 'Operation Thunderstorm'.

In October 1944, Roland Freisler, the Gestapo's judge

of choice, was a busy man. Many of those arrested, interrogated and tortured by the Gestapo in the wake of the plot were finally hauled before Freisler to receive their inevitable death sentences. Among those condemned to the firing squad were senior German officers Colonel Karl Heinz Engelhorn, Major Adolf Friedrich Graf von Schack and Lieutenant Colonel Wilhelm Kuebart. Even the notorious Freisler did not convict 100 per cent of those brought before him, however. Some, such as Albrecht Fischer, who offered to serve as commissioner for Stuttgart if the coup succeeded, were found not guilty at trial. It made little difference to the Gestapo: Fischer was simply re-arrested and deported to Sachsenhausen concentration camp. Though he survived and was liberated, most Gestapo prisoners were shot as the Nazis retreated in the face of the Allied troops in 1945.

Many other conspirators chose not to wait for the Gestapo to break down their doors. Wessel Freiherr Freytag von Loringhoven, the man who supplied Stauffenberg with the explosives packed into the briefcase, committed suicide in woods in East Prussia five days after the failed plot, aware the Gestapo was closing in on him.

Even torture and death were not enough to satisfy the Gestapo chief's thirst for revenge in the wake of the 20 July plot, though. On 4 August 1944, Heinrich Himmler ordered that the remains of one of the plotters executed on the night of the failed coup, Friedrich Olbricht, be exhumed. His body was then burnt and his ashes dispersed so that no physical trace of the traitor remained. The families of those involved in the assassination attempt were also targeted. Relatives of those executed after the 20 July plot were taken into custody and held in concentration camps. A total of 50 children related by blood to the conspirators were held in a 'children's home' in Bad Sachsa, where they remained until liberated by Allied forces in May 1945.

The Warsaw Uprising

As July 1944 drew to a close, Poland was in its fifth year of German occupation. The Red Army's spring offensive on the Eastern Front was driving Hitler's forces back to Warsaw's eastern suburbs, and the liberation of the country seemed close. In order to show that Poland was in solidarity with those fighting the Nazi tyranny, the Polish Underground Home Army decided to attack German forces in Warsaw. The offensive began on 1 August 1944, with some 40,000 Polish underground fighters, led by General 'Bor' Komorowski, taking part. The German garrison facing them numbered 15,000, but was better armed and better trained. The Poles believed they could drive the demoralized Germans from Warsaw. They were unaware that a decision had already been made to hold

A German staff car captured by the Polish Home Army during the Warsaw Uprising of 1944.

Warsaw at all costs, and that the city was critical in a German plan to counter-attack the Red Army.

German reinforcements poured into the city once the Polish insurgency began, and the defending garrison soon doubled in size to 30,000. Crucially, the Poles had only enough arms to support 2,500 of their fighters and enough ammunition to last for just one week of fighting. The Germans, on the other hand, were supported by tanks, planes and heavy artillery. The Soviet offensive halted 19 km (12 miles) from Praga, a suburb in east Warsaw, and as a consequence the Luftwaffe had the skies over the Polish capital to itself. The small and lightly armed

Polish Home Army would have to take on the might of the German military machine alone.

Over 180 German military installations were attacked by the insurgents, including the main military and police buildings, bridges, airports and train stations. In fierce and bloody fighting, the Germans managed to hold the most strategically important of their bases, but were forced to cede some significant strongholds in the city's west districts. By nightfall, the main post office and the high-rise Prudential building were in Polish hands, along with several key gas, electric and water works. Around 2,000 insurgents and 500 Germans lay dead. Crucially, the Germans had held out long enough for their reinforcements to arrive and for their forces to reorganize. The Poles no longer had the element of surprise on their side, and the battle for Warsaw would now enter a tragic new stage. The man in personal charge of the Warsaw operation from here on would be the head of the SS and Gestapo, Heinrich Himmler. Police and military units from all across the area were drafted in and given their orders: Warsaw was to be levelled, and the entire city's inhabitants slaughtered, as a warning to the rest of occupied Europe.

The German counter-offensive centred initially on the Wola and Ochota districts of Warsaw. German forces, primarily SS men and the Gestapo, rounded up 65,000 civilians in the captured districts. Under the supervision of the senior Gestapo officers, every man, woman and child was shot. Oskar Dirlewanger's homicidal SS *Sonderkommando* unit was one of those most heavily involved. The most notorious war crimes perpetrated during this stage of the campaign occurred at the district hospitals, where an estimated 1,360 patients and staff were murdered. The Radium Institute Hospital was attacked at just after ten o'clock on the morning of 5 August. The female staff were dragged into the hospital gardens and raped, while the male staff and all patients capable of walking were kept outside at gunpoint for four days in freezing conditions. They were then transported to concentration camps in Germany. The patients unable to move were shot in their beds, and the mattresses set on fire beneath them. Many not killed by the gunfire were burnt alive. The Germans then burnt the entire hospital to the ground, leaving the 70 or so patients trapped on the upper floors to die amidst the flames. Others captured were lined up in threes, and a Gestapo officer shot them, one by one, in the back of the head.

Drunken German troops also burst into the Wola hospital and machine gunned all those within sight. The remaining patients and staff were marched to a nearby house and relieved of any of their valuables. Around 500 were shot in batches of 12 or so. The dead included patients, staff, priests and nuns. Grenades were thrown into the pile of bodies and the house then burnt to the ground. The following day, tanks levelled the site. Himmler's orders to murder everyone in Warsaw and destroy every building were methodically carried out as the German troops moved remorselessly through the city. Some unfortunate civilians were hung from lampposts after having been beaten, whipped and raped. Photographs were taken of the events so that the Nazi elite would be satisfied at the level of murder and destruction.

One woman who miraculously survived the slaughter despite being shot in the head later described how the Germans sang and drank amidst the piles of bodies. They kicked the lifeless corpses to check for any signs of life, before taking any valuables that had hitherto been missed. Later, in order to save ammunition for the battle against the Polish Home Army, the Germans developed a new tactic for their mass murders: burning the residents of Warsaw alive. Houses and large buildings were surrounded from all sides, and then gasoline and grenades were thrown into them. Those who rushed out to flee the flames were mown down with machine guns. Most of those not killed in the initial fireball died of smoke inhalation, or later in hospital from their severe burns.

There were widespread reports of the Germans using large groups of civilians as 'human shields'. Mostly women, children and the elderly, they were forced to stand or kneel across Warsaw's streets so that the German troops could fire on the insurgents from behind them. The Germans had learned to their cost on the Eastern Front just how bloody street-to-street fighting could be and were determined to minimize their losses. Their brutal tactics made the job of the Polish Home Army far more difficult, yet many later testified to the almost miraculous accuracy of the Polish snipers. German troops were bewildered by the fact that their own side appeared to be struck with bullets from all directions, while their Polish hostages remained unharmed.

The insurgents battled on, despite the odds and their dwindling ammunition supplies. Communication between the various pockets of Resistance was maintained through the city's network of sewers. The British made over 200 sorties to air-drop vital supplies to the Resistance, but Prime Minister Winston Churchill's pleas to Franklin Roosevelt and Stalin for co-ordinated Allied assistance fell on deaf ears. Until the middle of September, all captured Polish Resistance fighters were executed on the spot rather than treated as prisoners of war. Stukas dive-bombed all areas under Polish control, including clearly marked hospitals.

Despite the Germans' determination to crush Polish morale through their brutality, the Poles managed to capture the ruins of the Warsaw ghetto and free 350 Jews from the Gesiówka concentration camp. Many of the city's residents were evacuated through the sewer system, which the Home Army used themselves in order to gradually fall back in the face of the German onslaught. The Red Army reached the east bank of the Vistula river in mid-September, but the retreating German army blew up all the bridges to prevent further progress. The Soviets provided only sporadic artillery and air support to the Resistance. On 18 September Stalin rescinded the ban on the Western Allies landing on Soviet territory, and the United States Air Force dropped supplies to the Resistance for the first time. But it was too little too late: by now the Polish forces were too thin and too widely dispersed to do anything but withdraw.

Capitulation finally came on 2 October, with the Germans agreeing to treat the combatants according to the Geneva Convention in return for their surrender. Around 15,000 of them were disarmed and sent to prisoner-of-war camps in Germany. The entire civilian population of Warsaw was expelled from the city and sent to a transit camp. Up to half a million people were sent from the transit point to labour camps, concentration camps and assorted other holding facilities throughout Germany. Then German demolition squads moved in. Flamethrowers were used to burn all the major buildings left standing, and the rest of the city was dynamited into rubble. Around 85 per cent of the buildings in Warsaw were destroyed.

The casualty figures on both sides can only be estimated, but it is widely believed that around 20,000 combatants died on each side. Due to the brutality of the Gestapo and SS forces, the Polish civilian casualties were far higher – some put the figure as high as 200,000.

The Betrayal of Anne Frank

On 4 August 1944, four Gestapo officers raided a canal warehouse at 263 Prinsengracht, Amsterdam. Inside they found eight Jewish people hiding in an annexe: Otto Frank, his wife and two children; the three members of the van Pels family; and a dentist by the name of Fritz Pfeffer. The Gestapo took them first to Westerbork camp and then on to the notorious concentration camp at Auschwitz. Of the eight people arrested, only Otto Frank survived the war. His daughter, Anne Frank, would later become one of the most widely known victims of the Gestapo, thanks to the diary she kept during her time in hiding.

It is believed the famous Anne Frank diary was dumped from Otto's briefcase when a Gestapo officer emptied it in order to fill it with the fugitives' valuables. It was later picked up by Miep Gies, one of the Dutch citizens who helped the Frank family hide, and she returned it to Otto Frank after the end of the war.

The diary chronicles Anne's life from her 13th birthday in 1942 until the moment of her capture. Though extraordinarily powerful thanks to Anne's personal style, the story of the Frank family is typical of thousands of other Jewish families during the Second World War. Born in Germany, Anne Frank moved with her family to the Netherlands when the Nazis came to power in 1933. They then became trapped when the Nazis occupied the country in 1940. When the persecution of the Jewish population by the Gestapo intensified, the family went into hiding. From 1942 until their arrest in 1944, they hid in an annexe hidden behind a bookcase in the building where Otto Frank worked.

Who, exactly, betrayed the family is a mystery. In truth, there is no shortage of candidates. The Gestapo relied heavily on its network of informants in all the territories it policed. Many collaborated because they were double agents, 'turned' by the heavy-handed interrogation techniques of the secret police. Others gave the Gestapo information in return for favourable treatment or black-market goods. After their arrest, the Franks were taken to the RSHA headquarters and interrogated. Having been caught hiding, they were considered criminals and shipped to Auschwitz, where Otto was separated from the rest of the family. It was here that

Anne became aware of the full horror of the gas chambers, though she herself was not selected for immediate execution. Instead, she and her sister Margot were transferred to the concentration camp at Belsen, leaving behind their mother, who was by that time too ill to be moved. Edith Frank died shortly afterwards.

Little is known of Anne and Margot's time in the concentration camps, but they both died before the Allies liberated the camps in 1945. It is most likely that Anne died in February 1945, of typhus, starvation or a combination of both. When last seen she was bald, emaciated and demoralized by the death of her mother – she believed her father was also dead, though in fact he survived his period in Auschwitz. Anne Frank was one of an estimated 107,000 Jews deported from the Netherlands during the Nazi occupation. Tragically, she was also one of the estimated 102,000 who perished in the German concentration camps. Like most of these, she was unceremoniously buried in a mass grave.

In 1963, Karl Silberbauer was identified as the commander of the Gestapo raid that arrested Anne Frank and her family. He was not prosecuted for his role in the death of the war's most famous diarist, however. Anne Frank's father Otto stated that Silberbauer had 'only done his duty and behaved correctly' during the arrest.

CHAPTER SIX

BREAKING THE CHAIN

The chain of command from the RSHA down to the provincial Gestapo offices rapidly fell apart as the Allies overran occupied territories and finally Germany itself. Relentless Allied bombing shattered the Nazi command and control structure. Prior to the war, the regional offices had always had far greater autonomy, but in the war years they had come to rely on orders from above. When that culture changed, the Gestapo struggled to adapt. Confusion rapidly turned to panic in the areas farthest from Berlin, and in regions where adherence to the Nazi philosophy was less fanatical than in the capital. Information often arrived too late to be of use to officers, or could not be acted upon even if it did arrive in time due to increasing shortages of staff. The ruthless efficiency that had characterized the Gestapo ebbed away, and with it its air of invincibility.

When Germany surrendered, the key figures of the reviled Gestapo were hunted down remorselessly by the Allies, and many of their stories are included here. The 'rank and file' members of the organization were rarely punished harshly, however. Thousands of former SS and Gestapo men found employment in the intelligence services and the civil services of both West and East Germany. A law passed in 1948 in West Germany granted amnesty for all crimes committed before 15 September 1949 for which the punishment was less than six months. As many as 700,000 convicts and suspects benefited as a result.

The Demise of Roland Freisler

By 1945, the Allies had forced the Luftwaffe onto the back foot and begun to take control of the skies over Western Europe: even the German capital was no longer safe from attack. One particular raid on 3 February was to have a major impact on the Gestapo, killing one of its best-known and most flamboyant associates, Judge Roland Freisler.

It was 'Raving Roland' Freisler who routinely handed down death sentences to the defendants brought before him by the Gestapo, often without any evidence of guilt being offered. A fanatical Nazi, Freisler was known for his angry outbursts at those in the dock, and for ruthlessly punishing anyone who dared to show disloyalty to Hitler. In one especially memorable instance, a young woman named Marianne Elise Kürchner was arrested by the Gestapo for making a joke about the Führer. She reportedly said, 'Hitler and Göring are standing atop the Berlin radio tower. Hitler says he wants to do something to put a smile on Berliners' faces. So Göring says, "Why don't you jump?".'

Freisler's judgement upon her? 'Her honour has been

permanently destroyed,' he said in his adjudication, 'and therefore she shall be punished with death.' As far as Freisler was concerned, the war was no laughing matter.

It is perhaps fitting that the Gestapo's chief judge lost his life while in the process of sitting in judgement on one of those arrested in the wake of the 20 July plot to assassinate Hitler. The wave of arrests that followed the attempted coup was one of the most notorious Gestapo operations. One of those interrogated and tortured was Fabian von Schlabrendorff, who had been a member of the German Resistance for several years and had unsuccessfully tried to assassinate Hitler in March 1943. A primed bomb he passed to one of Hitler's associates was supposed to blow his plane out of the sky, but it was left in the drawer of his desk, where in any case it failed to detonate.

Schlabrendorff was facing a certain death sentence from Freisler when an Allied air raid caused the trial to be halted. The unsentenced defendant was hurried away to a cell and spent the rest of the war being shuffled between detention camps, before being liberated by the Allies. Judge Freisler, however, deemed that he had time enough to pick up his paperwork before evacuating the court building after the suspension of Schlabrendorff's trial. It was a fatal mistake.

A direct hit on the building caused a roof beam to fall

on Freisler, who subsequently died of his injuries. The bombing raid was led by US Air Force pilot Robert Rosenthal, a Jew who later worked as an assistant to a prosecutor at the Nuremberg trials. A hospital worker who received Freisler's body was reported to have remarked, 'It is God's verdict.' It was certainly a verdict that Freisler himself had handed down to others on thousands of occasions during the war.

'Operation Carthage'

The Danish Resistance movement (*Modstandsbevægelsen*) had long requested that the Allies target the Gestapo headquarters in the 'Shell House' (*Shellhus*) building in Copenhagen. By March 1945 the British had both the means and the will to carry out such a raid, having perfected the art of high-speed, low-level bombing runs with Mosquito aircraft. Even so, it was an incredibly audacious and high-risk attack, involving a flight in broad daylight right into the heart of a major city that was heavily defended with anti-aircraft guns.

The Gestapo, however, was holding dozens of high-level Danish Resistance fighters and the building was packed with dossiers that could lead to the execution of hundreds more. The Shell House was notorious as a centre of torture and depravity, and as a symbol of Nazi oppression in Denmark. The plan was to badly

The Shellhus, Copenhagen headquarters of the Gestapo in Nazi-occupied Denmark, on fire in the aftermath of the 'Operation Carthage' bombing raid by the RAF, 21 March 1945.

disrupt the Gestapo's operation in the country while freeing the Resistance prisoners. The Gestapo held the majority of the prisoners on the top floor of the building, as 'human shields' against bombers, so the RAF decided to precision-bomb only the lower floors.

Three waves of six RAF Mosquitoes took part in the raid, supported by 30 American-supplied Mustang fighters. The latter's role was not only to provide cover against enemy aircraft but also to attack and draw fire from the anti-aircraft guns positioned all across the city. Given the Shell House's location in the centre of a densely populated area, the bombers would have to fly as low as possible. Indeed, as testament to this, one of the Mosquitoes crashed after its wing clipped a 30 m (100 ft)-high lamppost. Tragically, it spun out of control into the nearby Jeanne d'Arc School and burst into flames. Some of the following waves of bombers, seeing the flames, mistook the burning school for their target and dropped their bombs there. As a result, 86 schoolchildren and 18 adults (most of whom were nuns) were killed.

Many of the bombers, however, did score direct hits on the Gestapo HQ, and caused massive damage to the building. As it burnt, 18 Resistance prisoners took the opportunity to escape. A total of 55 Germans were killed, along with 47 Danish Gestapo employees and eight prisoners. One of the prisoners killed was Morgens Prior, who was being beaten by the Gestapo when the raid interrupted the torture. The badly wounded Prior died after jumping from the window of his fourth-floor interrogation room. The RAF lost four Mosquitoes and two Mustangs in the raid, which left nine airmen dead.

The role of the Danish Resistance has long been a source of historical debate, with many suggesting that Denmark did little to resist the Nazi occupation, while others point to the high quality of the information the Danes supplied to Britain. The most celebrated Danish Resistance fighter, Bent Faurschou Hviid (nicknamed 'Flammen' or 'the Flame' due to his bright red hair), was certainly a thorn in the side of the Gestapo. Widely believed to have personally executed 22 Nazi collaborators and double agents, Flammen was the most wanted man in Denmark until his death in October 1944. The bounty on his head led to his betrayal, and though he fled across a roof, he soon realized he was surrounded. Faurschou Hviid swallowed cyanide rather than face the Gestapo torture chambers. His lifeless body was dragged off the roof and down the stairs by its feet, with the arresting officers cheering each time his head struck a stair.

The remaining Danish Resistance fighters later succeeded in disrupting the Danish railway network in the days following D-Day, preventing German troops stationed in the country from reinforcing the Nazi defences in Western Europe.

The Case of Wernher Von Braun

The Gestapo's arrest of Germany's chief rocket scientist, Wernher von Braun, in March 1945, would arguably change the entire world. Throughout the war, von Braun was in charge of developing advanced rocket-based weapons that Hitler hoped would give the Reich a decisive military edge. Von Braun's brilliance resulted in the V-2 rocket, the world's first long-range guided ballistic missile. As the tide of war turned, the V-2 rockets were increasingly viewed as the wonder-weapon that might force the Allies to make peace with Germany rather than force the country to unconditionally surrender. More than 3,000 of the rockets were launched between September 1944 and the spring of 1945, initially targeted at London but later also at Antwerp and Liège. The number of people killed by the weapons is estimated at between 5,000 and 9,000.

Though the V-2 was effective as a terror weapon, it was too inaccurate to bring the kind of devastation of which Hitler dreamed. In addition, the production of the V-2 was horribly expensive, in terms of both treasure and blood. The Reich spent the equivalent of around £3 billion ($4.6 billion) in today's terms, and in excess of 10,000 forced labourers were killed while working on the project, from exhaustion, sickness, malnutrition and mistreatment.

Senior members of the Gestapo believed that von Braun was more interested in the potential for rockets to travel into space than he was in rocket-powered weaponry. Himmler had a burning personal desire to get his hands on the technology and pushed to be allowed to take control of the entire operation. When this route brought him no joy he planted the suggestion that von Braun was deliberately dragging his feet on the rocket project. A rumour was also spread that von Braun was in fact a British spy about to betray the secret technology to the British.

Hitler was unnerved enough to allow Himmler to arrest von Braun and interrogate him. The entire team behind the V-2 was raided at 2 am and hauled into Gestapo headquarters while their homes and workplaces were searched. Von Braun remained in 'protective custody' for over two weeks, but no evidence of the supposed plan to flee to England was discovered by the Gestapo investigation. Eventually Hitler ordered his release, and von Braun returned to work. He was still involved in the V-2 project when he surrendered to Allied forces in 1945, along with his brother Magnus and the rest of his team.

Because of Himmler's accusations and von Braun's imprisonment by the Gestapo, the German scientist was treated favourably by the United States army. He and his team were flown to America, where he eventually became technical director of the US army Ordnance

Guided Missile Project in Alabama. Von Braun designed the Saturn V booster that in 1969 sent Apollo 11 to the moon. By then he was a US citizen, and his past close association with the Nazi regime was a distant memory. His rehabilitation after the war was undoubtedly helped by Himmler, whose paranoid accusations provided von Braun with an anti-Nazi cover story that he never really had. As a result, the Gestapo inadvertently helped the United States win the space race, 25 years after they raided their chief rocket scientist's home.

Justice for Hermann Fegelein

Hermann Fegelein was a career opportunist who took advantage of his close links to those in power in order to rise up through the ranks of the Nazi military machine. He was the brother-in-law of Hitler's partner (and future wife) Eva Braun, and thus part of Hitler's inner circle. In addition, he cultivated a close friendship with Heinrich Himmler, who ensured that he received the positions he most coveted in the Reich.

When Fegelein faced court-martial charges in 1940 after stealing food and luxury goods, Himmler stepped in to ensure all charges against his friend were dropped. Gestapo head Reinhard Heydrich tried on several occasions to have Fegelein brought to justice for a variety of crimes, including 'murder motivated by greed'. That

Hermann Fegelein, who benefited from his acquaintance with Hitler through Eva Braun, Hitler's partner and subsequently his wife.

charge related to Fegelein ordering the execution of several prisoners held in a Gestapo prison so that he could take possession of their valuables. However, Fegelein was too well connected for any of the charges to stick.

Fegelein's SS *Totenkopf Reiterstandarte* ('Death's-Head Horse Regiment') worked closely with the German state police forces, including the Gestapo. While his unit was deployed in Poland it took part in the Kampinos Forest massacre that saw 1,700 Polish intellectuals shot dead. When the unit later moved to the Eastern Front, it assisted the Gestapo in rounding up partisans, Jews and suspected communists and executed them without trial. In offensive action Fegelein was daring to the point of recklessness, and was wounded by a Red Army sniper before being more severely wounded on 30 September 1943 during defensive actions against the Soviets.

Following his convalescence, Fegelein was moved from frontline duties and Himmler made him liaison officer and chief representative of the SS at Hitler's headquarters. He was one of those seated round Hitler's table during the failed assassination attempt on 20 July 1944. Fegelein, like Hitler himself, escaped with only minor wounds. For the rest of his life he kept photographs of those rounded up by the Gestapo and hanged in the wake of the failed coup. As the Allied and Soviet forces encircled Berlin in April 1945, Fegelein was at Hitler's side in the Führerbunker, but ever the opportunist, he saw the writing on the wall and was determined not to go down with the sinking ship.

On 27 April 1945, it was noticed that Fegelein was not in the Führerbunker as usual. One of Hitler's bodyguards, Peter Högl, was sent out to see what had happened to him. Upon arriving at Fegelein's Berlin apartment, Högl found him dressed in civilian clothes. Fegelein had been drinking heavily and was seemingly planning to flee to Switzerland or Sweden. His packed bags were found to contain large amounts of cash and jewellery – some of which belonged to his wife. Even worse, a briefcase in Fegelein's possession revealed evidence of Himmler's attempts to negotiate peace with the Western Allies.

Himmler's relationship with Hitler had been strained ever since the Führer had placed the Gestapo chief in charge of halting the Red Army's advance into Pomerania, a region today split between Poland and Germany. Himmler proved to be a disastrous military commander and was easily defeated by his opposing number, Marshal Georgy Zhukov. As the German forces desperately tried to flee across the Baltic Sea, Himmler began to send increasingly incoherent reports back to Hitler. He eventually suffered a nervous breakdown and fled to a sanatorium, further eroding Hitler's confidence in him.

The two men met for the last time on Hitler's birthday, 20 April 1945, when Himmler learned that Hitler intended to stay in Berlin and fight to the death rather than attempt to escape. Himmler swore loyalty to his leader but had no intention of joining his suicide pact. Instead he began secret negotiations with Count Folke Bernadotte, the head of the Swedish Red Cross, about a possible German surrender. Without Hitler's knowledge, Himmler agreed to the repatriation of thousands of concentration camp prisoners to the safety of neutral Sweden. Then, claiming to be the provisional leader of Germany, Himmler signed a surrender document, seeking to ensure that it was the Allies rather than the Soviets who entered Germany.

Himmler's negotiations would not be made public until a BBC news item the day after Fegelein's arrest. Once Himmler's treachery was confirmed, his represent-ative, Fegelein, was doomed. Hitler was enraged at what he saw as disloyalty all around him, and ordered Himmler to be stripped of all military ranks and arrested. Fegelein, who for so long had worked hand in hand with the Gestapo, was now to face one of its most feared interrogators, Heinrich Müller.

According to most accounts, a tearful and intoxicated Fegelein claimed merely to be Himmler's messenger and not to be directly involved in his peace plans. At least one report suggests that Hitler's partner, Eva Braun, pleaded on behalf of her brother-in-law, and as a result Hitler reversed a decision to sentence Fegelein to death. This account states that Hitler wanted Fegelein demoted and ordered him to prove his loyalty by fighting the Soviet invasion of Berlin. When others pointed out that Fegelein would simply desert and flee, Hitler changed his mind again.

Fegelein was brought out of his makeshift cell at the Führerbunker to face a hastily arranged court martial. Waffen-SS General Wilhelm Mohnke presided over the trial and, sympathetic to Fegelein's plight, concluded that the petrified defendant was in no fit state to stand trial. He ordered the proceedings to be closed and handed Fegelein over to General Rattenhuber and his security squad, with instructions that he be detained.

Exactly what happened thereafter is the subject of much debate. All accounts agree that at some point on 28 April Fegelein was taken into the garden of the Reich Chancellery and shot. Some reports suggest that this was done on Hitler's orders, others that a further court martial found him guilty of treason and sentenced him to death. The last survivor from the Führerbunker, body-guard Rochus Misch, later claimed to know the identity of Fegelein's executioner, but refused to reveal his name.

He stated that Fegelein was 'shot like a dog' and killed by a single bullet to the back of the head.

By the time Fegelein met his bloody end, the Soviets had advanced to Potsdamerplatz, just 300 m (330 yd) from the Reich Chancellery. News of this, combined with Himmler and Fegelein's disloyalty, prompted Hitler to write his last will and testament. Two days later, he shot himself in the head. The Germans surrendered unconditionally to the Allies on 7 May. After six catastrophic years, the war in Europe was finally over.

CHAPTER SEVEN

LAST DAYS OF THE GESTAPO

With the collapse of the German army on both the Eastern and Western Fronts came the collapse of the Gestapo from within. Gradually the chain of command, which throughout the war had been so rigid and dependable, dissolved. The Reich Security Main Office (RSHA) was obliged to pass responsibility for key decisions further and further down the Gestapo ranks. From February 1945 onwards, newly appointed 'Commanders of Security Police' (*Kommandeure der Sicherheitspolizei*) had the power to condemn almost anyone to death without trial. Middle-ranking officers were suddenly faced with momentous decisions they had no experience of dealing with. They reacted, in general, by copying the actions of their superiors – and often even outdoing them in terms of inhumanity. The result was a wave of mass executions as the Gestapo units retreated back towards Berlin.

In the Ruhr region of north-west Germany, a particular problem for the Gestapo was foreign workers. Most of these were forced into work after having been captured in the occupied territories of the east. Many were from the Soviet Union, and as such were associated with the very forces now threatening the future of the Reich on its eastern border. As the Western Allies and Red Army remorselessly rolled towards the German capital, revenge was in the air. Workers from the east bore the brunt of the Gestapo's frustrations, as they were considered to be of an inferior bloodline, and the Soviet armed forces had a not-undeserved reputation for brutality against captured Germans. Hundreds of such foreign workers were rounded up by the Gestapo and executed with a bullet to the back of the neck.

The most commonly cited reason for the executions related to maintaining public order. As the iron grip of the Gestapo began to weaken, groups of workers banded together to form armed gangs. They looted shops and factories and were frequently involved in shoot-outs with the security forces. With food and other supplies running critically short, there was little choice for some but to steal what they could. Many entirely innocent workers were thus tarred with the same brush and accused of looting or belonging to the burgeoning Resistance movement. The standard Gestapo response of an excessive show of force was deployed to try to prevent a slide into chaos.

The Gestapo's prisons were overflowing with prisoners even before the panic induced by the Allied armies' approach. Moving large numbers of inmates farther east, away from the frontline, was a logistical nightmare. Instead, large numbers were simply executed. Between the end of March and mid-April, almost all of the large cities in the Ruhr region saw mass executions. The best-documented examples serve here merely as an illustration of the widespread carnage wrought by the Gestapo in its final days.

In early February, 24 members of a group known as the 'Kovalenko gang' were shot in Duisburg, although many other prisoners there accused of minor offences were released. The chief of police decided who would live and who would die. Those in the latter category included 29 prisoners (including several women) who had allegedly provided shelter for the gang. They were marched to a nearby bomb crater and mown down by Gestapo officers with machine pistols. Though the Ruhr region was not short of bomb craters by this point in the war, soon the Gestapo would run out of these for use as execution sites. A further 38 eastern workers and German inmates were shot in Duisburg alone before the Gestapo fled the area.

In Essen, a 'special police court' was convened by the local Gestapo chiefs and 35 prisoners were condemned to death. They were taken to the 'Monday hole' near Gruga Park the next day and executed. The head of the Gestapo in Essen, Peter Nohles, ensured that those who pulled the triggers were police officers who had never previously been involved in executions. He wanted all of his underlings to be complicit in the bloody crimes in order to establish their loyalty. Doubtless he feared that anyone not directly involved might testify against him in future. Nohles was one of the main architects of the transport of Jews out of Essen and must have known that he would soon be brought to account for his actions. In the end he could not evade justice and elected to die by his own hand in 1947.

Similar scenes took place in other cities in the area, with the wave of executions reaching its climax in Dortmund, where the Gestapo's main office was located. In its prisons the Gestapo held hundreds of prisoners, including members of the local Resistance movement and those accused of spying. The overwhelming majority, however, were prisoners of war and labourers, mostly from Russia. Though no one knows exactly how many were executed in Dortmund in the final weeks of the war, the Gestapo's own meticulous records indicate that at least 230 were shot in the back of the neck and buried in bomb craters. The last executions took place in open fields where they could easily be witnessed, as the more discreetly located bomb craters were by this time already full of bodies. Many of the executed workers were females. The last three were shot close to the railway station on 8 or 9 April, just before the Gestapo officers boarded trains out of

Dortmund, as the first Allied troops entered the fringes of the city.

The chosen rendezvous point for the retreating Gestapo in the Ruhr region was the local high school at the garrison town of Hemer. A vast prisoner-of-war camp there held more than 200,000 inmates throughout the six years of the war, more than 24,000 of whom, as a result of the appalling conditions, ended up being buried close by. The Gestapo had always been a paranoid organization, but now that the writing was on the wall for the Nazi Reich, the secret police's mistrust spread to the German population in general, and even to fellow Gestapo officers. Gestapo men began to melt away and disguise themselves as civilians, or else to accuse one another of disloyalty or cowardice.

In the commandeered school house at Hemer, the mistrust reached almost farcical proportions. The staff of the various Gestapo offices in the Ruhr essentially found themselves guarding not prisoners but one another. Each office suspected that their colleagues in other offices were planning to run off rather than await instructions from their superiors. It became impossible to police the streets because all available officers were needed to watch one another for signs of desertion.

The thousands of executions carried out in the last weeks of the war cannot be fully explained in purely rational terms. There is no doubt that many of the kill-ings were simply down to the cold psychopathic logistics of the organization: prisoners could not be easily evac-uated, and so they were murdered. However, they could just as easily have been released en masse to be dealt with by the rapidly approaching liberation armies. Some may have been killed to prevent them testifying against members of the Gestapo, but again the rationale is flawed, as the Gestapo was well aware that no matter how many were killed there would still be plenty of witnesses to the organization's crimes left alive. It is difficult not to conclude that spite and vengeance moti-vated much of the slaughter. Senior Gestapo officers knew that they had no future after the war in a defeated Germany, and simply elected to take as many people as possible down with them.

The situation changed with Hitler's suicide and the subsequent surrender of Germany. Now, it was every man for himself. The hunters had become the hunted.

In Pursuit of the Gestapo

The Western Allies had specialist teams who sifted through prisoners of war looking for key members of the Gestapo. Those successfully captured would later stand trial at Nuremberg. The Soviets had a reputation for being more severe, and many Gestapo agents who fell into their hands were never heard of again. The majority were probably executed on the spot, though hundreds more were sent to Stalin's brutal Gulag camps. Those who had collaborated with the Gestapo often suffered summary justice at the hands of their fellow citizens or members of the local Resistance. It was not uncommon throughout occupied Europe for informants and collaborators to be paraded through the streets with signs hung around their necks before being hanged or shot.

In such an environment, many Gestapo men elected to seek out Allied forces and surrender willingly to them. The most senior figure to do so was Herman Göring, the man who for much of the war was second-in-command to Hitler and his chosen heir. He was taken into custody near Radstadt on 6 May after surrendering to the 36th Infantry Division of the US Army. Had Göring not done so, he may well have been executed by his own side: Hitler's private secretary, Martin Bormann, had sentenced him to death for treason. Göring had been stripped of all ranks and condemned as a traitor after attempting to assume control of the Reich shortly before Hitler's suicide.

Once in custody, Göring was flown to a prisoner-of-war camp in Luxembourg to be interrogated and weaned off the 320 mg of dihydrocodeine (a morphine derivative) he took daily. He would be the most high-profile official to stand trial at Nuremberg (though only the second-highest-ranking, after former Admiral Karl Dönitz was made Reich President in the wake of Hitler's suicide).

Heinrich Himmler was the next most senior figure on the Allies' wanted list, and on 22 May 1945 he was arrested along with two others at a British checkpoint at the Bremervorde Bridge. This was the only bridge left standing between Bremen and Hamburg, and Himmler intended to use it in order to reach the Bavarian mountains and escape. Himmler was using the name Heinrich Hitzinger, but drew attention to himself because of his curious appearance: he had a patch over one eye and several days of beard growth, and was dressed in an 'odd collection of civilian garments with a blue raincoat on top'. Under interrogation, the three prisoners contradicted one another's stories, and in due course Himmler removed his eye patch and admitted his true identity.

The British were well aware that many senior Nazis carried cyanide capsules to swallow as a last resort. Himmler was searched and two cyanide capsules were found on him and removed. He was then transferred to the British headquarters where a military doctor began a more thorough examination of the prisoner. It was at this point that Himmler bit down on a cyanide capsule that was embedded in one of his teeth. Despite frantic efforts to save him, he died 12 minutes later. Himmler's body was buried in secret by the British to prevent it ever becoming a Nazi shrine. To this day, nobody knows the location of his final resting place.

The Allies were deeply concerned about reports that certain fanatical Nazis intended to retreat to a 'National Redoubt' in the Austrian Alps and fight to the death. Intelligence suggested that tons of arms and ammunition had been taken to the redoubt, and that they would be used to launch attacks on Allied occupation forces in the weeks, months and even years after the war ended. These so-called 'werewolves' were to be led by Ernst Kaltenbrunner, the man who took over direct control of the Gestapo after the assassination of Reinhard Heydrich in 1942.

The hunt for Kaltenbrunner was intensified when his Gestapo chief in Vienna, SS Brigadier General Huber, was found in early May in a hospital in the Altaussee district of Austria. Huber admitted he had been sheltered by Kaltenbrunner, and soon local Resistance informants passed on the news that Kaltenbrunner had been spotted in a remote mountain cabin called Wildensee Huette. An American soldier dressed in traditional Austrian lederhosen and hat approached the cabin posing as a mountain hiker. When he discovered there were indeed

Germans hiding inside it, the cabin was surrounded by armed troops. Kaltenbrunner and three other SS men initially elected to fight but upon realizing the hopelessness of their situation decided to surrender. The Gestapo chief was carrying false papers and posing as a doctor, complete with full medical kit.

After interrogation by the Americans confirmed his true identity, Kaltenbrunner was flown to a British interrogation centre where he received harsh and unsympathetic treatment. As a consequence, he refused to co-operate with his questioners and denied all connections with the Nazi regime. His uncompromising attitude resulted in him being taken for trial at Nuremberg in handcuffs – the only one of the 21 major defendants to be treated in this manner.

Perhaps the greatest mystery left unsolved after the end of the war is the fate of 'Gestapo Müller', head of the organization and intimately involved in the very worst of their crimes. He is said to have been at Hitler's side in the Führerbunker just two days before the Nazi leader committed suicide. He remains officially missing, though a detailed report by the Americans concluded that he was probably killed in Berlin either shortly before the end of the war or very soon after it ended. However, a grave in Berlin said to contain his body was opened 30 years after the end of the war and found to contain two unknown soldiers rather than Müller.

The US records contain cryptic and conflicting hints of other possible fates. One former Nazi interviewed in December 1945 stated that Müller escaped Berlin via a secret underground passage. Reports from the Russian zone of Berlin suggested that he shot himself and his entire family two days before Hitler died. Remarkably, according to the US's own records, it appears that Müller was in their custody in a camp in Altenstadt in Upper Bavaria in December 1945. No details of what happened to him after this were recorded, though the card bore the words: 'Case closed 29th January 1946'. This has led some to speculate that Müller was secretly flown to the United States and employed by the American intelligence services.

This is less improbable than it first appears: the US Office of Strategic Services (OSS) was keen to prevent senior German scientific and military figures from being captured by the Soviets after the end of the war in Europe. Once key scientists such as Wernher von Braun had been debriefed, it became clear that their knowledge might help shorten the war in the Pacific, not least by potentially helping with the atomic bomb project. Stalin's Soviet military machine was already seen as a threat to the Allies, so senior German military leaders were highly prized for the intelligence they had on Soviet operations.

Ernst Kaltenbrunner

Ernst Kaltenbrunner took over as Chief of the Reich Security Main Office (*Reichssicherheitshauptamt*, or RSHA) after the assassination of Reinhard Heydrich in 1942. Born in Austria in 1903, he was physically imposing at 1.9 m (6 ft 4 in), and it is said that even Himmler feared him. His reputation for rounding up and executing suspects without trial reached its zenith after the failed plot to assassinate Hitler in 1944. He hatched his own plots to assassinate Churchill, Roosevelt and Stalin, and headed up an underground force of 'stay-behind' agents who were tasked with sabotaging Allied occupation forces in the event of Germany losing the war. He was executed in 1946 after being found guilty of war crimes.

The US officially launched 'Operation Paperclip' to round up a list of key German personnel in March 1946. This, however, was an extension of an operation that had begun even before the war had ended. Nuclear physicist Werner Heisenberg was arrested two days before Germany surrendered, in territory still controlled by German forces. He and countless others were captured during 'Operation Alsos', which directly targeted the Reich's nuclear scientists. The rocket scientists at the Baltic-coast German Army Research Centre at Peenemünde were taken into custody in July 1945 as a result of 'Operation Overcast'. Many more top figures willingly handed themselves over to the Allies rather than chance their luck with the Red Army. Others still used 'rat lines' to escape from Germany, often with the collaboration of Allied secret services.

The infamous Gestapo chief Klaus Barbie was one such escapee. The 'Butcher of Lyon' was employed by the US Counter Intelligence Corps despite having been tried *in absentia* in France and found guilty of crimes against humanity. At his trial, countless witnesses described how he had tortured them with his own hands, and he was implicated in the deaths of some 4,000 members of the French Resistance. Nonetheless, the United States aided him in escaping to Bolivia, where he was provided with a new identity and allegedly assisted in the capture and execution of Che Guevara.

It is a grim irony of the war that the Allied 'T-Forces' sent to capture German scientists adopted tactics unnervingly similar to those deployed by the Gestapo. They usually arrived in the dead of night and with no prior warning. Providing no evidence of their identity, the T-Force men would bundle their captives away and provide no information to relatives on where the men were being taken, or why. Around 1,500 Germans are estimated to have been abducted in such circumstances by the British alone.

Even some of the most infamous Gestapo war criminals were protected if they proved useful in the new 'Cold War' with the Soviet Union. Major Horst Kopkow was seized by British military policemen on 29 May 1945 in a village on the Baltic coast. Kopkow had been responsible for the Gestapo's counter-espionage and counter-sabotage operations and was implicated in the deaths of hundreds of SOE agents, including such famous names as Violette Szabo and Noor Inayat Khan. But he was also the 'desk murderer' who helped destroy the Soviet Red Orchestra espionage ring, and had crucial information relating to Soviet spies and double agents in the West. The British faked his death for him in 1948 and protected him from the war crimes tribunal in return for his intelligence. He was later given a new identity as a textile factory worker in the British zone of West Germany, and remained under the protection of British intelligence until his death in 1996.

Not all of those who escaped Germany after the war lived happily ever after, however. Adolf Eichmann, the man whom Heydrich entrusted to put into practice the 'Final Solution', adopted the name of 'Otto Eckmann' in 1945. He was arrested by the Americans and held in a camp for SS officers, but his captors had no idea of their prisoner's true identity. Before they could establish who he was, Eichmann escaped and fled to Austria. He lived there undetected for five years, posing as a forestry worker and later leasing a small parcel of land.

While the jury at Nuremberg was hearing testimony of the atrocities he had organized, Eichmann was busy conspiring to escape once more, this time to Argentina. With the help of Austrian cleric Bishop Alois Hudal, he obtained false papers under the name of 'Ricardo Klement'. Hudal was a known Nazi sympathizer who organized one of the key 'rat-lines' used by senior figures of the Third Reich to escape justice. In addition to Eichmann, he also assisted Josef Mengele (the 'Angel of Death' at Auschwitz), Captain Eduard Roschmann (the 'Butcher of Riga') and countless others.

Eichmann took a ship from Genoa to Argentina in

1950 and became department head at Mercedes-Benz in Buenos Aires. Confident of his safety, he began to give interviews to sympathetic journalists and his son Klaus boasted publicly of his father's exploits during the war. Via the dogged Nazi-hunter Simon Wiesenthal, news of Eichmann's whereabouts reached the Israeli secret service, Mossad. On 11 May 1960 they kidnapped him, returned with him to Israel and put him on trial. On 15 December 1961 he was found guilty of war crimes and crimes against humanity, and sentenced to death. He was hanged on 1 June 1962.

Martin Bormann, Joseph Goebbels and countless others elected to follow Hitler's lead and commit suicide rather than stand trial for their crimes. But many of the key Gestapo figures were arrested in due course and would stand trial in public at Nuremberg. Rudolph Diels, one-time head of the Gestapo, surrendered to American troops on 10 April 1945. He had been arrested by his former colleagues in the wake of the 1944 assassination plot against Hitler and held in 'protective custody' for several months. In March 1945 he was released to an SS Punishment Battalion and sent to the Western Front near Mainz. He became ill with tuberculosis and was moved to a hospital in Hanover, where he remained until the war came to an end. Diels would become a chief witness for the prosecution in Nuremberg.

Adolf Eichmann

Eichmann was the 'Jewish Specialist' employed by Reinhard Heydrich to investigate solutions to the Nazis' 'Jewish Problem'. Born in 1906, he was one of the chief architects of the 'Final Solution', which involved the extermination of Jews in concentration camps. Originally, he conceived of sending the Jewish population abroad to Poland or Madagascar, but the plan was never implemented. When Nazi leaders witnessed first-hand the initial mass executions of Jews by firing squads, they determined to find a more 'humane' method of murder, and settled upon the idea of gas chambers. Eichmann proved himself to be horribly efficient at organizing the transportation of hundreds of thousands of Jews to such chambers at Sobibor, Chelmno, Treblinka and Auschwitz. His enthusiasm for the task became legendary – even after Himmler had ordered him to cease deportations, Eichmann sent a further 50,000 Hungarian Jews on an eight-day death march to Austria.

After the war, Eichmann fled to Argentina and lived under the assumed name of Ricardo Klement until he was captured by Mossad agents in 1960. He was kidnapped and taken to Israel, where he was tried and sentenced to death for crimes against humanity. He was hanged at Ramleh Prison in 1962.

Rudolf Diels

A protégé of Hermann Göring, Rudolf Diels was head of the Gestapo during 1933 and 1934, having been head of the Prussian Political Police when Hitler came to power. He was the main interrogator in the investigation into the Reichstag Fire in 1933. Though considered competent, he was never ruthless or fanatical enough to hang on to power and fell victim to the political machinations of Himmler, who took control of the Gestapo in 1934. Diels survived the war and worked in local government until his retirement in 1953. He died in a hunting accident four years later.

The Nuremberg Trials

It was not just senior individuals such as Göring and Kaltenbrunner who went on trial in Nuremberg in 1945 and 1946: the entire Gestapo organization was alleged to be criminal, along with the SD, SA and SS. Described as 'the greatest trial in history' by Norman Birkett, one of the British judges who presided over it, the military tribunals that began on 20 November 1945 saw 23 of the most senior figures of the Third Reich called to account for their actions. Martin Bormann was tried *in absentia* and Robert Ley committed suicide just a week into proceedings, while Kaltenbrunner was absent for long periods due to illness.

Göring blamed Himmler for most of the Gestapo's atrocities and repeatedly attempted to distance himself from the organization he himself had founded. He bombastically presented himself as a patriotic German and was defiant, even brilliant, when defending his own record and the aims and objectives of the Third Reich. But his defence was undone by his own frank admissions of criminal behaviour and he became more subdued when confronted with images from the concentration camps, and the hundreds of pages of testimony on mass executions carried out by the Nazis. He was also badly shaken by the evidence of prosecutor David Maxwell-Fyfe, who proved beyond doubt that Göring knew about the executions of the Stalag

Senior Nazis on trial in 1946. The Gestapo's creator
Hermann Göring is seated at the left of the front row.
Beside him are Rudolph Hess, Joachim von Ribbentrop,
Wilheim Keitel and chief of the RSHA Ernst Kaltenbrunner.

Luft III escapers and did nothing to prevent them. The
trial lasted 218 days and, given the overwhelming evidence
against him, the verdict was inevitable:

*There is nothing to be said in mitigation. For Göring was
often, indeed almost always, the moving force, second only
to his leader. He was the leading war aggressor, both as
political and as military leader; he was the director of the
slave labour programme and the creator of the oppressive*

programme against the Jews and other races, at home and abroad.... His guilt is unique in its enormity. The record discloses no excuses for this man.

He was sentenced to hang, and the court refused his request to be shot instead. In the event, Göring did indeed get to choose the manner of his death: he swallowed potassium cyanide the night before he was due to be executed. How he obtained the poison remains a mystery, but the most likely explanation is that he bribed one of his American guards.

The evidence against Kaltenbrunner was more directly associated with the evidence against the Gestapo itself. Colonel Robert G. Storey put forward compelling evidence of the horrific crimes committed by the organization under the stewardship of first Heydrich and later Kaltenbrunner. He outlined the scale of the operation, indicating that 40,000 to 50,000 people were employed as Gestapo agents by the end of the war. Given that the Gestapo worked hand in glove with the Kripo and SD for many of its functions, and that each office had hundreds of informants on its books, it is clear that it cast a net very widely over the Reich.

The infamous *Einsatz* groups or *Einsatzkommandos* were clearly demonstrated to have been controlled by the Gestapo, and details of the hundreds of thousands of civilian murders for which they were responsible were heard. Even the Nazi commissioner of the territory of Sluzk, it was revealed, objected to the behaviour of the *Einsatz* groups in his territory, and wrote a scathing report on the matter to the Commissioner General of Minsk. The report was read aloud to the tribunal, to provide a snapshot of just one operation carried out in 1941:

... As regards the execution of the action, I must point out, to my deepest regret, that the latter almost bordered on sadism. The town itself during the action offered a picture of horror. With indescribable brutality on the part both of the German police officers and particularly of the Lithuanian partisans, the Jewish people, and also with them White Ruthenians, were taken out of their dwellings and herded together. Everywhere in the town shots were to be heard, and in different streets the corpses of Jews who had been shot accumulated.... To have buried alive seriously wounded people, who then worked their way out of their graves again, is such extreme beastliness that this incident as such must be reported to the Führer.

The details of how prisoners at Mauthausen camp were executed were also revealed: those condemned were 'measured' in a specially designed machine, which fired a bullet into the victim's neck as soon as the moving plank determining his height touched the top of his head. If a lack of time prevented this method being used, then prisoners were taken to a shower room that allowed either water or gas to be passed through its pipes. Colonel Storey's closing remarks to the tribunal can hardly be improved upon as a summary of the organization's brutality:

Its methods were utterly ruthless. It operated outside the law and sent its victims to the concentration camps. The term 'Gestapo' became the symbol of the Nazi regime of force and terror. Behind the scenes operating secretly, the SD, through its vast network of informants, spied upon the German people in their daily lives, on the streets, in the shops, and even within the sanctity of the churches. The most casual remark of the German citizen might bring him before the Gestapo where his fate and freedom were decided without recourse to law. In this government, in which the rule of law was replaced by a tyrannical rule of men, the Gestapo was the primary instrumental of oppression.

The Gestapo and the SD played an important part in almost every criminal act of the conspiracy. The category of these crimes, apart from the thousands of specific instances of torture and cruelty in policing Germany for the benefit of the conspirators, reads like a page from the devil's notebook:

They fabricated the border incidents which Hitler used as an excuse for attacking Poland.

They murdered hundreds of thousands of defenceless men, women, and children by the infamous Einsatz groups.

They removed Jews, political leaders, and scientists from prisoner-of-war camps and murdered them.

They took recaptured prisoners of war to concentration camps and murdered them.

They established and classified the concentration camps and sent thousands of people into them for extermination and slave labour.

They cleared Europe of the Jews and were responsible for sending hundreds of thousands to their deaths in annihilation camps.

They rounded up hundreds of thousands of citizens of occupied countries and shipped them to Germany for forced labour and sent slave labourers to labour reformatory camps.

They executed captured commandos and paratroopers and protected civilians who lynched allied fliers.

They took civilians of occupied countries to Germany for secret trial and punishment.

They arrested, tried, and punished citizens of occupied countries under special criminal procedures, which did not accord fair trials, and by summary methods.

They murdered or sent to concentration camps the relatives of persons who had allegedly committed crimes.

They ordered the murder of prisoners in Sipo and SD prisons to prevent their release by Allied armies.

They participated in the seizure and spoliation of public and private property.

They were primary agencies for the persecution of the Jews and churches.

Kaltenbrunner was found guilty and executed, along with nine other senior Nazis, on 16 October 1946. The entire Gestapo organization was also found to be criminal in nature. At the Nuremberg trials, thousands of victims of the Gestapo had their stories told to the world, and received a measure of justice. Hundreds of thousands more, however, lie in unmarked graves having suffered untold horrors at the hands of Hitler's secret terror police.

As the French Resistance hero Georges Bidault said after the war was over:

Freedom is when one hears the bell at seven o'clock in the morning and knows it is the milkman and not the Gestapo.

Index